# Integration of Cloud Computing with Emerging Technologies

This book gives a complete overview of cloud computing, its importance, its trends, innovations, and its amalgamation with other technologies. It provides content for reference.

Key features:

1 In-depth explanation of emerging technologies utilizing cloud computing
2 Supplemented with visuals, flow charts, and diagrams
3 Real-time examples included
4 Caters to beginners, as well as advanced researchers, by explaining implications, innovations, issues, and challenges of cloud computing
5 Highlights the need for cloud computing and the true benefits derived by its application and integration in emerging technologies
6 Simple, easy language

# Integration of Cloud Computing with Emerging Technologies
## Issues, Challenges, and Practices

Edited by
### Sapna Sinha
### Vishal Bhatnagar
### Prateek Agrawal
### Vikram Bali

CRC Press
Taylor & Francis Group
Boca Raton London New York

CRC Press is an imprint of the
Taylor & Francis Group, an **informa** business

Front cover image: Banlai/Shutterstock

First edition published 2024
by CRC Press
2385 NW Executive Center Drive, Suite 320, Boca Raton FL 33431

and by CRC Press
4 Park Square, Milton Park, Abingdon, Oxon, OX14 4RN

*CRC Press is an imprint of Taylor & Francis Group, LLC*

*British Library Cataloguing-in-Publication Data*
A catalogue record for this book is available from the British Library

ISBN: 978-1-032-37236-5 (hbk)
ISBN: 978-1-032-37693-6 (pbk)
ISBN: 978-1-003-34143-7 (ebk)

DOI: 10.1201/9781003341437

# Contents

## Section A  Recent and Future Trends in Application of Cloud Computing

# Section B  Integration of Cloud Computing with Technologies like AI, ML, IoT, Mobile, and Big Data

# Section C  Security and Challenges Associated with Cloud Integration

# Editors' Biographies

**Dr. Sapna Sinha** is an professor in Amity Institute of Information Technology, Amity University Uttar Pradesh, Noida. She has more than 20 years of experience in teaching UG and PG computer science courses. She received a PhD in computer science and engineering from Amity University. She has authored several book chapters and research papers in journals of repute. Machine learning, big data analytics, artificial intelligence, networking, and security are her areas of interest. She is a D-Link certified switching and wireless professional; she is also Microsoft technology associate in database management system, software engineering, and networking. She is an EMC academic associate in Cloud Infrastructure Services. She is lifetime member of the Institution of Electronics and Telecommunication Engineers (IETE). She has edited several books.

**Prof. Vishal Bhatnagar** holds BE, MTech, and PhD degrees in the engineering field. He has more than 21 years of teaching experience in various technical institutions. He is currently working as a professor in the Computer Science & Engineering Department at Netaji Subhash University of Technology East Campus (Formerly Ambedkar Institute of Advanced Communication Technologies & Research), Delhi, India. His research interests include data mining, social network analysis, data science, blockchain, and big data analytics. He has to his credit more than 130 research papers in various international/national journals, conferences, and book chapters. He is currently working as associate editor of a few journals of IGI Global and Inderscience. He has to his credit, experience in handling special issues of Scopus, ESCI, and SCIE journals. He is series editor for three book series of the CRC Press, Taylor & Francis Group. He has also edited many books of Springer, Elsevier, IGI Global, and CRC Press. He is lifetime member of the Indian Society for Technical Education (ISTE). He has also worked as an editor of many edited books of Springer, IGI Global, CRC Press to name a few.

**Dr. Prateek Agrawal** is working as a professor and Dy. Dean at the School of Computer Science & Engineering at Lovely Professional University, Phagwara, Punjab, India. He has received his PhD degree from IK Gujral Punjab Technical University, Kapurthala, Punjab (India) in 2018 and Postdoc from May 2019–April 2021 from University of Klagenfurt, Austria. He cleared the GATE exam in 2006. He received his BTech degree from Uttar Pradesh Technical University, Lucknow, Uttar Pradesh, India in 2007 and MTech degree from ABV Indian Institute of Information Technology & Management, Gwalior, Madhya Pradesh, India in 2009. His research areas include natural language processing, computer vision, video processing, expert systems, deep learning applications, etc. He worked on three European Union–funded agency projects during his postdoctoral research. He is also a member of different reputed organizations like IEEE, IET, MIR lab, IAENG society, etc. He has won the Research Appreciation Award in the years 2016, 2018, 2019, and 2021 at Lovely Professional University. He has published more than 65 numbers of research papers in Scopus/SCIE-indexed journals and conferences, three national patents, four edited books, and seven book chapters. He is co-inventor of South Africa patent grant. He is a book series editor of the IOP series on next generation computing. He chaired eight sessions in various international conferences. He is a reviewer of many SCIE journals like IEEE TCSS, IEEE TPDS, *Multimedia Tools and Applications*, New Generation Computing, *PloS One*, *PeerJ*, *IEEE Access*, *Journal of Ambient Intelligent and Humanized Computing*, *CMC*, etc.

**Dr. Vikram Bali** is a professor and head of the Computer Science and Engineering Department at JSS Academy of Technical Education, Noida, India. He graduated from REC, Kurukshetra – BTech (CSE), Postgraduation from NITTTR, Chandigarh – ME (CSE), and Doctorate (PhD) from Banasthali Vidyapith, Rajasthan. He has more than 20 years of rich academic and administrative experience. He has published more than 50 research papers in international journals/conferences and edited books. He has authored five textbooks. He has published six patents. He is on the editorial board and on the review panel of many international journals. He is a series editor for three book series of CRC Press, Taylor & Francis Group. He is a lifetime member of IEEE, ISTE, CSI, and IE. He was awarded the Green Thinker Z-Distinguished Educator Award 2018 for remarkable contribution in the field of computer science and engineering at the third International Convention on Interdisciplinary Research for Sustainable Development (IRSD) at the Confederation of Indian Industry (CII), Chandigarh. He has attended faculty enablement program organized by Infosys and NASSCOM. He is member of board of studies of different Indian universities and member of organizing committee for various national and international seminars/conferences. He is working on four sponsored research projects funded by TEQIP-3 and Unnat Bharat Abhiyaan. His research interests include software engineering, cyber security, automata theory, CBSS, and ERP.

# Contributors

**Prateek Agrawal**
Lovely Professional University
India

**Sandhya Arora**
Cummins College of Engineering
    for Women
India

**Vishal Bhatnagar**
NSUT East Campus
India

**Harshit Bisht**
Doon University
India

**Sover Singh Bisht**
NIET
India

**Priyanka Chandani**
NIET
India

**Vikas Chaudhary**
Greater Noida Institute of Technology
India

**Nutan Hemant Deshmukh**
Cummins College of Engineering for
    Women
India

**Deepali Goyal Dev**
ABES Engineering College
India

**Mahendra Kumar Garanayak**
BPUT
India

**Amrita Jyoti**
IMS Engieering Colllege
India

**Vinod M Kapse**
NIET
India

**Shatakshi Kokate**
G. H. Raisoni College of Engineering
India

**Aditya Kumar**
NSUT East Campus
India

**Sandeep Kumar**
Maharaja Surajmal Institute of
    Technology
India

**Satendra Kumar**
Doon University
India

**Vishu Madaan**
Lovely Professional University
India

**Jatin Madan**
Deloitte USI
India

**Suman Madan**
Jagan Institute of Management Studies
India

**Kishore Mane**
G. H. Raisoni College of Engineering
India

**Sonali Mathur**
Maharaja Surajmal Institute
 of Technology
India

**Sameer Mehra**
Amity University
India

**Preeti Mishra**
Doon University
India

**Mohit Mittal**
IMS Engieering College
India

**Mohit Mittal**
Maharaja Surajmal Institute
 of Technology
India

**Aditya Nautiyal**
Doon University
India

**Varsha Sujeet Pimprale**
Cummins College of Engineering
 for Women
India

**Mamata Rath**
DRIEMS Autonomous College
India

**Taksheel Saini**
Amity University
India

**Subhangi Saklani**
Doon University
India

**Ravi Shankar**
Lovely Professional University
India

**Amit Sharma**
Maharaja Surajmal Institute
 of Technology
India

**Vandana Sharma**
Amity University
India

**Sonali Shinge**
G. H. Raisoni College of Engineering
India

**Vikrant Shokeen**
Maharaja Surajmal Institute
 of Technology
India

**Urmila Shrawankar**
G. H. Raisoni College of Engineering
India

**Pawan Kumar Shukla**
NIET
India

**Shyla**
NSUT East Campus
India

**Laxman Singh**
NIET
India

**Yaduvir Singh**
NIET
India

**Ankit Singhal**
Jagan Nath Institute of Management
  Studies
India

**Sapna Sinha**
Amity University
India

**Niva Tripathy**
DRIEMS Autonomous College
India

**Subhranshu Sekhar Tripathy**
DRIEMS Autonomous College
India

# Preface

*Greetings!*

The COVID-19 pandemic has taught the world to get themselves adapted to digital world. Almost each process or services offered has been digitized, and some are still on the way of full digitization. Digital transformation has brought a lot of challenges, too, such as 24 × 7 availability, overnight procurement of infrastructure, and software and experts to manage the services.

Among all the technologies, cloud computing technology opened the avenue for most of the modern applications to increase customer experience with solution to all the challenges to be faced. On-demand service and 24 × 7 availability have made its adoption easier. New types of cloud computing like hybrid cloud have also raised some concerns like its security and compliance, tools and technology, business implementations, and IT landscapes. Other than this amalgamation of cloud with other technologies like artificial intelligence, machine learning, Internet of Things, and mobile computing, cloud computing needs serious attention from practitioners to find a proper use of these technologies and taking maximum benefit out of it.

Cloud computing practice using a network of remote server hosted on the Internet to store, manage, and process data, while AI has to struggle to gain footholds in other niches, it is finding its place in the world of cloud computing. The revolution is that it could rapidly change the face of businesses using cloud computing solutions over the next few years. The three areas of cloud computing AI that have taken long strides are parallel processing, ML and ML algorithm, and big data. This convergence also allowed IoT application to leverage the benefits of the cloud challenges' conflicting properties. In integration of cloud computing with mobile or mobile cloud computing, the brain of services in the cloud are easier to share content and assets are easier to maintain the data and are more immune to crashes and deletion.

The book aims to include different case studies or real-life scenario, where this integration of cloud and other technologies has made the huge difference. This book, *Integration of Cloud Computing with Emerging Technologies: Issues, Challenges, and Practices*, includes a chapter on technological advancement of cloud computing, its trends, and ongoing status of each as per perception of the contributors to help in its easier adoption in the areas where it is yet to be implemented.

Chapter 1 covers how cloud computing is an increasingly maturing model, for provide the request service like software, information data, resource, and other cloud devices are shared based on the user demands. Cloud computing model encourage their business, infrastructure, and change their environment and accelerate the time to market. This model can increase the cloud users, to move their request to cloud. Moreover the clouds are dived into three groups of clouds namely public, private, and hybrid. This chapter also describe the cloud computing service architecture with applications, advantages, and challenges.

Chapter 2 discusses about different vulnerabilities of cloud computing environment. It also discusses about use of Internet and ICT tools that have made routine work of organization easy but at the same time it has also made all data and whole infrastructure vulnerable and susceptible. Vulnerabilities of cloud computing make it susceptible from attack, which leads losing trust in the techniques.

Chapter 3 investigates and introduces an efficient resource scheduling technique that has a positive impact on computational cloud performance. The algorithm is proposed for scheduling algorithm to achieve and demonstrate two types of resource management techniques viz. priority-based algorithm and algorithm based on dynamic workload. The proposed solutions have been implemented using the CloudSim tool with a random workload generation system. The experimental analysis done shows that these approaches are useful for dealing with the cloud's increasing workloads and also demonstrate the improvement in the cloud's computational performance.

In Chapter 4, the authors covered federated learning as a holistic approach to collaborative and distributed learning, facilitating security and privacy of users and their data by training the base model copy on edge devices while keeping data on the edge devices themselves and further aggregated and integrated centrally on cloud base model, its various types based on feature space and the model used underneath as a base model, current challenges and limitation, and a basic algorithm for simulation of federated learning using two edge devices for classification on the CIFAR 10 data set.

Chapter 5 discusses about the cloud computing and different cloud security setting, and misconfiguration in them can easily lead to cloud data breaches. With the advancement in the technology, there also rises the security risk. Cloud computing is referred to as the new era of computing. Unlike previous computing methodologies like a physical server, where organization had to store all their data on the on-premise server for storage, networking organizations had to buy networking equipment like routers and switches for communicating safely over the Internet, still after spending too many companies were vulnerable to threat.

In Chapter 6, the authors have explored various attacking possibilities and defensive tools, specially focusing on network layer of cloud computing. Various traditional security solutions such as Network Intrusion Prevention System (NIPS) and Network Intrusion Detection System (NIDS) are used by researchers to protect cloud from network attacks. To effectively secure network layer, these traditional tools are no longer sufficient. One has to relentlessly search for tools that specifically focus on virtualization layer of cloud. In this chapter, we have discussed different security and attacking tools, providing a detailed study of the tools. Each of the categories is further classified based on the target layer of deployment at the virtualization layer. A case study on "Explainable Artificial Intelligence–based Network Intrusion Detection System" (XAI-NIDS) has been performed using UNSW-NB15 dataset to provide the practical demonstration on network attack analysis.

In Chapter 7, the IoT devices are currently being used extensively across several industries to collect data. Data traffic generated by the use and growth of IoT devices is huge. When data must be transferred to the cloud for storage, handling such a large amount of traffic becomes a significant problem. This in turn raises bandwidth and latency risks as well as risks linked to data security and confidentiality. The IoT network with heavy traffic can be readily attacked by hostile agents who threaten the security of information received from IoT. This problem can be solved using fog computing, which becomes more and more crucial to control the data flow. The fog computing is a branch of cloud computing. Processing now happens locally in a virtual platform as a result of the development of fog computing rather than on a centralized cloud server. Fog computing improves latency, transfer speed, veracity, safety, and protection by extending cloud services. Cloud computing and fog computing work better together since fog computing by itself is ineffective. The constraints of the current system use IoT and the cloud, the three-tier architecture, and benefits and challenges in fog computing; all these points covered in this chapter.

Chapter 8 discusses about cloud computing, challenges in cloud computing, blockchain technology, features of blockchain technology, the design of Blockchain-as-a-Service in the cloud and the challenges in front of the Blockchain-as-a-Service.

In Chapter 9, the author has provided an analysis of IoT and its applications, Indian government initiatives with respect to IoT and smart cities and its architecture and highlights essential components of smart city and attempts to establish relations between IoT and smart cities, issues and challenges, and then future opportunities that this new model brings to the areas of transportation and mobility, parking, defense, education sector, malls, hospitals, health, industries, and waste management.

Chapter 10 provides a study to show significant strategies used by AI and its future planning to improve the technology standard. This chapter is intended for technologists who need to get a layout of a future vision that is needed for how artificial intelligence may be used for the growth of advanced knowledge, such as cloud figuring and IoT.

Chapter 11 provides a brief outline of big data implementation, its uses in cloud computing, and four pillars of big data – performance, input detail, insights, and reliability and security – that can be leveraged in cloud computing to obtain these benefits at comparably reduced costs. This chapter also discusses various analytics, the technologies required in linking big data with cloud computing, the difficulties associated with this process, trends in applications of the area, and security considerations. This study also reviews the benefits and drawbacks of employing cloud computing resources to convert big data. It focuses on the connections among big data, cloud computing, storage technologies, and Hadoop technology.

Chapter 12 discusses how intrusion detection systems are important for systems security. A key part of any security system helps find threats before they do real damage. IDS is a mix of hardware, software, methods, or both, and its job is to find expected changes in network information. In the cloud environment, the API logs and authentication are monitored apart from implementing IDS for network layer and host-based security.

Chapter 13 discusses how technology has made it easier to make modern supply chains more complicated. This chapter aims to investigate and analyze blockchain technology, IoT, and cloud computing applications for SCM. Organizations must innovate and maintain their information systems (IS) up to date due to the ever-changing nature of information technology (IT), including numerous software and infrastructure technologies. Cloud computing could optimize the supply chain network by providing infrastructure, platform, and software solutions via the Internet. Cloud-based supply chain management has financial and operational benefits, but stakeholders should consider risks and constraints.

Chapter 14 discusses how the cloud enables previously unachievable tasks when combined with IoT, which accelerates corporate growth. Numerous cloud services and solutions serve a wide range of purposes in an IoT ecosystem. To manage the complex tasks required for IoT, several cloud computing systems come with integrated business intelligence tools, SQL engines, and machine learning. Many IoT cloud platforms, their characteristics, and how they operate are covered in this chapter. This chapter elaborates on a case study for a temperature-humidity monitoring, visualization, and alarm system using the ThingSpeak IoT platform.

Chapter 15 discusses the limitations of the currently available platforms, the design of the tribal e-store model based on the distributed indexing and content retrieval, results, advantages, and the challenges in front of the e-store. This discussed model will be the first step toward lifting the life standards of tribes.

In Chapter 16, we offer an approach for accurately identifying bogus news. The framework's three main components are machine learning, natural language processing, and information retrieval. Data gathering and the development of machine learning models are the components of this study.

Chapter 17 discusses how universities and institutions can use the cloud to improve their teaching and learning environments. It also looks at how the cloud can be cost-effective, efficient, and reliable. Authors have compiled a list of educational cloud case studies from some of the leading providers of cloud services.

Chapter 18 discusses the concept of smart rural structures using IoT and cloud computing. It involves integrating various technologies to create efficient and sustainable living environments in rural areas. The aim of this chapter is to know about the use of IoT devices and cloud computing to provide essential services such as smart energy management, agricultural monitoring, and remote healthcare.

We wish all our readers and their family members good health and prosperity.

Editors

**Dr. Sapna Sinha**
**Dr. Vishal Bhatnagar**
**Dr. Vikram Bali**
**Dr. Prateek Agrawal**

# Section A

*Recent and Future Trends in Application of Cloud Computing*

# 1 Cloud Computing Service Architecture

*Amrita Jyoti and Mohit Mittal*

## 1.1 INTRODUCTION

With the advancements in the processor and storage technologies, there is a big boom in cloud computing (CC). The success of the Internet, along with dynamic allocation and cheaper cloud resources, prompted many people to move to CC. The CC model allows cost-effective access to the network, which is used to share some resources such as data storage, applications, services, servers, etc. The main purpose of the CC is to provide a flexible online environment to manage prolonged work volume without affecting the execution time of framework. Based on five functionalities, cloud provides users access to resource pooling, on-demand self-service, quick elasticity, broad network access, and measured service. Measured services are provided with the help of four models (public, private, hybrid, and community), called cloud deployment models, and three service models infrastructure-as-a-service (IaaS), platform-as-a-service (PaaS), and software-as-a-service (SaaS), providing a flexible and direct approach to information maintenance and recovery. Due to the increase in the number of cloud providers (CPs) and the variety of services offered, the user has to face a number of challenges [1,2].

## 1.2 SERVICE OF CC

In the CC model, the software, hardware, storage services, computing model, and platform are distributed as per demand to several users in access to the Internet. In CC, the users basically use the pay-per-use technique. This method of CC is known for capability and access [3], in which the capability of cloud service (CS) models and access method are called deployment models. CC is a process of providing IT services by which the cloud resources are obtained by the Internet in web-based tools and applications, as opposed to the direction of the server connection and keeping the files on the proprietary hard drive, cloud-data storage makes the database very safe [4]. The CC service architecture is shown in Figure 1.1.

As long as the communication devices (PC, mobile, etc.) have access to the web, they also have access to the data and software programs to execute them. Consequently, the capabilities are based on three models, whereas the access method consists of four models. The deployment model is further classified as private and public cloud; the capability is further divided into SaaS, IaaS, and PaaS [5].

DOI: 10.1201/9781003341437-2

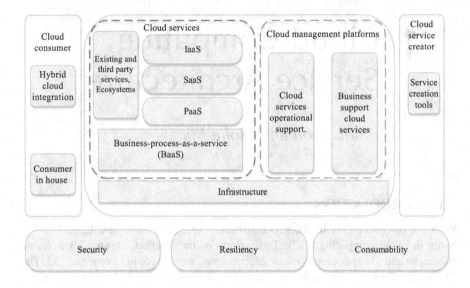

**FIGURE 1.1**   Cloud computing service architecture.

## 1.2.1   INFRASTRUCTURE-AS-A-SERVICE

IaaS is the lowest layer of the CC system in which the virtualization technique is used. Meanwhile, it provides all types of services, such as storage, network equalities, and backup process. In IaaS, people have to pay for the application software for their needs [6]. The structure of IaaS is shown in Figure 1.2.

A case study on the migration of a corporate IT system to IaaS is talked about in the third-party CC environment. According to this, if the cloud party is introduced, it presents many opportunities to develop the revenue of IT companies and expenditure management for both financial and customer personnel [7]. These are the advantages of the internal data center, along with low service cost. Therefore, the third party is responsible for not executing the data center. During this process, the infrastructure of the cloud is more helpful for companies to reduce the administrative burden. It allows the organizations to develop and extend their network infrastructure on the demand basis. IaaS has computing capabilities and basic storage function, which is used to standardize the CSs over the network. In this service, the information storage systems, data center, networking equipment, etc., are available to handle the user's workloads [8].

Moreover, IaaS provides different types of services, storage, network, and backups of the system. Figure 1.2 shows the IaaS infrastructure. A few examples of IaaS are as follows:

- *Amazon Simple Storage Solution (AS3)*: It provides the user with a dynamic storage system.
- *Amazon Elastic Compute Cloud (AEC2)*: It possesses a special virtual machine for users.
- GoGrid: It uses dedicated servers based on the dynamically scalable computing system.

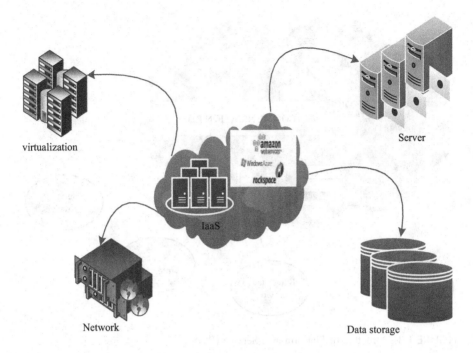

virtualization

Server

IaaS

Network                                            Data storage

**FIGURE 1.2**   Structure of Infrastructure-as-a-Services (IaaS).

*Benefit of IaaS*

- Customers can scale up and down based on their needs at any time.
- Customers can reduce the total CS cost of capital expenditure and ownership.
- Customers can access the enterprise grid of IT infrastructure and resources.

### 1.2.2 PLATFORM-AS-A-SERVICE

The PaaS provides the platform of the web to the users. Search encryption and cloud software are some of the platform services, which provide a stack or platform for software solutions to the users. Moreover, it will help the user to save system investment with the help of Google engine and Force.com. PaaS is a development of software design, testing, and hosting [9]. Figure 1.3 shows the PaaS infrastructure.

PaaS is mainly used for individual use of business purposes. Moreover, it provides a stack or platform for software solutions. It will help the user to access the system. Here, the software level is encapsulated and offered as a service, on which other higher service levels can be built. The customer has various ways to build their applications, which run on the provider's infrastructure [10].

Google app engine: It allows the user to run their application in the infrastructure and store the complete development stack. Force.com: This provides the user to run and build the applications of users in AppExchange6.

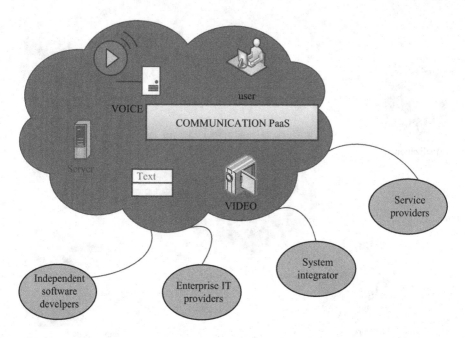

**FIGURE 1.3**   Structure of Platform-as-a-Service (PaaS).

*Benefit of PaaS*

- *Lower cost*: IT companies face less risk because they do not have to make an initial investment in software and hardware.
- *Simplified development*: The development team can focus on improving the application of CS without having to worry about the infrastructure of organization.
- *Community*: Nowadays, many users are involved in cloud application (PaaS service). It strongly supports the community, which is used to develop the business.

### 1.2.3 SOFTWARE-AS-A-SERVICE

SaaS is the topmost layer of CC, which was consumed by end users. In addition, it provides the user to use their software, particularly any type of application software, e.g., Google, Salesforce.com. Application of SaaS is suggested in video conferences, accounting, and customer resource management [11]. Figure 1.4 represents the SaaS infrastructure.

SaaS is the main type of the CS model in CC and mainly focuses on users' capabilities, such as user management or email. Moreover, it is based on the customer service management. In this model, the services are provided to the customer applications and the user demands. On the user side, there is no need for front-end investment in software and server. Therefore, the service cost is low and easy for service providing [12].

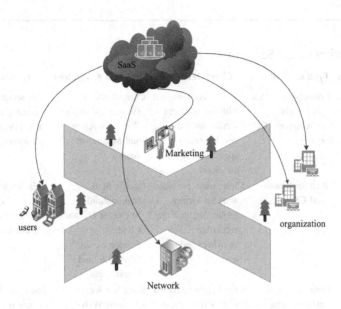

**FIGURE 1.4**    Structure of Software-as-a-Service (SaaS).

An example of services of SaaS is as follows:

*Google apps*: Its document management provides a web-based system such as e-mail and calendar.

***Benefit of SaaS***

- Neglect the infrastructure concerns
- Access from any location with cloud network service
- Fast scalability
- Provide online service well known in Microsoft Office
- Used in a short-term manner, e.g., cooperation software for all project

The performance of different types of CSs is shown in Table 1.1.

## 1.3   DEPLOYMENT SERVICE MODELS

The CC contains two deployment models such as public and private models. In addition, it has two other perspectives that are hybrid and community cloud [13]. The developed CC services are shown in Figure 1.5.

### 1.3.1   PUBLIC CLOUD

In the public cloud, the user can access the cloud openly through interfaces using a web service, web browser, etc. The service provider of this public cloud can manage the software and hardware's process [14]. In public cloud resources, a payment

**TABLE 1.1**

**Classification of CC Services**

| CC Services | Type of Products | Characteristics | Products & Vendors | Disadvantage |
|---|---|---|---|---|
| PaaS | Framework, APLs programming, development CC system | Cloud users provided with the platform service for the development of application hosts in the cloud | Computer wire, Google app engine, Windows Azure, and Manjrasoft Aneka | This service control required different and new security measures. |
| SaaS | Web application and CS | Cloud users provided with the service application that are accessible anywhere and anytime | Google Mail (automation), Microsoft Dynamic CRM, Saleforce.com, ORACLE, and Clarizen.com | This service control required different and new security measures. |
| IaaS | Data storage management, VM management, and service management | Cloud users provided with VM hardware and data storage on the top of infrastructure | Rock Service, Amazon Web Services, Verizon, Microsoft, and GoGrid | The large productivity depends on the vendor's capability, business efficiency is low. This service control required different and new security measures. |

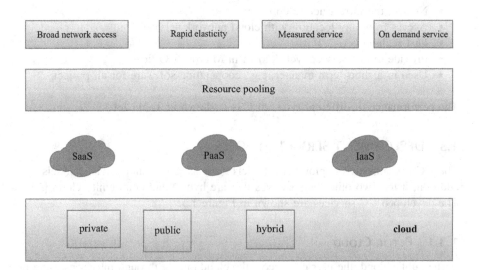

**FIGURE 1.5**   Developed cloud computing services.

commission is offered as a service through an Internet connection. The public cloud can sell CS and servers to a diverse pool of users. So, the user can access the public cloud anywhere in the world. This service is helpful for small- and medium-business users. But its major issue is that it is less secure than other types of CSs [15,16].

*Advantages of Public Cloud*

- In this service, there is no need to buy a new hardware device. The virtual service and host are accessed by a third party, which is used to reduce the cost of the service.
- The public CS ID is more effective and simple.
- If any CS is offered, it will not take any service cost for system maintenance.
- The service reconfiguration time is less.

## 1.3.2 PRIVATE CLOUDS

The private cloud is designed for a single tenant. This cloud can manage the software and hardware services. The main use of this model is that it can be easy to manage, upgrade, and secure. The public cloud has two main processes: first, on-premise private cloud (internal cloud) can provide more standard processes and protection, but this cloud has low storage and scalability; second, external hosted private cloud is performed with CP for privacy computing. The private cloud don't prefer the public cloud because of sharing the physical resources by many users [17,18].

*Advantages of Private Cloud*

- The private CS can be used by the single organization because it offers more security for a user's information.
- This service can control more organization data.
- The private cloud is used to develop the organization.

## 1.3.3 HYBRID CLOUD

The hybrid cloud is the combination of both private and public clouds. It is a safer way to view the data on the Internet [19]. The solution of this hybrid cloud is used to integrate various kinds of clouds, namely community cloud, partner cloud, internal cloud, and external cloud [20]. The structure of the hybrid cloud is shown in Figure 1.6.

*Advantages of a Hybrid Cloud*

- The hybrid cloud is used to develop the infrastructure of every organization; this makes a better virtualization of the infrastructure.
- This service helps the organization to reduce their service cost than the other two types of CS.

The comparison of the development service model in CC is shown in Table 1.2.

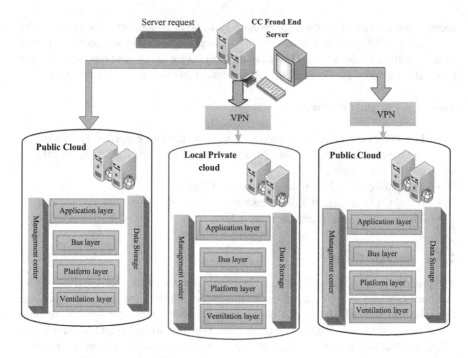

**FIGURE 1.6**   Structure of hybrid cloud.

**TABLE 1.2**

**Comparison of Development Service Model in CC**

| Service Development Model | Service Manage | Service Security | Goal of Service |
|---|---|---|---|
| Public cloud | The private cloud is managed by service provider. | Low security | 1. This service is used by general public users and large number of industry groups.<br>2. Unlimited scalability.<br>3. Service cost is low. |
| Private cloud | It is managed by service organization (IT enterprise) | High security | 1. The scalability of this service is limited.<br>2. The service level of private cloud is IT specific. |
| Hybrid cloud | The hybrid CS is managed by both public and organization. | Medium security | 1. It controls both service provider and IT enterprise.<br>2. The service cost is medium.<br>3. The scalability of this service is burstable and base. |

## 1.4  CC SYSTEM KEYS

The CC has some key techniques, e.g., Google file system (GFS), Big Table (BT), Map-Reduce Programming Model (MRPM) [21].

### 1.4.1  METAL-AS-A-SERVICE DISTRIBUTED STORAGE

In CC, the Metal-as-a-Service (MaaS) distributed storage is used to develop the economy and credibility to store the user data by using redundancy storage to confirm the reliability of data storage. The storage process is performed by software; this software has two types of storage files, namely Hadoop Distributed File System (HDFS) and Google File System (GFS) [22].

#### 1.4.1.1  Google File System

GFS is a distributed data system for efficient, reliable resources to access the data for a large number of clusters in commodity hardware. It is used to optimize the CC core, data memory, and usage needs. Based on this process, there are many features, such as scalability, performance, reliability, and availability. These are performed with the distributed system and are also influenced by Google's technological environment and workload application. It is used for core data storage and usage needs, which can generate the enormous amount of data to be retained. This key is developed by the IT vendor, containing Intel, and Yahoo in cloud environment plan; it is also used in HDFS data storage technology. The file size of GFS is not equal to the system file size; the size of the GFS is G byte. When the files are in the read-and-write model, the GFS system is not able to do any long transparent operations. But the flexibility of co-design applications and application programs interface file system has improved [23]. The structure of GFS is given in Figure 1.7.

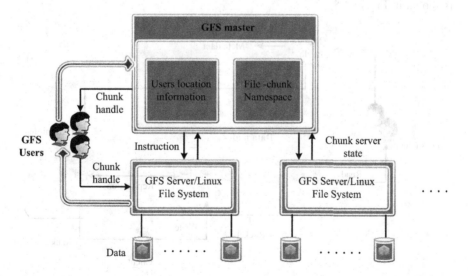

**FIGURE 1.7**  Google file system (GFS) structure.

The nodes of GFS are divided into master nodes and chunk server that are used to operate the multiple users. Then the files are separated into fixed chunks that have 64 megabytes, which are overwritten or rewritten, usually appended to the read format. The logical mapping must be maintained for each chunk server and then based on the redundancy of the data. The master nodes will not store the data, but will store the metadata associated with the chunk's location and also the table mapping. Then the location of the copies of the chunk process is written, which is maintained by the master node. In this GFS, the application programs interface is used to make communication between the server and master to read and write the data. It can achieve more performance and better results for its own applications [24].

## 1.4.1.2    Hadoop Distributed File System

The Hadoop Distributed File System (HDFS) is developed to store the user's data. It has many distributed file storage systems, but the size of each storage file is different. The HDFS can provide user information into several clusters to access high throughput, so this process is applied to large-scale data sets. The storing process of HDFS is divided into master and slave. The task tracker is known as the master node. The clusters of HDFS create two nodes: data node and name node. First, the name node is placed at the center of the server, which is used to manage the client access file and namespace of the file storage system. Normally, the data node is responsible for managing data storage. Second, the clustering part the data is divided into many parts, which are used to save the data node. The data node and master node are run by slave node because the master node and data nodes are communicated with each other.

The slave node receives instructions from the master node and stores the data based on their instructions. The name node is mainly responsible for managing and preserving all metadata in the file storage system [25]. The basic structure of HDFS is shown in Figure 1.8.

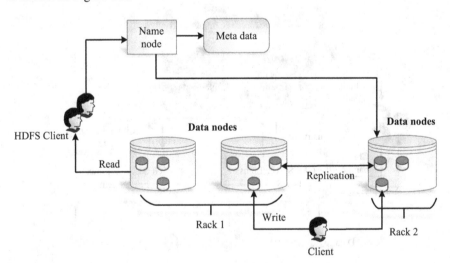

**FIGURE 1.8**    Structure of Hadoop Distributed File System (HDFS).

## 1.4.2   Big Table

Big data is used in GFS applications for generating a data table and modifying the data contents in the table. It is mainly used in the Google application, Orkut, Gmail, Google map, etc. It is a sort, distributed, multidimensional map, which contains the timestamp, column key, and row key. It consists of a highly available locking service called chubby service. This service consists of some types of models – one acts as the master and serves the request. The service is alive, and then the majority of the locations can communicate with each other. The big table uses the majority of the table servers to begin and finalize the table server death – to ensure there is always an active master.

Each table has multidimensional tablet segments with 200 megabytes. The first level is the location where the file is saved. Each meta-table data contains the information about the root level [21]. The basic functional structure of the Big Table in CC is shown in Figure 1.9.

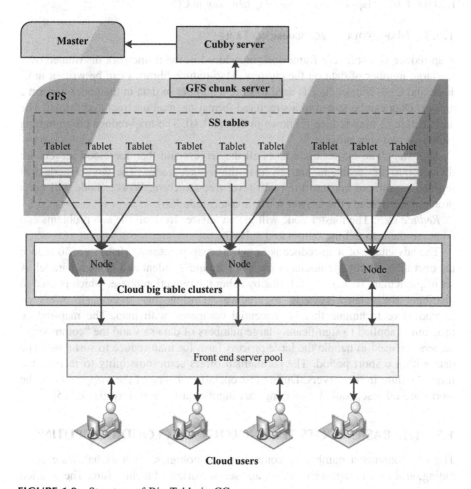

**FIGURE 1.9**   Structure of Big Table in CC.

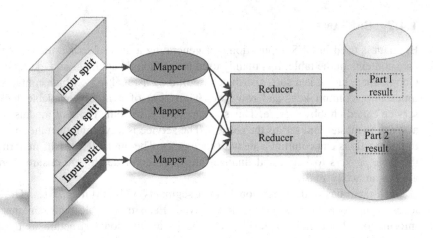

**FIGURE 1.10**   Map-reduce programming table key in CC.

### 1.4.3   Map-Reduce Programming Table

Map-reduce is a software framework introduced in the framework distributed over the large number of data on the clusters. Map-reduce libraries can be written in C, Java, and C++. Map-reduce is used to store a number of data in the nodes to form a cluster. Data can be stored in a structured format or in an unstructured format. The architecture of map-reduce is shown in Figure 1.10. The map-reduce programming table is a two-step process.

*Map step*: The master node takes all the servers and then the cloud servers are divided into sub-problems and given to the worker nodes. The worker node will repeat it again and get into the multi-level tree structure. Worker node will get a problem, so it sends the answer to the master node [26].

*Reduce step*: The master node will get an answer from all the sub-problems and combine them to get the output and solve it.

The advantage of map-reduce is to get the map processing distributed to reduce the operation. So all operations of mapping are independent and make it parallel. A set of particular "reducers" performs by using the reduction phase, which is used to distribute the related keys to the reducer. During this process, it offers an unproductive technique that is sequential compared with map. The map-reduce program is applied to significantly large numbers of data sets and the "commodity" servers are used to handle the large process farm for map-reduce to sort a pet-type data within a short period. The parallelism offers some possibility to recover the limited failure in the servers. During this operation, if one of the mappers fails, the works are all rescheduled, assuming that input data were still available [25].

## 1.5   THE BASIC ROOTS TECHNOLOGY OF CLOUD COMPUTING

The CC contains a number of computing technologies, such as hardware computing, grid computing, web service, and service-oriented architecture. The detailed explanation of these technologies is given next.

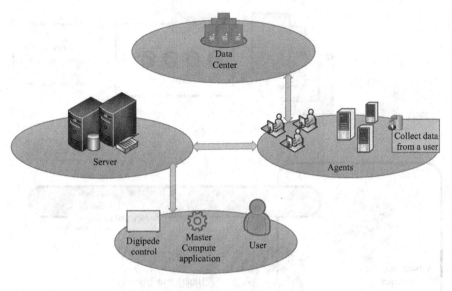

**FIGURE 1.11**   Basic structure of grid computing (GC).

## 1.5.1 GRID COMPUTING

Grid computing (GC) is generally a concept of huge potential in an organization. The GC is widely used for several service orientations to provide fast throughput, seamless sharing, and flexibility of heterogeneous networks for user data intensive and compute intensive processes. The main benefit of GC is high reliability, scalability, resource utilization, virtualization, and data management. The GC environment provides more complexity and increases the energy efficiency of the grid infrastructure. In many industries, the GC applications are used for computer intensives and more resource efficiency. The basic structure of GC is shown in Figure 1.11.

In a GC environment, the single computer interference is used to manage the heterogeneous network and makes a strong computer infrastructure through the use of decentralization and fault tolerance, and fails to make a better computer environment to react to minor or major disasters. The main goal of GC is used to provide a signal view for each user and single mechanism, which is used to utilize the large number of tasks. The main key components of GC are security management, resource management, service management, and data management [27].

## 1.5.2 VIRTUALIZATION

Virtualization is one of the important large computing technologies; this virtualization environment provides a virtual hardware environment in a CC operating system. This service plays a fundamental role in CS (SaaS, IaaS, and PaaS). The virtual technology is mainly used for data storage, networking, and memory process. The basic phenomena of virtualization are to develop the performance of computing capacity, software resources, and underutilized hardware. Rise of administrative costs, lack of

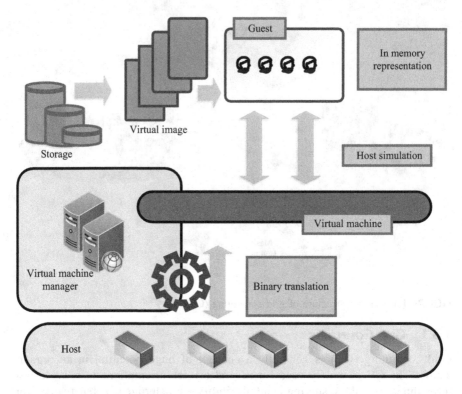

**FIGURE 1.12**   Structure of hardware virtualization (HV).

space, and greening initiatives. These phenomena can cause hardware virtualization and also cause other kinds of virtualization [28].

### 1.5.2.1   Hardware Virtualization

The hardware virtualization (HV) is mainly used to control and manage the virtualization layer in CC; this process is called VM manager (VMM). The virtual host is denoted by physical hardware systems. In this hardware model, the guest is denoted by operating system. In this HV service, the VMM is operated by a hypervisor. The hypervisor is a combination of hardware and software. This virtualization has two main functions. (1) The hypervisor running process is directly applied on the top of the hardware. The overview structure of hardware virtualization (HV) is shown in Figure 1.12.

It mainly operates in instruction set architecture (ISA); this interference is used to manage the guest operating system. This process is called a native virtual machine. (2) In the second process, the hypervisor supports the operating system, which provides the virtual service. This service can manage the programming operating system. This process is known as a hosted virtual machine [29].

### 1.5.3   Web Service Architecture

In a CC environment, the web service provides the interconnection operation between various software, and preforms on different platforms. The file of Web

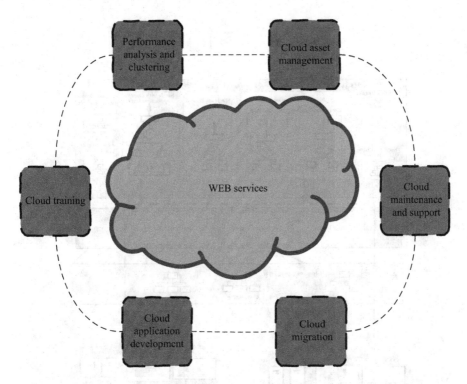

**FIGURE 1.13**   Architecture of Web Service Architecture (WSA).

Service Architecture (WSA) provides the common web service for a large web service framework community. The WSA context is used to understand the web service and makes a relationship between the different component models. This WSA service is used to exchange the document in the machine for web service interference. This interference contains transportation protocol, massage formats, transportation serialization, and data type. The architecture of WSA is shown in Figure 1.13.

These interferences are performed between the provider agent and request agent. This service can provide the specific network service to any location and provide the data about the user message exchange pattern [30].

## 1.5.4   SERVICE-ORIENTED ARCHITECTURE

The general function of Service-Oriented Architecture (SOA) is based on the technology of the Organization for the Advancement of Structure Information Standard (OASIS). The SOA architecture is based on the specific service and it focuses on service implementation. The basic function of SOA and its result adaptation are as follows: increase the performance speed of the user and improve the flexibility of the system, which is used to develop the requirement and its performance [31]. The structure of SOA in CC is shown in Figure 1.14.

**FIGURE 1.14**    Architecture of Service-Oriented Architecture (SOA).

It allows the CS to manage the organization's boundary level. The SOA provides new effective service for multiple activities. The metadata should offer the service to manage the cost and effort. In order to add SOA in CC, add a layer and self-provision has to be made. Moreover, the service layer has to be placed above the cloud resources.

## 1.6    APPLICATION OF CLOUD COMPUTING

The term CC means that customers' information is stored online and is accessed through the Internet, so the traditional hard drive computers are not required. The CC services originate on days when flow charts and presentations represent the infrastructure of the Internet server. In CC, the local storage data are stored and its programs are run from the hard drive by using load balancing (LB) and cloud service brokering

(CSB) services. So, the users can access the data fast. This is possible by a dedicated cloud server in a residence; however, it does not mean that there is a computing. CC is an important standard for providing distributed access, such as software, hardware infrastructure, and the Internet to the users. The users can access the database assets anywhere in the CC environment. It has both hardware and software service systems. Consequently, it is flexible, incurs reducible costs, achieves economic scale, etc. The main benefit of CC applications is no constraints to a certain kind of mobile devices, PCs, or operating systems. Furthermore, there is no need to worry about storage capacity and calculation speed limits.

### 1.6.1 THE MOBILE DEVICE

The mobile device (MD) viewpoint refers to both data processing and storage in the mobile device. The major reason is that MDs (smartphones, tablets, etc.) are more intelligent and highly developed in today's environment. The advantage of MD is to provide the user with an ownership. One significant illustration of CC system is webmail, which maintains the server system and protects the access control. The goal is to utilize CC techniques for processing and storing the data in mobile devices. MD computing provides benefits to the users and applications enterprises. In CC, the MD industries have expanded swiftly and constantly. Nowadays, the MD users have increased rapidly, so the service ranges of all users are almost needed. According to cloud computing.com, the CS is spending 20% on services all over the world. But nowadays, most systems work with the cloud system. Thus, it becomes an important need of today's life [32].

### 1.6.2 BUSINESS CLOUD COMPUTING

The customers who need the fast and high level of service protection choose Virtual Private Network (VPN) and Internet Service Provider (ISP). This approach is used for proper communication. The major benefit of business computing is to make the CS ability high or low, which is used to access a wide variety of applications. There is no license required to access computing services, and the user has to pay only for the used service. Major cloud service providers (CSPs) have invested billions of dollars in their infrastructure with plenty of redundancy built in for higher reliability [33].

### 1.6.3 MEDICAL HEALTH CARE

In the medical field, the CC plays a vital role such as it is used to provide strong health service and collect the patient detail and their daily activities. The collection of daily detail is used to give better service to patients and correct healthcare system behavior. The human details and their activities are monitored using CC, which is used to share the patient's conditions among the doctors from the CS. To access the CS, it has some basic procedures: first, the user should authenticate the CS, and second, approve the cloud access permission. Accelerometer and gyroscope collect data from the human body and make predictions based on the Semi Markov

Condition Random Field. The human health monitoring using CC has some advantages that it can transfer the Voice over IP service through this and the patient can communicate with a doctor in any kind of situation [34].

### 1.6.4 Modern IT Organization

In modern IT organizations, workplace has been developed by using a CC service, which is used to provide decision-making information and share the document and collaboration. The cloud technology can remove unwanted information and the burden of purchasing costly devices (server and networking devices) and any software license. This is used to develop their organization by employing less CC resources and improve their organizational needs. It also develops the company's capacity and provides more opportunities for fast growth [33].

### 1.6.5 Amazon Web Service

The Amazon Web Service (AWS) provides comprehensive IaaS CS, ranging from storage, networking, and virtual computing stacks. AWS can compute and store the service demand, namely simple storage service (SSS) and elastic compute cloud (ECC). The ECC can provide the user with virtual hardware; it is used as basic infrastructure for organizing the computing system. It can select the variety of virtual hardware configured with cluster instances and GPUs. These ECC patterns are saved in SSS and deliver the storage template based on the user's request [35].

## 1.7 CHALLENGES OF CC

CC technology has been used by lots of companies, business organizations, etc. The CC brings more profits to the organizations, but the user requests and CS traffics damage the performance of CS. If the capacity of CS is more than 80%, the cloud user systems will be irresponsible. This makes crashes between users and servers and there are higher chances of losing the important organizational data, customer information, etc. The cloud federations also create more challenges than other type of models. There is a chance to damage the distributed resources, service descriptions, service level arrangement (SLA) negations, data portability, and monitoring [36].

In CC, there are so many challenges that affect the performance of task LB and CSB among various nodes. Balanced workload planning requires a series of complex problems due to the heterogeneous and dynamic nature. However, in CC, there are many parameters such as cost accessibility and flexibility to evaluate the condition of CC. But these merits underlie the requirements for CSs. Being the main concern in these problems, LB allows CC to "balance the user request." These are the major issues with CC, and some challenges are given as follows.

### 1.7.1 Data Protections

Confidentiality was one of the main criteria for secure communication and data encryption methods. The data encryption should be confidential secure communication.

If the cloud system was confidential, then the third party will not intrude into the cloud system. The data's mitigating and segregation in the cloud system are the privacy issues. They mainly focus on data storage issues in the CC environment and how to secure the user data in a private and confidential way. The cloud segregation gives the accurate segregated information, and allowed desired storage space in the cloud environment. Furthermore, these segregated data should be stored at one secure place in the cloud system for the user to whom it belongs to and prevents a breach in a private section. When many users' data is stored, the actual locations of the data are not identified clearly. So the data are balanced and allotted to the CS.

### 1.7.2  DATA AVAILABILITY AND RECOVERY

In CC, the organization has many users and information to arrange the service so each demand is stringently followed. The service control team plays an important role in data control and manages the service-level agreement and run-time application [37]. The data availability is performed by using some operation teams given below:

- Data replication
- Run-time maintenance
- System monitoring
- Capacity and performance management
- Disaster recovery

### 1.7.3  RESOURCE PRICING AND MARKETING

In CC, the resource marketing and pricing is a major challenge to federate CPs. The user should understand resource allocation for each demand. The key factors of this barrier can influence their revenues, such as resource share and in-resource price for new users. These two berries are considered together to achieve better results. The LB and the service broker policy are used to solve this problem and give more efficiency for federation resources in CC [38,39].

### 1.7.4  ECONOMIC AND ENABLE STANDARD CHALLENGE

These challenges are different from the traditional cloud model. These challenges contain security, distribution resource provision, data probability, monitoring, billing, cloud networking, and accounting [38].

### 1.7.5  CHALLENGES OF LB AND CSB

The LB can overcome these problems and improve the features wider adopted in the cloud federation [44]. The above-mentioned challenges are overall CC challenges. Based on these issues, some problems in LB and CSB are discussed next.

### 1.7.5.1   VM Migration

The entire machine can seen with the virtualization as a set of files. The VM migration can move the running VM or application between the disconnected clients without a physical machine. If the running process gets overloaded, it transfers the load to another machine with low interruption to users. This transfer process makes the interconnection between one machine and another machine [40]. It is used to shut down the VM; it will develop the performance of network application and related location communication. It is a geographically distributed data center among various CP for multicloud, and allocate the resource to another physical host, this transaction process may create problem in LB in CC. In the last few years, the container-based virtualization is used to avoid VM migration [41].

### 1.7.5.2   Stored Data Management

The data storage management in many organizations and enterprises is a major problem due to the huge data quantities. The size of the data plays a major role in industries, but the value of the data is evaluated based on the large data set. Based on this evaluation, the organization can estimate the future data rate and increase the storage capacity and network.

### 1.7.5.3   Energy Management

The energy management of the CC is one of the challenging issues. In many organizations, energy savings is a major problem for proper communication. The energy consumption analysis is a major challenge for many data centers because the energy requirement comes from various areas such as networking equipment, servers, operations, and cooling infrastructure [36]. In a CC environment, the energy management can be tackled at various levels from virtual resources to workload distribution across various data center. The data distribution of data centers brings more challenges, based on the global resource management. This distribution problem is created based on the irregular users' requests and ability of data efficiency [42].

### 1.7.5.4   Automatic Service Provision

In CC, the CSs are accessed by software service used in cloud resources. The CC service contains some software components to improve the set of dynamic resource allocation. The main objective of ASP is to enable the resource allocation and de-allocation automatically. The key feature of this provision is to release the resource on request. The automatic service provision (ASP) complexity challenges are faced by the end user; these challenges also occur due to the current location of the users [43].

### 1.7.5.5   Service-Level Agreement

The Service-Level Agreement (SLA) defines the functional and non-functional characteristics of CC services, the services are arranged by CPs and cloud users. The overall parameters of SLA are monitoring, price model, and resource metering. When the CSP is not able to meet the stated term in SLA, the violation occurs. For example, a SaaS provides the user task agreement in minimum response time, low storage space, and data reliability. But, if the user cannot get the service at a desired response time, the frequent error will occur. The flexibility of task pricing is taken into account when SLA violation has been developed and orders to create the low price model in the CC scenario.

### 1.7.5.6  Quality of Service (QoS)

The basic concept of QoS varies among the cloud users, each and every user has its own requirement. The common parameters of QoS are minimum bandwidth, arrange the number, size of input/output devices (hardware, storage volume), and medium response time. If the number of customer task is increased, these parameter values are reduced. At that time, the CS will never provide the service arrangement of all these metrics. But the provider point of view is the challenges to manage, provision, and forecast the CS in long run.

### 1.7.5.7  Energy Efficiency

The working process of data center in CC is based on the data center provisioning and the hardware usage by software (VM management) depends on the users demand. This process is required to maintain the data center in normal condition. Hence, the performance of service energy consumption in data center is directly interconnected to each other. But, if the energy level increases, the service cost also increases. This service cost may transfer to the users to balance the energy consumption.

## 1.8  CONCLUSION

The function of a CC model has developed day by day. The CC development is useful for the growth of IT companies and many organizations. Therefore, the organizations in the competition offer a large space, which is used to store the user information along with quality service and various features. The services offered by CC have some characteristics, which bring more benefits to both CS user and CSP [44]. The capability of CC is available over the Internet and access is provided through the mechanism. This standard mechanism is promoted by thin, heterogeneous platforms or users such as personal digital assistants, laptops, and mobile phones.

In CC, some computer services such as network, application, email, and server services are provided without any human actions and interaction with each CSP. The CSP provides the self-service request with AWS, IBM Microsoft, and Google. Based on this process, the consumer can provision the computing capability.

The CC resources are pooled together, which are used to serve multiple customers by using multiple-tenant model, with various dynamica virtual resources and physical resources assigned. After theta, the resources are reassigned based on the user's request. The resource service has memory, processing, storage, email service, and network bandwidth. The resources are pooling together to create resource-build economies of scale. In CC, the resources are controlled and measured, and are transparent to both consumer and provider for service utilization. The CC has a service measure meter; the capability of service measuring is to optimize and control process. This denotes that time, air, water, and IT service are charged per usage metrics. In CC, the CS is rapidly elastically provisioned, based on the user request the process can scale out and scale quickly. For the user, the features available for provisioning often seem to be unlimited resources and acquire any quality of service at any period.

## REFERENCES

[1] Qian L, Luo Z, Du Y, Guo L, Cloud computing: An overview. In IEEE International Conference on Cloud Computing 2009 Dec 1 (pp. 626–631). Springer, Berlin, Heidelberg.

[2] Zhang LJ, Zhou Q, CCOA: Cloud computing open architecture. In 2009 IEEE International Conference on Web Services 2009 Jul 6 (pp. 607–616). IEEE.

[3] Wang C, Wang Q, Ren K, Cao N, Lou W, Toward secure and dependable storage services in cloud computing. *IEEE transactions on Services Computing*. 2012 Apr; 5(2): 220–232.

[4] Doelitzscher F, Sulistio A, Reich C, Kuijs H, Wolf D, Private cloud for collaboration and e-Learning services: From IaaS to SaaS. *Computing*. 2011 Jan 1; 91(1): 23–42.

[5] Chun SH, Choi BS, Service models and pricing schemes for cloud computing. *Cluster Computing*. 2014 Jun 1; 17(2): 529–535.

[6] ur Rehman Z, Hussain OK, Hussain FK, Multi-criteria IaaS service selection based on QoS history. In 2013 IEEE 27th International Conference on Advanced Information Networking and Applications (AINA) 2013 Mar 25 (pp. 1129–1135). IEEE.

[7] Morais FJ, Brasileiro FV, Lopes RV, Santos RA, Satterfield W, Rosa L, Autoflex: Service agnostic auto-scaling framework for IaaS deployment models. In 2013 13th IEEE/ACM International Symposium on Cluster, Cloud, and Grid Computing 2013 May 13 (pp. 42–49). IEEE.

[8] Kovari A, Dukan P, KVM & OpenVZ virtualization based IaaS open source cloud virtualization platforms: OpenNode, Proxmox VE. In 2012 IEEE 10th Jubilee International Symposium on Intelligent Systems and Informatics 2012 Sep 20 (pp. 335–339). IEEE.

[9] Boniface M, Nasser B, Papay J, Phillips SC, Servin A, Yang X, Zlatev Z, Gogouvitis SV, Katsaros G, Konstanteli K, Kousiouris G, Platform-as-a-Service architecture for real-time quality of service management in clouds. In 2010, Fifth International Conference on Internet and Web Applications and Services 2010 May 9 (pp. 155–160). IEEE.

[10] Ojala A, Helander N, Value creation and evolution of a value network: A longitudinal case study on a Platform-as-a-Service provider. In 2014, 47th Hawaii International Conference on System Sciences 2014 Jan 6 (pp. 975–984). IEEE.

[11] Kang S, Myung J, Yeon J, Ha SW, Cho T, Chung JM, Lee SG, A general maturity model and reference architecture for SaaS service. In International Conference on Database Systems for Advanced Applications 2010 Apr 1 (pp. 337–346). Springer, Berlin, Heidelberg.

[12] Wu L, Garg SK, Versteeg S, Buyya R, SLA-based resource provisioning for hosted Software-as-a-Service applications in cloud computing environments. *IEEE Transactions on services computing*. 2014 Jul; 7(3): 465–485.

[13] Hoefer CN, Karagiannis G, Taxonomy of cloud computing services. In 2010, IEEE Globecom Workshops 2010 Dec 6 (pp. 1345–1350). IEEE.

[14] Shin DH, User centric cloud service model in public sectors: Policy implications of cloud services. *Government Information Quarterly*. 2013 Apr 1; 30(2): 194–203.

[15] Wang Q, Wang C, Li J, Ren K, Lou W, Enabling public verifiability and data dynamics for storage security in cloud computing. In European symposium on research in computer security 2009 Sep 21 (pp. 355–370). Springer, Berlin, Heidelberg.

[16] Hofmann P, Woods D, Cloud computing: The limits of public clouds for business applications. *IEEE Internet Computing*. 2010 Nov; 14(6): 90–93.

[17] Li M, Yu S, Cao N, Lou W, Authorized private keyword search over encrypted data in cloud computing. In 2011, 31st International Conference on Distributed Computing Systems 2011 Jun 20 (pp. 383–392). IEEE.

[18] Bittencourt LF, Senna CR, Madeira ER, Scheduling service workflows for cost optimization in hybrid clouds. In 2010, International Conference on Network and Service Management 2010 Oct 25 (pp. 394–397). IEEE.

[19] Bittencourt LF, Madeira ER, Da Fonseca NL, Scheduling in hybrid clouds. *IEEE Communications Magazine*. 2012 Sep; 50(9): 42–47.

[20] Chen Q, Deng QN, Cloud computing and its key techniques [J]. *Journal of Computer Applications*. 2009 Jul; 9(29): 2562–2567.

[21] Tien JM, Manufacturing and services: From mass production to mass customization. *Journal of Systems Science and Systems Engineering*. 2011 Jun 1; 20(2): 129–154.

[22] Hsiao HC, Chung HY, Shen H, Chao YC, Load rebalancing for distributed file systems in clouds. *IEEE Transactions on Parallel and Distributed Systems*. 2013 May; 24(5): 951–962.

[23] Adamov A, Distributed file system as a basis of data-intensive computing. In 2012, 6th International Conference on Application of Information and Communication Technologies (AICT) 2012 Oct 17 (pp. 1–3). IEEE.

[24] Kim M, Cui Y, Han S, Lee H, Towards efficient design and implementation of a hadoop-based distributed video transcoding system in cloud computing environment. *International Journal of Multimedia and Ubiquitous Engineering*. 2013 Mar; 8(2): 213–224.

[25] Gunarathne T, Wu TL, Qiu J, Fox G, Map reduce in the clouds for science. In 2010, IEEE Second International Conference on Cloud Computing Technology and Science 2010 Nov 30 (pp. 565–572). IEEE.

[26] Erwin DW, Snelling DF, UNICORE: A grid computing environment. In European Conference on Parallel Processing 2001 Aug 28 (pp. 825–834). Springer, Berlin, Heidelberg.

[27] Luo S, Lin Z, Chen X, Yang Z, Chen J, Virtualization security for cloud computing service. In 2011, International Conference on Cloud and Service Computing 2011 Dec 12 (pp. 174–179). IEEE.

[28] Sun D, Chang G, Guo Q, Wang C, Wang X, A dependability model to enhance security of cloud environment using system-level virtualization techniques. In 2010, First International Conference on Pervasive Computing, Signal Processing and Applications 2010 Sep 17 (pp. 305–310). IEEE.

[29] Avetisyan AI, Campbell R, Gupta I, Heath MT, Ko SY, Ganger GR, Kozuch MA, O'Hallaron D, Kunze M, Kwan TT, Lai K, Open cirrus: A global cloud computing testbed. *Computer*. 2010 Apr; 43(4): 35–43.

[30] Tsai WT, Sun X, Balasooriya J, Service-oriented cloud computing architecture. In 2010, Seventh International Conference on Information Technology: New Generations 2010 Apr 12 (pp. 684–689). IEEE.

[31] Dinh HT, Lee C, Niyato D, Wang P, A survey of mobile cloud computing: Architecture, applications, and approaches. *Wireless communications and mobile computing*. 2013 Dec 25; 13(18): 1587–1611.

[32] Marston S, Li Z, Bandyopadhyay S, Zhang J, Ghalsasi A, Cloud computing—the business perspective. *Decision Support Systems*. 2011 Apr 1; 51(1): 176–189.

[33] Rolim CO, Koch FL, Westphall CB, Werner J, Fracalossi A, Salvador GS, A cloud computing solution for patient's data collection in health care institutions. In 2010, Second International Conference on eHealth, Telemedicine, and Social Medicine 2010 Feb 10 (pp. 95–99). IEEE.

[34] Chang V, Walters RJ, Wills G, The development that leads to the cloud computing business framework. *International Journal of Information Management*. 2013 Jun 1; 33(3): 524–538.

[35] Ren K, Wang C, Wang Q, Security challenges for the public cloud. *IEEE Internet Computing*. 2012 Jan; 16(1): 69–73.

[36] Bojanova I, Samba A, Analysis of cloud computing delivery architecture models. In 2011, IEEE Workshops of International Conference on Advanced Information Networking and Applications 2011 Mar 22 (pp. 453–458). IEEE.

[37] Feng Y, Li B, Li B, Price competition in an oligopoly market with multiple IaaS cloud providers. *IEEE Transactions on Computers*. 2014 Jan; 63(1): 59–73.

[38] Guzek M, Gniewek A, Bouvry P, Musial J, Blazewicz J, Cloud brokering: Current practices and upcoming challenges. *IEEE Cloud Computing*. 2015 Mar; 2(2): 40–47.

[39] Stieninger M, Nedbal D, Characteristics of cloud computing in the business context: A systematic literature review. *Global Journal of Flexible Systems Management*. 2014 Mar 1; 15(1): 59–68.

[40] Cheraghlou MN, Khadem-Zadeh A, Haghparast M, A survey of fault tolerance architecture in cloud computing. *Journal of Network and Computer Applications*. 2016 Feb 1; 61: 81–92.

[41] Li XY, Zhou LT, Shi Y, Guo Y, A trusted computing environment model in cloud architecture. In 2010, International Conference on Machine Learning and Cybernetics 2010 Jul 11 (Vol. 6, pp. 2843–2848). IEEE.

[42] Wang C, Wang Q, Ren K, Cao N, Lou W, Toward secure and dependable storage services in cloud computing. *IEEE transactions on Services Computing*. 2012 Apr; 5(2): 220–232.

[43] Doelitzscher F, Sulistio A, Reich C, Kuijs H, Wolf D, Private cloud for collaboration and e-Learning services: From IaaS to SaaS. *Computing*. 2011 Jan 1; 91(1): 23–42.

[44] Ghomi EJ, Rahmani AM, Qader NN, Load-balancing algorithms in cloud computing: A survey. *Journal of Network and Computer Applications*. 2017 Jun 15; 88: 50–71. (60,118)

# 2 Vulnerabilities in Cloud Computing

*Vikas Chaudhary and Sapna Sinha\**
*Amity University, Noida

## 2.1 INTRODUCTION

As we know, an organization has a limited budget for IT infrastructure, and out of that, 70% is used for running IT infrastructure and 30% is used for expansion. Data is also being generated in abundance due to the explosion of apps. A limited budget and time for acquisition and installation, respectively, do not give flexibility to acquire or update IT infrastructure frequently. There are also many issues like globalization, aging data centers, storage growth, application explosion, cost of ownership, and acquisition acting as a catalyst behind the popularity of cloud computing. None of the sector is untouched by the use of cloud computing. The recent era of the pandemic of COVID-19 is proof of how cloud computing has helped keep services going.

### 2.1.1 WHAT IS CLOUD COMPUTING?

As per NIST [1–3], cloud computing is a ubiquitous, convenient, and on-demand network access model to a shared pool of configurable computing resources such as networks, servers, storage, applications, and services with the feature of rapid elasticity, automatic provision, metered service, and broad network access. The essential characteristic of cloud computing includes the following:

*On-demand self-service*: Customer must pay only for the resources used by them.
*Broad network access*: Since all the resources are available and accessible via the Internet, broad network access is needed.
*Resource pooling*: Resources should be arranged in a pool, and an abstraction layer is added over the physical pool to make it abstract/virtual pool.
*Rapid elasticity*: There should be a facility of auto-provisioning so that the customer can scale up and scale down as per their own requirement.
*Measured service*: Metering service should be built in so that the tariff can be calculated to charge between the customers accordingly.

The cloud services can be offered using different service and deployment models. The different service models of cloud services are the following (Figure 2.1):

1. *IaaS*: Infrastructure-as-a-Service (The customer subscribes to the infrastructure, such as server, storage, and network only; the rest of the things,

DOI: 10.1201/9781003341437-3

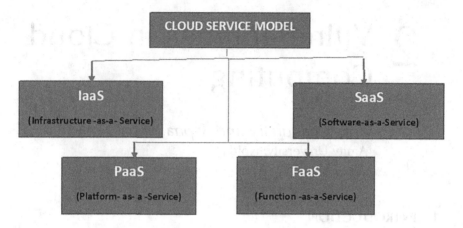

**FIGURE 2.1** Cloud service models.

such as operating system and software installation over the subscribed infrastructure, are managed by the customer.)

2. *PaaS*: Platform-as-a-Service (The customer subscribes to the platform and, along with it, the infrastructure is part of the bundle; customer uploads software of its own choice above it.)

3. *SaaS*: Software-as-a-Service (The customer subscribes for a software and infrastructure, and a platform is also provided along with software, too.)

4. *FaaS*: Function-as-a-Service (The developer is relieved from the infrastructure and the server selection issues are required to execute the function.)

The cloud services are provided by different service providers or organizations that can build their own cloud infrastructure. The deployment model defines the cloud environment, ownership, and its nature. It also defines the resources and management issues related to proper functioning of cloud services.

Different types of cloud computing deployment models are as follows (Figure 2.2):

1. *Public cloud*: Cloud is owned by public, and usually it is free for use; however, security issue is there.

2. *Private cloud*: Cloud is owned by an organization, it is not available for the people outside the organization; hence, more secure in nature.

3. *Hybrid cloud*: Cloud is a combination of both public and private clouds. The service provider decides which part can be made public and which part can be kept private and out of bounds.

4. *Community cloud*: Cloud is available for a group of people who belong to the same ideology.

5. *Multi-cloud*: There are multiple cloud service providers available; the customer can subscribe to multiple vendors.

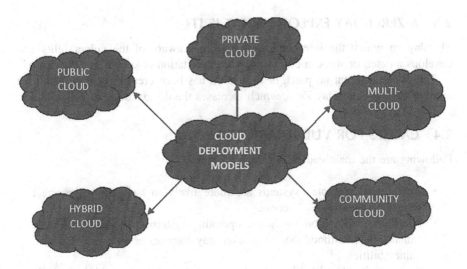

**FIGURE 2.2**   Cloud deployment models.

## 2.1.2 VULNERABILITY IN THE CLOUD

Vulnerability in the cloud is a weakness or flaw that could be used by hackers to break into a computer network without authorization. A hack can run harmful code, install malware, and even steal sensitive data after exploiting a vulnerability. Any vulnerability, which has at least one vector, is an exploitable vulnerability.

Cross-site scripting (XSS), SQL injection, buffer overflows, and open-source exploit kits are just a few of the techniques that can be employed to take advantage of web application flaws.

A popular software has multiple vulnerabilities, which increase the danger of a data leakage or supply chain assault for the many users of the software. These zero-day exploits are listed as a common vulnerability exposure by the Massachusetts Institute of Technology Research and Engineering (Common Vulnerabilities and Exposure) (MITRE [CVE]).

## 2.2   WHAT DISTINGUISHES VULNERABILITY FROM RISK?

Consider risk the likelihood and consequences of a vulnerability being used against you.

A vulnerability poses little risk if its impact and likelihood of being exploited are both modest. On the other hand, there is a high risk if a vulnerability's impact and likelihood of being exploited are both high.

An exploitable vulnerability is one that has at least one verified, functional attack vector. The period between the disclosure of the vulnerability and its patching is known as the window of vulnerability.

## 2.3   A ZERO-DAY EXPLOIT: WHAT IS IT?

The day on which the interested party becomes aware of the vulnerability and develops a patch or workaround to prevent exploitation is known as "Day Zero."

The possibility that no patch or mitigation has been created increases with the number of days after Day Zero, which increases the danger of an effective attack.

## 2.4   CAUSES FOR VULNERABILITIES

Following are the main causes of vulnerabilities:

- *Complexity*: Complex systems are more likely to have flaws, incorrect setups, or unauthorized access.
- *Familiarity*: Common hardware, operating systems, software, and code enhance the likelihood that an attacker may discover or be aware of known vulnerabilities.
- *Connectivity*: The likelihood of a vulnerability increases with a device's level of connectivity.
- *Password management issues*: Brute force may be used to crack weak passwords, and using the same password repeatedly increases the risk of data breaches.
- *Flaws in the operating system*: Operating systems are software, and software has bugs. Operating systems that are insecure by default and let any user log in, possibly allowing the introduction of malware and infections.
- *Internet usage*: Adware and spyware that may be loaded on computers automatically are abundant on the Internet.
- *Software bugs*: Software bugs can be intentionally or unintentionally left by programmers. End users occasionally neglect to update their software, leaving it unpatched and open to exploitation.
- *User input is not checked*: Your website or code may execute undesired SQL instructions if it considers that all input is secure.

## 2.5   CLOUD INFRASTRUCTURE VULNERABILITIES

- *Unauthorized use of the administrative interface*: On-demand self-service in the cloud requires a management interface that is accessible to cloud service users. Because of this, unauthorized access to the administration interface is a vulnerability that is particularly important to cloud systems.
- *Internet protocol weaknesses*: Because of the cloud's constant network access, cloud services are accessible across a network utilizing established protocols. This system is often the Internet. For cloud computing, Internet protocol vulnerabilities like man-in-the-middle attacks are important.
- *Recovery of data vulnerability*: Resources assigned to one user may later be redistributed to another user due to the flexibility and individuality of the cloud. It could be feasible to recover data that was previously written by another user from memory or storage.

- *Transferring data safely*: As we transfer our data to and from the cloud, it may be exposed to prying eyes. As a result, we shouldn't transfer sensitive or private information over an unsecured wireless network or a haphazard public Wi-Fi network. Utilizing our home network and making sure that our data is encrypted is preferable. Our wireless router needs to be password-protected; therefore, we must check. The web URLs of the websites we visit should always be HTTPS rather than HTTP. Encryption is used on HTTPS sites to transport information securely.
- *Session riding and hijacking*: Using a legitimate session key to obtain unauthorized access to the data or services stored on a workstation structure is known as session hijacking. It is related to online application technology and refers to the stealing of a cookie that is used to authenticate a user to a remote server. Vulnerability in the web appliance setup at their disposal offers hackers the chance to carry out a number of nefarious activities. Session riding alters system and network configurations, deletes client data, performs online transactions such as bids and orders, distributes spam to intranet schemes over the Internet, and even opens the firewall.
- *Vendor lock-in*: Immature service providers and novel business structures, which increase the danger of failure and industry extinction, are to blame for this susceptibility. Lock-in makes a customer dependent on a provider for goods and services, making it impossible for them to interact with another provider without incurring high switching fees.
- *Virtual machine (VM) escape*: As contained VMs and physical servers, cloud computing servers employ the compatible OS, business, and web applications. Virtualized cloud computing environments are seriously threatened by the potential for malware or attackers to slightly exploit weaknesses in these systems and applications.
- *Accessing data*: Since the data of customers are stored on the remote servers, it is the responsibility of the service provider to ensure data is available as and when required. Assurance of data accessibility leads to sticking of customer with big giant.
- *Data backup*: In cloud computing, data backup is stored on remote a server; what will happen in case of any disaster and how will data be recovered?
- *Password use*: Multiple hacks and data breaches expose the password through well-known websites and companies due to not using strong and unique passwords.
- *Privacy*: One has to be careful about information that is accessed because some mobile applications and services have access to key accounts such as Facebook and Twitter. For privacy, the customer should review admission grants to server connection, eliminations, and the option of utilization or mistreatment.

References [4,5] stated seven vulnerabilities in cloud computing [5]. They are as follows:

1. *Lack of multifactor authentication for users*: Due to poor passwords and hacking of authentication details most data breaches take place. The stolen log-in details are used by hackers for monetizing by using it or selling it on the dark web. By using multi-factor authentication (MFA), an additional log-in security layer can be added to reduce risk. For exploiting log-in credentials, hackers use various techniques such as phishing, credential stuffing, prior data breaches, reused passwords, reset password spraying, keystroke logging, brute force, and local discovery. Therefore, a multilayer of security is needed to ensure security; multifactor authentication adds an extra layer [6].

2. *No-multifactor authentication for connecting device*: Multifactor authentication for connecting devices can prevent hackers from using the authentication details of others in their devices, because in it, beside using ID and password, a verification code is sent to the trusted device of the user. In this, only the actual user can log in to their account from any other device.

3. *S3 bucket is open and freely available for access*: It is one of the popular storage services of Amazon, but these buckets are unprotected and open because they are accessible by using scripts and tools. Anyone can access these buckets from anywhere using HTTP. As it contains customer sensitive data, it is a critical security risk. For security, very restrictive policies are needed; strict access control policies should be defined in access control lists (ACLs) [7].

4. *Visibility of stored data is not there, so data deletion is incomplete*: On the cloud, customers have reduced visibility of the place where their data is stored physically and they can't verify the secure deletion of their data. Unsecured deletion of data can result in the spread of data across multiple storage devices and the procedure used for deletion of data; remnants of data can be security risk. The risk rises more when multiple cloud service providers are used by one organization [8].

5. *Lambda Command Injection*: Especially in serverless computing, the user can execute arbitrary commands on the host. A lambda function allows running code without provisioning, taking care of administrative issues.

6. *Insecure API*: Application Programs Interfaces (APIs) are used by one software to communicate another software over an unsecure communication channel. These APIs provide open access to data and infrastructure to others.

7. *No clear separation of multitenants*: As thecloud is a multitenant model in which data and applications of multiple customers coexist on the same infrastructure. Multitenancy has its own complexities and needs a clear separation between virtual machines so that data breaches and overlapping of resources are not there.

## 2.6   EFFECTIVE CLOUD SECURITIES

- *BYOD*: Security risks due to the use of BYOD can be mitigated by the use of a centralized management tool.

- *Data management*: Effective data management can help the user to manage their data; the right data is available for all employees.
- *Potential loss of data*: Carefully analyzing the potential cause of a data breach in advance and adopting mitigation strategy will avoid it in future.
- *Implementing security regulations*: Proper use of security regulations and enforcing proper access controls via ACLs is also a good strategy for ensuring security.
- *Access to all infrastructure resources' visibility*: Having access to visibility into all infrastructure resources in the cloud is essential for managing, monitoring, and optimizing cloud-based environment. Cloud services offer various tools and approaches to achieve this visibility, allowing user to monitor performance, track usage, detect issues, and ensure security. While cloud visibility is essential, it's also crucial to balance it with security and compliance considerations. To ensure that only authorized individuals have access to the visibility tools and that sensitive information is protected. Regularly review and adjust to monitoring strategy to align with evolving cloud environment and business needs.
- *Examination of log data in real-time*: Real-time examination of log data can prevent the occurrence of an unusual event handle in advance.
- *Reporting on compliance*: Regular auditing will help in ensuring that all the regulatory compliances are ensured.

## 2.7 VULNERABILITY MANAGEMENT

Vulnerability management [8] can help in dealing with vulnerabilities. It is a cyclic process that includes various steps, such as:

- Vulnerability detection
- Vulnerability assessment
- Vulnerability remediation

The vulnerability detection phase has three sub-phases. (1) Vulnerability scanning in which tools are used to scan the system for vulnerabilities. Penetration testing is used to check the IT test. It can be done manually or automatically or both. Besides these security policies, security awareness, compliance, and how the system responds to security incidents are also checked. Google hacking can also be used through Google advanced search. (2) In the vulnerability assessment phase, different types of vulnerabilities are identified, verified, mitigated, and remediated. Assessment of different types of vulnerability is done, such as network based, host based, wireless network based, application based, and database based. (3) In the vulnerability remediation phase, the code is checked, vulnerabilities are prioritized, and on the basis of priority the vulnerabilities are fixed.

## 2.8   CONCLUSION

The cloud is evolving and it's the same for the security issues. Issues of the past are resolved by now, and the industry is struggling to deal with new surfacing issues. Along with the cloud, the types of attacks are also evolving. Organizations and service providers are to take measures in securing the data and infrastructure in all aspects. Understanding probable risks, threats, and vulnerabilities and mitigating them by using effective tools and techniques is not enough. Due to continuous advancement in technology, forms of threats and vulnerabilities are also evolving. Being vigilant, updated, and adopting suitable measure on time are the keys to ensure the data security of customers. An amalgamation of security concerns and mitigating them at the same time as development will be more appropriate in the future.

## REFERENCES

[1] Mell, P., & Grance, T. NIST SP 800-145, The NIST Definition of Cloud Computing. Available at https://nvlpubs.nist.gov/nistpubs/Legacy/SP/nistspecialpublication800-145.pdf
[2] Cloud Deployment Models – GeeksforGeeks
[3] Mitre.com
[4] https://www.kratikal.com/blog/cloud-vulnerabilities/
[5] Saxena, R., & Gayathri, E. (2021, October). A Study on Vulnerable Risks in Security of Cloud Computing and Proposal of Its Remedies. In Journal of Physics: Conference Series (Vol. 2040, No. 1, p. 012008). IOP Publishing.
[6] Amazon S3 Bucket Security: How to Find Open Buckets and Keep Them Safe. Available at https://bluexp.netapp.com/blog/aws-cvo-blg-amazon-s3-buckets-finding-open-buckets-with-grayhat-warfare
[7] Morrow, T. (2018). 12 Risks, Threats & Vulnerabilities in Moving to the Cloud. Available at https://insights.sei.cmu.edu/blog/12-risks-threats-vulnerabilities-in-moving-to-the-cloud/
[8] Navedita James (2022). Cloud Vulnerability Management: The Detailed Guide. Available at https://www.getastra.com/blog/security-audit/cloud-vulnerability-management/#:~:text=Cloud%20vulnerability%20management%20refers%20to,ensure%20data%20and%20application%20safety

# 3 Cloud Computing Security Issues and Challenges

*Taksheel Saini and Sapna Sinha\**

*Amity University, Noida

## 3.1 INTRODUCTION

Project MAC was given to MIT by DARPA (the military advanced research projects agency) in 1963. This project describes the capability of allowing two or more people to utilize a single computer concurrently, which after several advancements is today known as cloud computing (CC) [7–11].

Cloud computing paradigms and private clouds (this is where the framework is facilitated to provide service to a single user or single-user organization) are designed to cater specifically to the computing needs of a single user or organization, ensuring tailored control and security. Even though it was first made available in 2008, it was still in its development and not very well liked. The public cloud, which is a cloud type where resources are owned or managed by single entity or organization and by that operator, was provided and shared with different tenants (since the cloud is a service like a condo or a house on rent) over our priceless network of networks known as the internet (it has raised concerns regarding poor security). The difficulties that CC and its services encountered included these and several more complex security problems.

In 2011, the idea of hybrid computing (as used by AWS or Microsoft Azure) was introduced. This made it possible to move workloads alternating through the two clouds (public and private), as well as reduce the utilization time and heavy workload or heavy demands of services on both private and public clouds.

The process of delivering a service that includes storing a server, databases, software, etc. online in order to come up with quicker innovation with resource flexibility is known as cloud computing. Activities like using social networking websites are supported by CC. However, the primary goal of CC and the majority of its time are spent on data storage, management, and processing through the global network system known as the internet.

Cloud computing evolved over the several recent years from a potential idea for a commercial advantage to one of the IT industry's fastest-growing segments. Software developers describe the cloud in a different way than a system administrator (SA). Every category or stage of human growth has seen a considerable increase in the demand for secure data storage over the past year, and this trend is expected to continue in the years to come. These needs will also include speedy and

DOI: 10.1201/9781003341437-4

efficient data transfer. More security worries brought on by our increasing reliance on cloud-based services have hampered their uptake in a number of different businesses. Security is seen as the main barrier to CC.

If we look at it from the opposite perspective, cloud security might be enhanced by gathering all the data, or centralizing it, as we say in the IT industry, and then focusing more security resources on that technique. On the other side, we may also envision losing control of the private information. This study consists of research that is specifically focused on the many security-related difficulties [2,11–15].

## 3.2 LITERATURE SURVEY

According to analyst Gartner, there are security vulnerabilities associated with CC. In the June research, titled "Assessing the Security Risks of Cloud Computing," Gartner claims that smart clients would raise difficult questions and take into consideration having a security assessment from an unbiased third party before choosing a cloud vendor [2,15].

According to Gartner, before choosing a certain cloud service provider, clients should raise a few security concerns with the suppliers of cloud-based services. Some of those issues are as follows [2,15].

### 3.2.1 PRIVILEGED USER ACCESS

In this case, if we find ourselves in need of a cloud-based service and bring in a stranger from outside our company, we will want to learn the most about the person who would be handling or managing the data. "Ask providers to supply specific information on the hiring and oversight of privileged administrators, and the controls over their access," Gartner says [2,15].

### 3.2.2 REGULATORY COMPLIANCE

Even when their data are stored by a third party, customers are still accountable for maintaining the security and integrity of their own data. Cloud computing providers who refuse to undergo this scrutiny are "signaling that customers can only use them for the most trivial functions," according to Gartner [2,15].

### 3.2.3 RECOVERY

Our cloud service provider will describe what would happen to the service and the data in the case of a disaster, supposing we lost our data and don't know where it is. "Any offering that does not replicate the data and application infrastructure across multiple sites is vulnerable to a total failure," Gartner says. The cloud service provider (CSP) will describe how to obtain our data in the aforementioned case [2,15].

### 3.2.4 DATA LOCATION

When making use of our cloud service, we will most likely be unaware of the location or country in which our data are stored. "Ask providers if they will commit to storing and processing data in specific jurisdictions, and whether they will make a contractual commitment to obey local privacy requirements on behalf of their customers," Gartner advises [2,15].

## 3.3 CLOUD COMPUTING DEPLOYMENT MODELS

Cloud security issues stem from its service delivery and deployment technologies. Although many MNCs, including AWS, have adopted and used these different cloud model methods. There has been a delayed uptake due to the numerous security concerns that have been identified in both the clouds as well as certain hybrid clouds. The CC deployment models are what determine how our cloud framework or structure will appear, what we may alter, and whether we will be provided with certain services or whether we must construct everything from scratch. The kinds of cloud deployment also determine the relationship between the user and the framework [3,16].

Various cloud deployment models include the following.

### 3.3.1 PUBLIC CLOUD

This open cloud approach allows anybody and any system to access the data. Since everyone on the globe may access its data, it is less secure. Instead of the user, who is the client, this cloud deployment model type is owned by the service provider. It is advantageous since it requires very little upfront investment and no money to set up, and the service provider, not the user, is responsible for maintenance. Privacy and data security issues are major drawbacks, which slow down or prevent the use of the technology [2,3,16].

### 3.3.2 PRIVATE CLOUD

The private cloud differs greatly from the public cloud. It is a one-on-one service, where the relationship between the user or client and the service provider is maintained. For example, if we wanted to rent a house for three months, we would pay the owner three months' worth of rent. In a similar way, when using a private cloud deployment model, we will compensate the service provider for the specific service and the time it took to complete. It is advantageous since it offers more control over the service. It's also excellent for keeping company data that is only accessible to certain individuals or under their management. It's negative because of the greater price, more advantages we obtain, increased investment, and increased maintenance costs (Figure 3.1) [2,3,16].

### 3.3.3 HYBRID CLOUD

Private and public clouds can coexist in a hybrid cloud environment. It offers the best of both cloud worlds for cloud computing. By employing this tactic, we can take use of the public cloud's cost-saving capabilities while hosting the data in a safe setting. Since the hybrid model combines the private and public sectors,

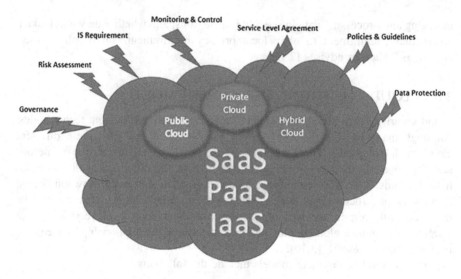

**FIGURE 3.1**   Deployment models in cloud computing [2].

**FIGURE 3.2**   Hybrid cloud deployment model.

businesses that use it can transfer data back and forth. Its affability and control over data transfer makes it preferable. Our data are also safeguarded as these are isolated, and the likelihood of data leak or theft is reduced, while costs are also reduced and extra is only paid when more services are needed. Its high maintenance makes it unpopular, which implies the organization that adopts it will incur large costs (Figure 3.2) [2,3,16].

## 3.4   CLOUD COMPUTING SERVICE DELIVERY MODELS

A specific pre-packaged combination of IT resources offered by a CSP is represented by the cloud computing service delivery model (CCSDM). There are three well-known models for delivering cloud services, and they all present security challenges (Figure 3.3).

These three cloud computing service delivery models are the following:

### 3.4.1   SOFTWARE-AS-A-SERVICE (SAAS)

It is a genuine product that is managed and operated by the service provider. It is a cloud service with a pay-per-use pricing model. The user can access it over the

**Cloud Clients** - Web Browser, Mobile
App, Thin Client, Terminal Emulator

**SaaS** - CRM, Email, VD (Virtual
Desktop), Communication Games, .........

**PaaS** - Database, Development Tools,
Execution Runtime, ..........

**IaaS** - Storage, Network, Virtual
Machines...

**FIGURE 3.3**   Cloud computing service delivery models [17].

internet. Since it provides the full package—infrastructure, OS, platform, and
time—it is a superset of PaaS and IaaS. Businesses support this concept in light of the
COVID-19 epidemic. Independent platform, on-demand service, and subscription-
based billing are its advantages (Figure 3.4) [1,3,16].

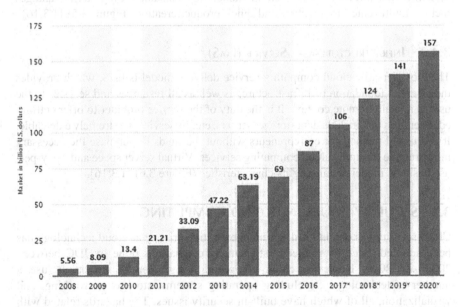

**FIGURE 3.4**   The total size of the public cloud SaaS market worldwide (in billions of U.S.
dollars).

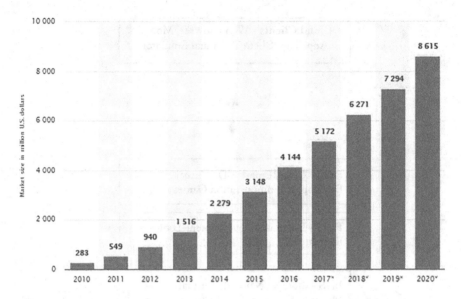

**FIGURE 3.5**   The total size of the public cloud PaaS market worldwide (in millions of U.S. dollars).

### 3.4.2   PLATFORM-AS-A-SERVICE (PAAS)

It is a subset, and the virtual construction of its architecture is comparable to IaaS. In this service delivery model, a vendor aids businesses with middleware, operating systems, web servers, and database management systems (database management system). This information is a cloud model for a distant setting. Its advantages include multi-renter architecture and quick product creation (Figure 3.5) [1,3,16].

### 3.4.3   INFRASTRUCTURE-AS-A-SERVICE (IAAS)

The most versatile cloud computing service delivery model is IaaS, which provides the essential foundation or infrastructure, as well as all resources and services to the user in a totally remote context. It is the duty of the service provider to offer cutting-edge services that include data storage, servers, etc. Its service is extremely extensible. It is a useful method for entrepreneurs without the funds to purchase the necessary infrastructure to supply cloud computing services. Virtual server space and a pay-per-use business model are among its characteristics (Figure 3.6) [1,3,16].

## 3.5   SECURITY ISSUES IN CLOUD COMPUTING

Cloud security has continuously been an executive priority as cloud technology has been adopted. Security ranked first in many evaluations done by IDC between 2008 and 2009. However, cloud computing conglomerates frequently use a number of technologies, including operating systems, storage, networking, and virtualization, all of which have built-in security issues. The hazards related with

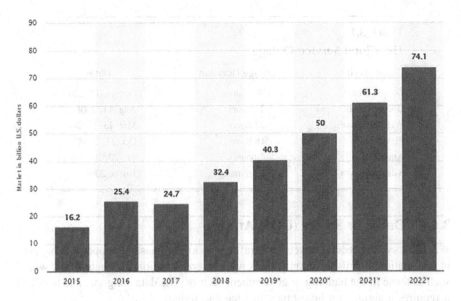

**FIGURE 3.6** The total size of the public cloud IaaS market worldwide (in billions of U.S. dollars).

cloud computing include network intrusions, denial of service assaults, and browser-based attacks. There is a potential that the digital platform may be subjected to a big wave of attacks.

## 3.6 FOLLOWING ARE THE SEVERAL PRESSING SECURITY PROBLEMS IN CLOUD COMPUTING

### 3.6.1 DATA LOSS

It is one of the problems with cloud computing. *Data leaking* is the term used to describe this problem. Our data or information may be disclosed by the hackers if they gain access to our cloud [16].

### 3.6.2 USER ACCOUNT SEIZING

Among the most critical problems, the hacker has complete authority to access any data and engage in unlawful actions if the user's or the company's account is compromised in any way.

### 3.6.3 LACK OF SKILL

These are the primary issues faced by an IT firm that lacks the necessary person with that sort of skill set, whether working, finding an extra feature, or knowing how to utilize it. Therefore, we require a worker with cloud computing expertise.

**TABLE 3.1**

**The Cloud Service Outage**

| Cloud Service | Outage Duration | Dates |
|---|---|---|
| Google Gmail | 30 hours | Oct. 16–17, 2008 |
| Google Gmail, Apps | 24 hours | Aug. 11, 2008 |
| Windows Azure | 22 hours | Mar. 13–14, 2009 |
| FlexiScale | 18 hours | Oct. 31, 2008 |
| Amazon S3 | 7 hours | Jul. 20, 2008 |
| Salesforce.com | 40 minutes | Jan. 6, 2009 |

### 3.6.4 DENIAL OF SERVICE (DOS) ATTACK

When the system receives excessive traffic, this kind of assault happens. It happens in multinational firms or organizations with several locations throughout the world, such as those in the banking or government sectors. The data are gone, and handling it requires a significant investment of time and money.

### 3.6.5 AVAILABILITY

This is close to making information available anytime it is required. This is one of the most pressing challenges for organizations whose missions and safety are crucial. In Table 3.1, you can find instances of well-known outages of top cloud providers discovered in various times of current cloud providers' viability. Availability concerns might also lead to the need to switch suppliers [16].

## 3.7 CLOUD COMPUTING CHALLENGES

There are various issues linked with cloud computing's current utilization since clients continue to have worries about its authenticity. According to many surveys and websites, the main obstacles to enterprises adopting or recognizing cloud computing include the following (Figure 3.7).

### 3.7.1 DATA SECURITY AND PRIVACY

When using cloud computing, it is one of the foremost worries. Data saved in the cloud by users or businesses are private. Cloud security risks include data theft through data leakage, virus infection to computers, system hacks, and cloud identity theft. As a result, that particular organization may suffer a possible loss of money, reputation, and respect (Figure 3.8).

### 3.7.2 PRIVATE CLOUD CREATION

The biggest difficulty with establishing or adopting the private cloud is that the business, organization, IT team, or service provider must develop, install, repair,

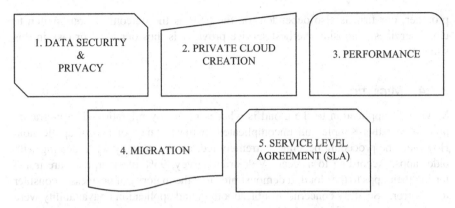

**FIGURE 3.7** Challenges in cloud computing (CC).

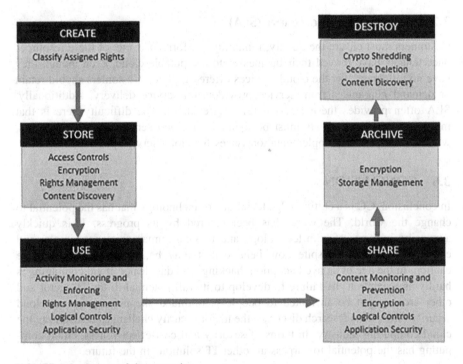

**FIGURE 3.8** Image of data security.

and manage everything on their own. Both the human work and the cloud's smooth operation must be checked by the IT staff. They must verify that duties are being carried out in the designated sequence.

### 3.7.3 PERFORMANCE

Assume that we have a business and that it has applications for the business. Now that those apps have been transferred to a third-party vendor or cloud service provider, our firm is also dependent on the CSP as the outcome of our switch to cloud services. Choosing the best service provider is thus our issue or task in this situation.

### 3.7.4 MIGRATION

Moving an application to the cloud is what is meant by migration. The migration process is rather simple and uncomplicated in the instance of a new application. However, the procedure becomes extremely tedious and lengthy when dealing with older apps. According to a recent Velostrata survey, 95% of enterprises are transferring their apps to the cloud. It demonstrated that the majority of businesses consider it a "horror." Security concerns, troubleshooting, and application unavailability were the most obvious difficulties [16].

### 3.7.5 SERVICE LEVEL AGREEMENT (SLA)

Customers must ensure the quality, reliability, performance, etc. of these resources once tenants have moved their businesses to a reputable cloud, even though they have no influence over the cloud services offered to them. Customers should retain or demand guarantees from service providers on service delivery. Additionally, SLA often provides these (service level agreement). The difficulty here is that multiple SLA requirements must be defined for cloud service delivery methods, which creates a lot of implementation issues for cloud service providers [2,16].

## 3.8 CONCLUSION

In conclusion, CC is a cutting-edge technique or technology that has the potential to change the world. The world has been altered by its progress. It is quickly advancing in terms of both technology and making human existence simpler and easier. Nevertheless, despite how beneficial it may be, we must also exercise caution. In the age of delayed adoption, hacking, and data leaks, cloud computing is hardly an exception. Its failure to develop to its full potential in the IT sector and other areas might be attributed to people's continued skepticism over its cloud security flaws. This research discusses the major security challenges confronting the cloud computing industry. In terms of security and cost-effectiveness, cloud computing has the potential to surpass all other IT solutions in the future.

## REFERENCES

[1] Sen, J. (2015). Security and privacy issues in cloud computing. In *Cloud Technology: Concepts, Methodologies, Tools, and Applications* (pp. 1585–1630). IGI global.
[2] Kuyoro, S. O., Ibikunle, F., & Awodele, O. (2011). Cloud computing security issues and challenges. *International Journal of Computer Networks*, 3(5), 247–255.
[3] Singh, S. K., & Singh, D. K. (2017). Cloud computing: Security issues and challenges. *International Journal of Advances in Engineering & Technology*, 10(3), 338.

[4] Singh, A., & Chatterjee, K. (2017). Cloud security issues and challenges: A survey. *Journal of Network and Computer Applications, 79*, 88–115.

[5] Nadeem, M. A. (2016). Cloud computing: Security issues and challenges. *Journal of Wireless Communications, 1*(1), 10–15.

[6] Popović, K., & Hocenski, Ž. (2010, May). Cloud computing security issues and challenges. In *The 33rd international convention mipro* (pp. 344–349). IEEE.

[7] Verma, A., & Kaushal, S. (2011). Cloud computing security issues and challenges: A survey. In *Advances in Computing and Communications: First International Conference, ACC 2011, Kochi, India, July 22–24, 2011, Proceedings, Part IV 1* (pp. 445–454). Springer Berlin Heidelberg.

[8] Alvi, F. A., Choudary, B. S., Jaferry, N., & Pathan, E. (2012). Review on cloud computing security issues & challenges. iaesjournal. com, 2. *Com, 1 (2)*.

[9] Jathanna, R., & Jagli, D. (2017). Cloud computing and security issues. *International Journal of Engineering Research and Applications, 7*(6), 31–38.

[10] Zissis, D., & Lekkas, D. (2012). Addressing cloud computing security issues. *Future Generation computer systems, 28*(3), 583–592.

[11] Harfoushi, O., Alfawwaz, B., Ghatasheh, N. A., Obiedat, R., Mua'ad, M., & Faris, H. (2014). Data security issues and challenges in cloud computing: A conceptual analysis and review. *Communications and Network, 6*(1), 15–21.

[12] An, Y. Z., Zaaba, Z. F., & Samsudin, N. F. (2016, November). Reviews on security issues and challenges in cloud computing. In *IOP Conference Series: Materials Science and Engineering* (Vol. 160, No. 1, p. 012106). IOP Publishing.

[13] Puthal, D., Sahoo, B. P., Mishra, S., & Swain, S. (2015, January). Cloud computing features, issues, and challenges: A big picture. In *2015 International Conference on Computational Intelligence and Networks* (pp. 116–123). IEEE.

[14] Majadi, N. (2013). Cloud computing: Security issues and challenges. *International Journal of Scientific & Engineering Research, 4*(7), 1515.

[15] Jothipriya, D., & Akila, A. (2016). Literature review: Cloud computing–security issues, technologies and challenges. *Engineering and Scientific International Journal, 3*(2), 1–15.

[16] Padhy, R. P., Patra, M. R., & Satapathy, S. C. (2011). Cloud computing: Security issues and research challenges. *International Journal of Computer Science and Information Technology & Security (IJCSITS), 1*(2), 136–146.

[17] Yang, Y., & Li, Z. (2016). Research on information security enhancement approaches and the applications on HCI systems. *arXiv preprint arXiv:1602.00804*.

# 4 Federated Learning as a Learning Strategy for Secure Cloud Architecture

*Aditya Kumar, Vishal Bhatnagar, and Shyla*

## 4.1 INTRODUCTION

It is evident that with the development in the field of artificial intelligence and machine learning, the potential influence is endless. And without cloud computing technology to handle the enormous volume of data and to supply the computational power necessary to train these algorithms to execute such amazing jobs, this would not have been possible. The most recent additions to the list are ChatGPT and DALLE.

However, because of incidents like the Cambridge Analytica Scandal, users became aware of privacy breaches, and as a result, many nations have already implemented rigorous data policies. How to learn from user data while respecting user privacy has therefore become a big problem for businesses in the industries; how to improve user-sensitive systems, or to learn from user data while maintaining user privacy [1]; or how to learn from user-sensitive data without even acquiring it [2,3].

Researchers at Google first proposed the idea of federated learning [4] in 2016. A comprehensive approach to dispersed and collaborative learning is referred to as federated learning. By training the base model copy on edge devices while maintaining data on the edge device itself, it facilitates security and privacy of users and their data [5–7]. The revised aggregated weights are then shared with edge devices, and these updated model weights from each edge device are then delivered back via encrypted communication to the cloud for aggregation and integration on the base model. And as seen in Figure 4.1, this training cycle will continue until the desired outcome is attained.

## 4.2 TYPES OF FEDERATED LEARNING

Based on the type of feature space they use and whether the base model is pre-trained or not, there can be three types of federated types of learning.

DOI: 10.1201/9781003341437-5

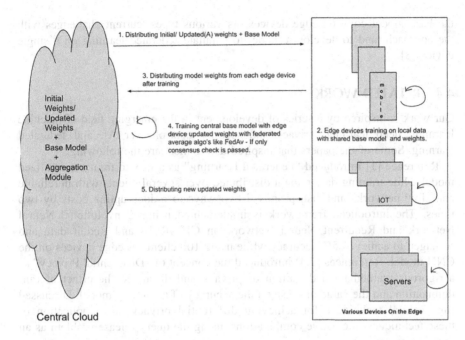

**FIGURE 4.1**  Basic working of a federated learning system [1,3].

### 4.2.1  HORIZONTAL FEDERATED LEARNING

In this type of federated learning, the data set is of the same feature space among the edge devices. Customer details have the same feature space data sets on different edge devices such as training image classification models using the same feature space image data sets.

### 4.2.2  VERTICAL FEDERATED LEARNING

In this type of federated learning, the data are of different feature spaces among the edge devices. For example, customer details have different feature spaces in different data sets on different edge devices but complementary in nature like Netflix customer data and IMDB customer data, which could be used to learn about customer preference.

### 4.2.3  FEDERATED TRANSFER LEARNING

It is a type of federated learning, in which a pre-trained architecture model is used to retrain on a similar problem either with existing weights or new weights. It could easily be understood as an extension of "transfer learning" but federated.

## 4.3  OBJECTIVE

To study federated learning [1,3] as a holistic approach to collaborative and distributed learning, facilitate security and privacy of users and their data by training the base model copy on edge devices, its various types, current challenges with the approach, and to develop a model to simulate federated learning on a single device [8].

## 4.4  RELATED WORK

Our work is inspired by a series of development in the emerging field of machine learning, deep learning, privacy and security control over AI, and federated learning. Some of the papers that inspired us the most are the following.

Reference [1] introduced "Federated Learning" as a way to train a centralized model while training data remain distributed over several clients with unreliable and slow networks and also proposed two ways to reduce uplink costs by two times. The introduced framework is implemented using Convolutional Neural Network and Recurrent Neural Network on CIFAR 10 and Reddit data and managed to achieve 85% accuracy while using 100 clients as edge devices on the CNN model. References [2,4] introduced the concept of "Differential Privacy" as a rigorous mathematical definition of privacy and discussed the effect of randomization and the value of noise on the accuracy of a learning model. Discussed fundamental techniques for achieving differential privacy, and application of these techniques in creative combinations, using the query-release problem as an ongoing example.

Reference [3] explained the concept of "federated learning," and discussed the current challenges while implementing, ideas, and relevant techniques using Gboard on Android as an example. Reference [5] systematically explained the existing work and development in federated learning and supporting technologies, and analyzed the currently used practical application of federated learning, the authors discussed technologies, challenges, and future research possibilities along with current ones. Reference [8] managed to develop the generic framework – Pysyft to implement SMPC, federated learning, and differential privacy on a familiar deep learning API to the end user, their design relies on the exchange of chains of tensors between local and remote workers facilitated using Pytorch API to combine MPC and DP functionalities with the same framework.

It is evident from [1–4,8] how technology evolves with the integration of old and new concepts.

## 4.5  CURRENT CHALLENGES IN FEDERATED LEARNING

There are various current challenges from the point of implementation to communication overhead reduction, communication security between edge devices and central cloud, and data quality control over the edge devices.

### 4.5.1  BALANCING PRIVACY – ACCURACY TRADE-OFF

The sole phase in federated learning, where a hacker might even attempt to obtain sensitive user data, is the phase where model and weights are transmitted back and forth between central cloud and edge devices, but with the aid of auxiliary data. And as it would be dealing with users' sensitive data, this kind of data sniffing cannot be treated carelessly. It is at this point that the principles of differential confidentiality and Secure Multi-Party Computation are necessary [4].

### 4.5.2 SECURE MULTI-PARTY COMPUTATION

Secure multi-party computation hides the model updated weights using various encryption schemes and shares some part of it with edge devices. Then each edge device will share its set of updated encrypted weights with the central server/cloud. And on the central cloud, as expected, it will need every scrambled encrypted part that edge devices shared with each other to decrypt and get average updated weights. But this security comes at a cost of extra computational overhead, along with the high and frequent communication cost among edge devices [4].

### 4.5.3 DIFFERENTIAL PRIVACY

It is a mathematical definition of privacy, and an algorithm can only be differentially private [2,4]. If by looking at the output, one can't tell whether individual data were included in the training set or not. This can be done by altering the values of random individuals' data points in the training data set, thus introducing noise. And this noise and randomization result in a differentially private algorithm at the cost of accuracy [9,10].

Based on requirements, we can adjust the trade-off between privacy and accuracy. As for medical diagnostics on images, priority would be given to privacy, and the algorithm can't suffice the need of a doctor, but initial and accurate results can be gained for initial diagnostics [2].

## 4.6  MANAGING COMMUNICATION OVERHEAD

In federated learning, the edge devices could be mobile devices, Internet of Things (IoT) devices, or even a server. And with these different operating specification and data pipeline which includes Wi-Fi as a medium in between is highly unreliable. The devices are high-latency devices with an unreliable data pipeline [11]. This creates the problem of how to train the model and exchange the updated weight and model efficiently. But with high-compression algorithms and pruning algorithms, the problem of sharing the updated weights and model gets addressed to a certain point. And for training, the model on these edge devices' ideal time is chosen, for example, when the mobile is idle or is in charge.

## 4.7  DATA QUALITY CONTROL AND HANDLING ITS IMPACT

By far, one of the most critical challenges, which could affect the outcomes of federated learning, is the quality of data. If the quality of data fed by the edge devices is not optimum, it could lead to serious complications or accuracy loss.

As the deep learning models are opaque in nature, it is not possible to pinpoint the host's updates and erase their impact on the shared model.

## 4.8 ALGORITHM USED FOR SIMULATION OF FEDERATED LEARNING

The algorithm we used to simulate federated learning is based on the use of virtual workers as edge devices to simulate edge devices and it is working, as shown in Figure 4.2 and explained step by step in Section 4.8.1.

where

Wi = initial weight
Wag = aggregate weight
Wa = updated weight by edge device A
Wb = updated weight by edge device B

### 4.8.1 STEPS

1. Central server/cloud shares the initial model and locally trained weights with virtual worker/edge devices A and B.
2. Virtual worker/edge devices A and B use their local data to train their shared model copy.
3. Then, these updated weights are shared back with the central server/cloud to aggregate.
4. Now, this updated aggregate weight is shared with virtual workers/edge device to train with freshly generated data and share the new updated weight back to the central server/cloud for aggregation.
5. Steps 1 to 4 will be repeated till the desired number of epochs or certain desired accuracy is achieved.

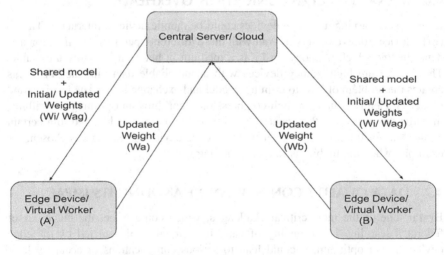

**FIGURE 4.2**  Learning cycle of the used algorithm [8,12–31].

## 4.8.2 Used Data Set

For the simulation purpose of federated learning, we chose the CIFAR 10 data set. The CIFAR 10 data set is made by using 60,000 images of 32 × 32 × 3 colored images of ten categories: bird, cat, airplane, automobile, deer, dog, frog, ship, horse, and truck. The data set is divided in the ratio of 83.34% and 16.66% for the training and testing set. Class-wise, the distribution is 5,000 to 1,000 of training to testing images.

## 4.8.3 Used Model Description

We have used a basic convolutional neural network with softmax activation in the last layer for the classification of ten classes as the shared base model. And the model description is as follows:

```
Net(
    (conv1): Conv2d(3, 64, kernel_size=(3, 3), stride=(1, 1), padding=(1, 1))
    (conv2): Conv2d(64, 128, kernel_size=(3, 3), stride=(1, 1), padding=(1, 1))
    (conv3): Conv2d(128, 256, kernel_size=(3, 3), stride=(1, 1), padding=(1, 1))
    (pool): MaxPool2d(kernel_size=2, stride=2, padding=0, dilation=1, ceil_mode=False)
    (fc1): Linear(in_features=4096, out_features=500, bias=True)
    (fc2): Linear(in_features=500, out_features=10, bias=True)
    (dropout): Dropout(p=0.25, inplace=False)
)
```

As our data are of image type and have the same feature space, which makes our learning model based on horizontal federated learning.

## 4.9 DATA PREPROCESSING

For data pre-processing, we simply convert the data to tensor and normalized image data. For pre-processing image data, we can also augment images using various filters and techniques such as rotation and flipping for increasing the amount of data. But for our simulation purpose, we didn't use any of the augmentation techniques.

### 4.9.1 To Tensor

*Tensors*: In machine learning and deep learning, matrices over the dimension of two are known as tensors. In Python, tensors are represented using an N-dimensional array (ndarray). In machine learning, tensors are used to represent input, output, and immediate product of a series of operations during learning and evaluation to representation.

The first step in pre-processing the CIFAR 10 data set is to convert it to a tensor, to work with it further.

**TABLE 4.1**

**Description of the Result Achieved Using Federated Learning on CNN Model Architecture Performed on CIFAR 10 Data Set**

| Model | Epochs | Training Loss | Test Loss | Test Accuracy |
|---|---|---|---|---|
| Proposed model for simulation | 40 | 0.4644 | −6.4542 | 76% |

### 4.9.2 NORMALIZATION

Normalization of an image consists of simple steps:

- Normalization of the image, i.e., scaling the image pixel between 0 and 1, this can be achieved by simply dividing the pixel values with a maximum value of the pixel.
- Pixel centering – in this, pixel values are scaled to have 0 mean.
- Pixel standardization – in this, pixel values are scaled to have unit variance and 0 mean.

In our model, images are normalized with the mean = (0.5,0.5,0.5) and std = (0.5,0.5,0.5).

These two steps are done for both training and testing data sets.

## 4.10 RESULT ANALYSIS

After training the used model with a learning rate of 0.01 with SGD as an optimizer for 40 epochs, we had the following results (Table 4.1).

One of the objectives of the study to simulate federated learning using the generic framework, Pysyft has been achieved successfully on the CIFAR 10 data set with a testing accuracy of 76%. The model accuracy can be improved with an increased number of epochs and varying hyperparameter values.

## 4.11 CONCLUSION AND FUTURE SCOPE

Federated learning provides edge devices a noble way to cooperate and create a shared prediction model while completely rejecting the idea of sharing any training data at all. In this study, the authors had investigated federated learning as an extensive technique for distributed and collaborative learning that promotes the security and privacy of users and their data by training the base model copy on edge devices while maintaining data on the edge devices themselves, and further aggregating and integrating centrally. The authors managed to use federated learning using deep learning on Cifar10 dataset CIFAR 10 data set with 0.01 of learning rate on SGD with 40 epochs. Deep learning models are quite known for the huge volume of data they require to get trained and infer successfully. The General Data Protection Regulation (GDPR) and strict laws regarding the use of user data made the companies hesitant to share and use users' sensitive data to make an uncertain AI model which is keeping the potential growth of AI. Federated learning is a boon for such heavy data-reliant industries to provide a private and secure way to learn from users' sensitive data without even accessing it. As it is still in the early stages, there are certain challenges with this approach. But with the current and upcoming advancements, it will get better and better. With the advancement of this approach, we may see it as a core concept of upcoming approaches, or its variant to perform learning on some of the most data-sensitive departments like medical and banking.

## REFERENCES

1. C. Dwork, "Differential Privacy", *International Colloquium on Automata, Languages, and Programming ICALP*, 2006.
2. B. McMahan and D. Ramage, "Federated Learning: Collaborative Machine Learning without Centralized Training Data", *Google AI Blog*, 2017.
3. C. Dwork and A. Roth, "The Algorithmic Foundations of Differential Privacy", *Foundations and Trends® in Theoretical Computer Science*, vol. 9, no. 3–4, pp. 211–407, 2014.
4. J. Konečný et al., "Federated Learning: Strategies for Improving Communication Efficiency", *NIPS Workshop on Private Multi-Party Machine Learning*, 2017.
5. C. Zhang et al., "A Survey on Federated Learning", *Elsevier – Knowledge-Based Systems*, vol. 216, p. 106775, 2021.
6. C. Xu et al., "An Intrusion Detection System Using a Deep Neural Network with Gated Recurrent Units", *IEEE Access*, vol. 6, pp. 697–707, 2018.
7. C. Yin et al., "A Deep Learning Approach for Intrusion Detection Using Recurrent Neural Networks", *IEEE State Key Laboratory of Mathematical Engineering and Advance Computing*, vol. 10, pp. 109–125, 2017.
8. T. Ryffel et al., "A Generic Framework for Privacy-Preserving Deep Learning", arXiv, 2018.
9. F. Chen, R. Dou, M. Li, and H. Wu, "A Flexible QoS-Aware Web Service Composition Method by Multiobjective Optimization in Cloud Manufacturing", *Computers and Industrial Engineering*, vol. 99, pp. 423–431, 2016.
10. F. Smarandache, "A Unifying Field in Logics. Neutrosophy: Neutrosophic Probability, Set and Logic", *American Research Press*, pp. 1–141, 1999.
11. H. Wang, F. Smarandache, and Y. Q. Zhang, "Interval Neutrosophic Sets and Logic: Theory and Applications in Computing", *Infinite Study*, vol. 5, 2005.
12. J. S. Dyer, "Maut—Multiattribute Utility Theory. In: Multiple Criteria Decision Analysis: State of the Art Surveys", *International Series in Operations Research & Management Science*, vol. 78, 2005. 10.1007/0-387-23081-5_7
13. J. Ye, "Multicriteria Decision-Making Method Using the Correlation Coefficient under Single-Valued Neutrosophic Environment", *International Journal of General Systems*, vol. 42, no. 4, pp. 386–394, 2013.
14. J. Ye, "Similarity Measures between Interval Neutrosophic Sets and Their Applications in Multicriteria Decision Making", *Journal of Intelligent & Fuzzy Systems*, vol. 26, no. 1, pp. 165–172, 2013.
15. J. Ye, "Single Valued Neutrosophic Cross-Entropy for Multicriteria Decision Making Problems", *Applied Mathematical Modelling*, vol. 38, no. 3, pp. 1170–1175, 2014.
16. J. Konečný et al., "Federated Learning: Strategies for Improving Communication Efficiency", *NIPS Workshop on Private Multi-Party Machine Learning*, 2016.

17. K. T. Atanassov and G. Gargov, "Interval-Valued Intuitionistic Fuzzy Sets", *Fuzzy Sets and Systems*, vol. 3, pp. 343–349, 1989.

18. K. T. Atanassov, "Intuitionistic Fuzzy Sets", *Fuzzy Sets and Systems*, vol. 20, pp. 87–96, 1986.

19. K. T. Atanassov, "Operators over Interval-Valued Intuitionistic Fuzzy Sets", *Fuzzy Sets and Systems*, vol. 64, pp. 159–174, 1989.

20. Kotian et al., "Realtime Detection of Network Anomalies Using Neural Network", In *IEEE International Conference on Smart Technologies in Computing, Electrical and Electronics*, pp. 240–245, 2020.

21. L. A. Zadeh, "Fuzzy Sets", *Information and Control*, vol. 8, no. 3, pp. 338–356, 1965.

22. L. Heilig, E. Lalla-Ruiz and S. Voß, "A cloud brokerage approach for solving the resource management problem in multi-cloud environments", *Computers and Industrial Engineering*, vol. 95, pp. 16–26, 2016.

23. N. Paulauskas and J. Auskalnis, "Analysis of data pre-processing influence on intrusion detection using NSL-KDD data set", in Proc. Open Conf. Elect., Electron. Inf. Sci. (eStream), pp. 1–5, 2017.

24. P. Liu and Y. Wang, "Multiple attribute decision-making method based on single-valued neutrosophic normalized weighted Bonferroni mean", *Neural Computing and Applications*, vol. 25, no.7, pp. 2001–2010, 2014.

25. R. Buyya, C. S. Yeo, S. Venugopal, J. Broberg and I. Brandic, "Cloud computing and emerging IT platforms: vision, hype, and reality for delivering computing as the 5th utility", *Future Generation Computer Systems*, vol. 25, no. 6, pp. 599–616, 2009.

26. R. R. Kumar, S. Mishra, and C. Kumar, "Prioritizing the solution of cloud service selection using integrated MCDM methods under Fuzzy environment", *The Journal of Supercomputing*, vol. 73, no. 11, pp. 4652–4682, 2017.

27. R. X. Nie, J. Q. Wang and H. Y. Zhang, "Solving solar-wind power station location problem using an extended weighted aggregated sum product assessment (WASPAS) technique with interval neutrosophic sets", *Symmetry*, vol. 9, no. 7, p. 106, 2017.

28. S. Chou, T. T. T. Duong and N. X. Thao, "Renewable energy selection based on a new entropy and dissimilarity measure on an interval-valued neutrosophic set", *Journal of Intelligent & Fuzzy Systems*, vol. 40, no. 6, pp. 11375–11392, 2021.

29. Shyla et al., "Machine Learning Algorithm Performance Evaluation for Intrusion Detection", *Journal of Information Technology Management*, vol. 13, no. 1, 2021.

30. T. L. Saaty, "How to Make a Decision: The Analytic Hierarchy Process", *European Journal of Operational Research*, vol. 48, no. 1, pp. 9–26, 1990.

31. Z. Ahmad et al., "Network Intrusion Detection System: A Systematic Study of Machine Learning and Deep Learning Approaches", *Wiley: Transactions on Emerging Telecommunications Technologies*, 2020. 10.1002/ett.4150

# 5 Data Breach in Cloud Computing Due to Misconfigurations

*Sameer Mehra, Sapna Sinha\*, and Vikas Chaudhary*
\*Amity University, Noida

## 5.1 INTRODUCTION

Cloud computing is based on the pay-as-you-go model. In cloud computing, the customer has to pay only for the resources that they use and only for the time it is used, i.e., when the resources are at their disposal.

Cloud computing has revolutionized everything. It helps in reducing the capital expenditure, i.e., the cost related to buying the infrastructure. Rather than capital expenditure, it focuses on the operational expenditure. Operational expenditure means the cost of the resources that customers are using. Cloud computing helps us in easily accessing the IT resources over the internet. IT resources include storage, networking, software, databases, analytical tools, and many more.

Cloud computing made everything so easy and effective. Cloud computing has many advantages but along with advantages, it provides us with a lot of resources, but it has limitations also.

As each and every resource is accessible only through the internet, it is important to understand that cloud computing also comes with the lot of security risks. To overcome this security risk, to take in proper consideration who possesses the security risk to the data saved in the cloud, and the services provided by the cloud, for these purposes, the cloud is based on the shared responsibility model. Both the customer and the vendor have their own responsibility.

## 5.2 LITERATURE REVIEW

In order to understand the cloud computing basics and services and cloud security, several resources were taken into consideration. This section provides a review literature to set the foundation on what we will be discussing.

Absa S. discussed cloud computing and the need for cloud computing. Along with this, there is discussion about different cloud services [1].

According to Ahmed Albugmi et al., cloud computing is simple and offers us a variety of IT resources. The model of cloud computing is based on pay as you go.

DOI: 10.1201/9781003341437-6

Along with many benefits of cloud computing, there are some risk and security concerns also [2].

Paul S. Wooley discussed cloud computing and security risks associated with cloud computing. He discussed the cloud services and examples of cloud services we are using, e.g., AWS Beanstalk, Google app engine, Google docs programs [3].

Qahtan Shallal and Mohammad Bokhari discussed in their paper the different cloud service models, including Iaas, Saas, and Pass. They have also discussed the shared responsibility model, which means in terms of cloud computing what type of responsibility is borne by the vendor and user [4].

B. Patel in his paper discussed the cloud services and different cloud computing deployment models that are public cloud, private cloud, hybrid cloud; he also discussed the comparison between each and every deployment model [5].

Deepak Verma and Rajesh Tyagi discussed the cloud computing services and deployment models, and also talked about the cloud computing security including the cloud data security [6].

## 5.3  MOTIVATION

The motivation behind this chapter is the authors' interest in the topics. Cloud computing fascinates me a lot. Being a cloud computing enthusiast I have gained the knowledge of different clouds, such as Microsoft Azure, Google Cloud Platform (GCP), and Amazon Web Services (AWS). The authors came to know that somehow every cloud computing platform offers the same things but has different names. They all have different cost structures. Irrespective of cost, in the end, the customer always looks for the security in the cloud and whether their data will be safe or not. During the configuration part, the author misconfigured the setting of shared access signature (SAS), which led to a data breach. This misconfiguration motivated the authors to write a chapter about all the misconfigurations in the cloud security setting leading to a data breach.

## 5.4  TYPES OF CLOUD DEPLOYMENT MODELS

### 5.4.1  PRIVATE CLOUD

In a private cloud, there is only a single tenant. The resources don't get shared with the other tenants. It is dedicated to only a single organization. It is basically on the premise. It includes benefits like scalability, elasticity, access control, and security.

In this, all the resources are accessed by only one customer. It is also known as isolated access.

### 5.4.2  PUBLIC CLOUD

In this, services are maintained by the third-party vendors, e.g., Microsoft Azure, AWS, GCP. In a public cloud, resources are available for anyone to purchase. Here we see the concept of resource pooling. Resource pooling means that the scalable services are being offered to serve multiple clients at the same time.

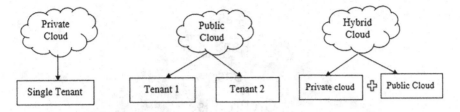

**FIGURE 5.1**  Cloud deployment models.

In the case of a public cloud, there comes a shared responsibility model about which we will discuss shortly.

### 5.4.3  HYBRID CLOUD

It is the combination of both the private and public cloud. If we talk in regards to application, then we can say the application is running in a combination of different environments.

The hybrid cloud helps us in securing our data in the way that an application is the one we should access over the internet. Therefore, the application needs to be deployed on a public cloud, whereas the database, which uses the application, can't be deployed over to the internet because of confidential data it holds, like information about the users, and thus the database needs to be deployed on a private cloud (Figure 5.1).

## 5.5  CLOUD COMPUTING SERVICES

### 5.5.1  IaaS (INFRASTRUCTURE AS A SERVICE)

This service allows the customer to access the storage, networking, virtual machine, server, and other resources. In IaaS, the user can decide about what type of OS is needed, number of cores, size of memory, data storage capacity, networking, and processing power.

Under the shared responsibility model in IaaS, the user is responsible for securing the OS, application configuration, application data storage, and networking. In IaaS, the user has access to a lot of OS images and one can choose from the pool and configure the infrastructure according to the need.

Some examples of IaaS are Aws EC2 instances, Google Compute Engine, and Microsoft Azure.

### 5.5.2  PaaS (PLATFORM AS A SERVICE)

PaaS actually provides the user with the platform. Unlike IaaS, the user first needs to configure the infrastructure and then carry out the work. In PaaS, the user will get the platform to carry out their task without worrying about the infrastructure. An example of PaaS includes AWS Beanstalk, which helps the user to easily deploy and manage their web application.

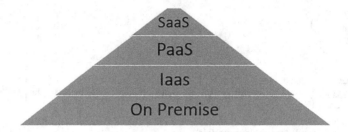

**FIGURE 5.2**   Cloud service models.

Under the shared responsibility model in PaaS, the user is responsible for securing the application and application configuration. Securing the identity and access control and application data storage is the responsibility of both the customer and vendor and securing the physical security, operating system, network flow control, and host infrastructure is the responsibility of the vendor.

### 5.5.3   SaaS (Software as a Service)

SaaS is a service in which the applications are delivered over the internet as a service. We don't need to worry about the software to be installed, or about the hardware requirement for downloading the software.

SaaS made it easy for developers to leverage the benefit of this service and carry out the main task, without worrying about the hardware.

SaaS can also be termed on-demand software. There is a marketplace in every cloud environment from where we can use any software we want to. Examples of SaaS are Microsoft 365, Eclipse, Zoom, Salesforce, etc.

Under the shared responsibility model in SaaS, securing the application configuration is the responsibility of the customer. Securing the identity and access control is the responsibility of both the customer and the vendor and securing the physical security, OS, application data storage, application, network flow control, and host infrastructure is the responsibility of the vendor (Figure 5.2).

## 5.6   CHARACTERISTICS OF CLOUD COMPUTING

### 5.6.1   Resource Pooling

Resource pooling is when multiple clients are being provided with provisional and scalable services. It is used to serve multiple clients at one time.

### 5.6.2   Large Network Access

Cloud computing has a large network access; cloud resources can be accessed from anywhere in the world. We can access the resources from any device, mobile, or laptop.

### 5.6.3  ON-DEMAND SELF-SERVICE

Cloud computing has offered us the ability to utilize or use the resources when their demand arises, thus giving us flexibility.

### 5.6.4  RAPID ELASTICITY

Capabilities can be elastically provisioned and released, and in some cases automatically, to scale rapidly outward and inward commensurate with demand.

### 5.6.5  PAY AS YOU GO

In cloud computing, we don't pay for the resources that we don't use. This is what makes cloud computing cost effective. Whatever the resources we use, we pay only for them, and as the demand grows, so does the amount.

### 5.6.6  SCALING

Scaling is the process where the cloud resources can be scaled down or scaled up as per the demand. When the demand will be less, resources will be scaled down automatically.

## 5.7  WHAT IS THE SHARED RESPONSIBILITY MODEL?

Every cloud computing platform is based on the shared responsibility model. This model is like a cloud security framework that states that the security obligation is both on the vendor and the user.

This model is related to securing everything within the cloud environment, which includes hardware, software, networking, storage, and many more.

Under this model, both parties, that is the vendor and the customer, have the responsibility of securing what lies inside the cloud environment. Both parties have a different responsibility in term of different cloud services being offered like IaaS, SaaS, and PaaS.

With every services, the customer chooses, the cloud comes with the responsibility. For some services, the customer is solely responsible, for some the cloud provider is solely responsible, and for some services both are mutually responsible (Figure 5.3).

## 5.8  CLOUD COMPUTING SECURITY

Cloud computing security includes the measure to prevent the resources from vulnerable attacks. There are a lot of security mechanisms available within the cloud to protect the data, storage, application, and resources.

There are different applications of cloud security and the role of each application is to prevent data, storage, networking, and resources from unauthorized access. Since all of our data are on cloud, we need to be more cautious and well advanced in

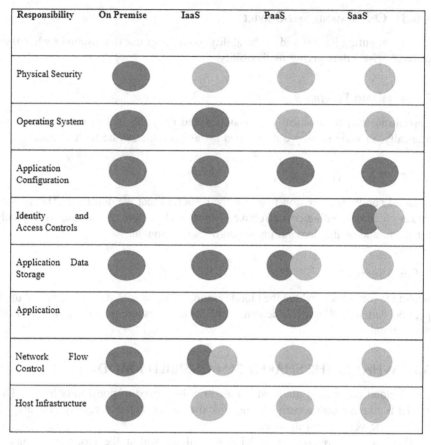

| Responsibility | On Premise | IaaS | PaaS | SaaS |
|---|---|---|---|---|
| Physical Security | | | | |
| Operating System | | | | |
| Application Configuration | | | | |
| Identity and Access Controls | | | | |
| Application Data Storage | | | | |
| Application | | | | |
| Network Flow Control | | | | |
| Host Infrastructure | | | | |

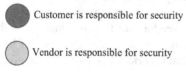

Customer is responsible for security

Vendor is responsible for security

Both the customer and cloud vendor is responsible for security

**FIGURE 5.3** Shared responsibility model.

terms of security mechanisms in order to protect our data and resources deployed on the cloud.

Cloud computing offers multifactor authentication service to secure the resources. In multifactor authentication, we don't only need to type the password to get access but other factors are also considered. In Microsoft Azure, there is an Azure active directory multifactor authentication service like scanning a finger print or typing the code to receive on a phone apart from the password; the aim is to keep the resources secure.

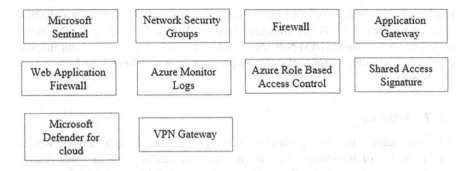

FIGURE 5.4  Cloud security mechanisms.

Other security parameters include implementation of user policies, group policies, IAM (identity and access management), security groups, and firewall settings.

If we talk about cloud computing security mechanisms available in Azure, then
we have (Figure 5.4):

- Microsoft Sentinel
- Microsoft Defender for Cloud
- Azure Monitor Logs
- Azure Role Based Access Control(RBAC)
- Shared Access Signature
- Network Security groups
- Firewall
- VPN Gateway
- Application Gateway
- Web Application Firewall

Encryption and decryption are the basic levels of cloud security mechanism; all data
in the cloud are secured using encryption. Cloud security mechanisms play an
important role in securing the resources and prevent any data breach.

Proper configuration of cloud security settings is vital to prevent unauthorized
access to the resources and prevent data breach. Any misconfiguration in any of the
cloud security settings can easily allow a third person to access our resources and
data and thus lead to a data breach.

## 5.9  HOW CAN A MISCONFIGURATION IN A CLOUD SECURITY SETTING LEAD TO A DATA BREACH?

As discussed earlier, in any kind of security mechanisms, misconfiguration in any
component can make it easier for the intruder to access available resources.

### 5.9.1  IAM (IDENTITY AND ACCESS MANAGEMENT)

IAM aims at finding what kind of role is being assigned to the particular user.
Different users have assigned different roles. Misconfiguration of IAM policies leads

to a breach of data security. An IAM misconfiguration could lead to catastrophe that once the hacker has found any vulnerability in the IAM policy, he can easily access the information related to IAM policies and roles and on the basis of which an attacker can easily find different roles of different people within the cloud, thus leading to a data breach.

### 5.9.2   FIREWALL

A firewall helps in preventing our cloud resources to be accessed by anyone who is not in the list of incoming addresses of who has access to these resources. A misconfiguration in the firewall security setting can result in unauthorized access to our resources.

### 5.9.3   VPN

A VPN is the sort of encrypted connection over the internet to communicate securely site-to-site. In a cloud environment, a VPN service is being provided by different name by different cloud vendors, e.g., Azure VPN, AWS VPN. Misconfiguration in the VPN can easily expose an internal corporate network, thus leading to a data breach.

### 5.9.4   OVER PERMISSION TO ACCESS

Giving excessive permission to the user puts the application at a higher risk of being authorized by a third person who doesn't have the proper credential to access it. Therefore, permission should be in limits and clearly defined.

### 5.9.5   MISCONFIGURATION IN THE STORAGE ACCESS

A misconfiguration in the storage access means not setting the boundaries of who have access to the storage and who does not have. In Azure, shared access signature is used to provide access to the storage to those people on whom we can't trust. Therefore, we should limit the access to the storage using proper configuration settings. Misconfigured cloud security settings always pose higher security risk to the resources.

Some of the risks that are caused by a misconfiguration of a cloud security setting include the following:

- *Data breach*:It refers to the incident where the information of the user gets stolen without his/her information. There can be may reason behind data breach, e.g., stolen or weak credentials.
- *Data loss*:Data loss means when sensitive information was leaked from the system due to theft, malwares, and viruses.
- *Leakage of data*:A leakage of data in the cloud occurs when the data on the private cloud exposed to the internet.

- *VM (virtual machine) theft:*Virtual machine theft occurs when the hacker gets unrestricted access to the VM contents.
- *Threat to APIs:*APIs are the primary resource that interacts with the cloud resource on request. They need to be secured, if left unprotected, and then can easily be exploited and hackers can gain access to the APIs.

## 5.10  PROPOSED

There are so many security mechanisms in place in order to secure the cloud infrastructure. Still, somehow hackers get access because of misconfigurations in security setting, which makes the hacking process easy.

What I have to propose is the use of the threat of an intelligence security mechanism, the honeypot technology. Even at every level of security settings, this technology needs to be in place, even if somehow a misconfiguration is there in the security settings, then cloud security mechanism should update the user of those misconfigurations and activate the honeypot technology. By the time the user makes a security configuration correct at that time, this technology makes the system safe from the hacker by luring them, by which they feel like they are gaining access, but in reality it will just be an illusion and by the time user can make the security configurations setting correct.

## 5.11  CONCLUSION

The cloud is being adopted by many organizations, even by the start-ups to not to incur the cost of capital expenditure, and with the belief that their data can be accessed from anywhere in the world. It is of utmost importance to configure the cloud security setting with efficiency and effectiveness.

Data are the new currency and no one would like their data to be accessed by others who don't even have the authority to access it. To secure resources, proper implementation of security settings should be done with precision and proper group policies, user policies, and security policies needed to be implemented. Resources in the cloud will always be at higher risk if a security setting will not be configured properly and effectively.

While configuring the security settings, the user must keep in mind what type of service should be accessed by the people over the internet and what services should not be accessed. Along with the access, the user must enable the different security policies, and never forget to enable the multifactor authentication.

## REFERENCES

[1] Absa, S. 2019, 'Performance analysis of cloud computing services'. Available at http://hdl.handle.net/10603/302800.
[2] Albugmi, A., Alassafi, M. O., Walters, R., Wills, G. 2016, 'Data security in cloud computing', F.ifth International Conference on Future Generation Communication Technologies.

[3] Wooley, P. S. 2011, 'Identifying cloud computing security risk'.
[4] Shallal, Q., Bokhari, M. 2016, 'Cloud computing service models: A comparative study', *IEEE Network*. 16–18.
[5] Patel, B. 2021, 'Cloud computing deployment models: A comparative study', *International Journal of Innovative Research in Computer Science & Technology*, 9. 10.21276/ijircst.2021.9.2.8.
[6] Verma, D., Tyagi, R. 2018. 'Cloud computing security: A review'.

# 6 A State-of-the Art Survey on Various Attacks and Security Tools at the Virtualization Layer of Cloud Computing
## A Virtual Network Security Perspective

Aditya Nautiyal, Shubhangi Saklani, Preeti Mishra,
Satender Kumar, and Harshit Bisht

## 6.1 INTRODUCTION

The pandemic has caused various organizations to upgrade their working model and shift toward opting for more cloud-based service platforms. It has introduced serious vulnerabilities and simultaneously created new opportunities for people working in the field of security. As a result, virtualization security has taken on the role of data security and network security, causing a great deal of enthusiasm among the people tackling these challenges. Google reported one of the most popular attacks, i.e., "Threat Horizon" in November 2021 that forced crypto mining techniques to hack 86% of user accounts [1]. As per the report of Amazon in 2021, various data breaches caused network service outages for weeks and disrupted business throughout the country [2]. Based on current trends, there are more chances of similar network-related threats in virtualization, such as a SQL injection [3], distributed denial-of-service (DDoS) attack, and man-in-the-middle (MITM) attack [3], etc.

MITM is a sort of attack that allows an attacker to gain control of a user's network without being discovered. A DDoS attack is comparable to a denial of service (DoS) attack in that it originates from several, coordinated sources. The growing number of network attacks on virtualization has increased the need for virtualization security. It is a combination of software and hardware-based security solutions for securing a virtualized IT environment. There exist various traditional

DOI: 10.1201/9781003341437-7

security solutions which are being used by various researchers in virtualization scenarios, such as Network-based Intrusion Prevention System (NIPS) [4]. NIPS is a software system that is used to analyze a network as well as preserve its confidentiality, integrity, and availability.

NIPS's main functionality includes protection of the network from threats like DoS, unauthorized usage, etc. An Intrusion Detection System (IDS) is a security tool that captures, analyzes the network traffic and system's log by scanning the network for unusual, suspicious activities. A Network-based Intrusion Detection System (NIDS) [5] is usually placed at network points such as gateways or routers to detect the security threats. In order to secure a virtualization layer effectively, the traditional tools are no longer sufficient. One has to relentlessly search for tools that are specifically designed for virtualization.

Moreover, there are various design constraints at different layers of virtualization. Therefore, the same tool can not be deployed at all virtualization layers. Hence, it is crucial to classify all the tools according to the layered architecture of virtualization. Some of the attacking tools that can be deployed at the virtual machine (VM) layer are SQLMap [6], Xerosploit [7], hping3 [8], HOIC [Cloudflare], and Tor's Hammer [9]. In addition, the attacking tools that can be deployed at virtual machine monitor (VMM) layer are HInjector [10], Xensploit [11], Blue pill, SubVirt [12], Canvas [13], etc. SQLMap is a penetration testing tool that is free of cost. Xensploit [11] is a MITM attacking tool at VMM level. The hping3 can be used as an attacking tool for sending custom TCP/IP packages to display target replies.

Furthermore, some network security tools that can be deployed at VM or network points are IronWASP [Ironwasp], Argus [14], and Inviciti [15–17]. Some of the tools that can be deployed at the hypervisor (VMM) layer are LibVMtrace [18], SolarWinds Virtualization Monitor [Solarwinds], V-Sight [19], and OpManager [Engine]. TLS prober [Kali] is an attacking tool, used to identify the implementation used by SSL/TLS services. The OwaspZAP [Zaproxy] is a open-source web scanner tool used to perform penetration tests and intercept vulnerabilities in the website with help of auto scanners. The specified tools have been classified at both VMM layer and VM layer. The major contributions can be summarized as follows:

- Detailed description and taxonomy of attacking and security tools at VM and VMM level.
- Detailed description and taxonomy of various attacking and attacking tools at VM and VMM level.
- Comparative description of mentioned attacking and security tools, respectively.
- Case study on eXplainable Artificial Intelligence (XAI) for network attack analysis tools.

The chapter is organized as follows. Section 6.2 shows the related work done in the virtual network environment. Section 6.3 discusses the taxonomy of network security and attacking tools in various virtualization layers. Section 6.4 describes different attacking tools, which are specific to the VM/VMM layer. Section 6.5 provides the detail of the network security tools based on the VM/VMM.

Section 6.6 includes the demonstration of case study on network traffic analysis using XAI libraries. Finally, we have concluded our paper in Section 6.7.

## 6.2   RELATED WORK

Recently, the cloud security issues and the security of the virtual network have become a key interest for researchers. During this phase of virtualization, issues such as network breaches, VM layer attacks, and hypervisor attacks have become more popular than earlier. Nevertheless, many researchers are working to find a better solution to the problem. There are many security tools provided for virtual network attacks.

Conti et al. [20] have offered a taxonomy of known cloud forensic solutions in order to better enlighten both the research and practical communities, as well as an in-depth review of present traditional digital forensic tools and cloud-specific forensic analysis tools.

Agarwal et al. [21] have primarily focused on network layer security by providing extensive information about various dedicated attacking and security technologies. The discussion of several tool kinds, such as WEP and WPA-PAK key crackers, wireless network detectors, password crackers, and packet analyzers, had enlightened us.

Repetto et al. [22] discussed various tools based on the extended Berkeley Packet Filter (eBPF) for comprehensive and efficient packet analysis in virtualized environments. He also exhibited vNetTracer, an eBPF-based network traffic tracer in a virtualized context.

Mishra et al. [23] have discussed a VM monitoring security model called Malicious Network Packet Detection (MNPD), which analyzes VMs from the outside at both the network and virtualization layers in a cloud setting. MNPD analyzes network traffic behaviorally at the Cloud Networking Server (CNS), providing key network-level defense against intrusions. This work's weakness is that it uses an obsolete statistical learning technique (Random Forest) to learn network activity behaviors, whereas more modern and accurate XAI-based algorithms are already available. To the finest of our awareness, no survey exists that categorizes security and assaulting tools at the network layer of distinct virtualization levels. We attempted to categorize various network layer tools in a virtualized environment based on their capabilities and security characteristics and had also organized them into further subgroups depending on their operation at different virtualization levels.

## 6.3   TAXONOMY OF NETWORK ATTACKS AND SECURITY TOOLS AT THE VIRTUALIZATION LAYER

This section discusses the taxonomy of several network-based tools at the virtualization layer, as shown in Figure 6.1. The monitoring tools are divided into two classes, i.e., attacking and security tools. Each category is further subdivided into two subcategories, i.e., VM-layer tools and VMM-layer tools. A comparative study on the tools is shown in Tables 6.1 and 6.2, respectively.

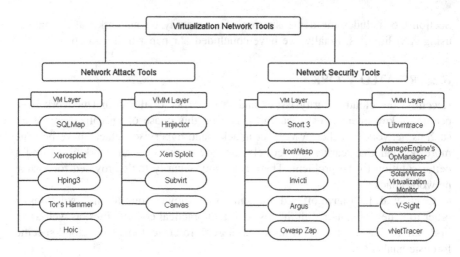

**FIGURE 6.1**  Virtualization network tools.

## TABLE 6.1
## Network Layer Attacking Tools

| Attacking Tools for VM | Year | Environment | Type | Cost of Service | Expertise Required | Virtualization Layer |
|---|---|---|---|---|---|---|
| SQLMap (penetrating tools) | 2006 | Linux, Windows, Mac | SQL injection | Free | Yes | VM |
| Xerosploit | 2016 | Ubuntu, Kali Linux, Parrot OS | DoS, DNS Spoofing | Free | No | VM |
| Hping3 | 2012 | Linux, Windows | DDoS | Free | No | VM |
| Tor's hammer | 2014 | Linux, Windows, Mac | DDoS | Free | Yes | VM |
| HOIC | 2012 | Linux, Windows | DDoS | Free | No | VM |
| HInjector | 2013 | Xen | Hyper-call attack | Free | Yes | VMM |
| Xensploit | 2008 | VMware, Xen | VMEscape | Free | Yes | VMM |
| Subvirt | 2006 | VMware, Xen, KVM, etc. | Root-Kit | Free | Yes | VMM |
| Canvas | 2008 | VMware | VMEscape, cloud burst ex- ploit | Paid | No | VMM |

These assaulting tools can be used to initiate virtual network attacks and acquire access to the system/guest machine in order to perform malicious operations. On the contrary, the security tools can be used as a defensive mechanism to analyze the malicious events occurring on the virtualization layer. Some security tools ensure the security of the data and prevent the unauthorized decryption of data to reduce the risks of eavesdropping by third parties. Each security tool has a specific

**TABLE 6.2**
**Network Security Tools**

| Network Security Tool | Year | Environment | Cost of Service | Expertise Required | Virtualization Layer | Features |
|---|---|---|---|---|---|---|
| Snort 3 | 2021 | Windows, Linux, Mac OS | Free | No | VM | Hyperscan, HTTP inspector, Port Scan, etc. |
| IronWASP | 2012 | Windows, Linux, Mac OS | Free | No | VM | Detection of XSS, SQL injection, Click-jacking, etc. |
| Invicti | 2022 | Windows, Linux | Paid | Yes | VM | Vulnerability assessment |
| Argus | 2013 | Windows, Linux | Free | Yes | VM | Monitors TCP + UDP applications, IP connectivity, SNMP OIDS, etc. |
| Owasp Zap | 2015 | Linux, Mac, Windows | Free | No | VM | Intercepting proxy server. |
| LibVMtrace | 2016 | XEN, KVM | Free | Yes | VMM | Network monitoring, packet capture, IPv4 tracing |
| SolarWinds Virtualization Monitor | 2009 | Nutanix AHV, Hyper-V and VMware vSphere | Paid | No | VMM | Device health monitoring, network monitoring |
| V-Sight | 2020 | OpenVirteX | Free | Yes | VMM | SDN/SDN-NV monitoring, per-VN flow metrics |
| OpManager by Manage Engine | 2016 | VMware vSphere | Both | No | VMM | Network mapping, WAN RTT monitoring, device health monitoring, etc. |
| vNetTracer | 2018 | Xen, KVM | Free | Yes | VMM | End-to-end network performance monitoring, optimized monitoring, programmable trace points |

mechanism to detect or analyze a specific pattern of an attack. Let us first discuss various types of network attacks that can be launched at the virtualization layer.

### 6.3.1  NETWORK ATTACKING TOOLS

Within the section, we have discussed some of the network attack tools that are capable of compromising hypervisor's virtual network layer in the cloud architecture, as mentioned in Table 6.1. These tools are used to perform assault at the application layer (VM) to get unauthorized access or exploit the resources of the target machine, they can even take over the whole system by targeting hypervisor's network layer (VMM). All the necessary details regarding system support, availability, features, etc. have been given below.

### 6.3.2  NETWORK ATTACKING TOOLS AT VM LAYER

Various network attacking tools at the VM layer are described in this section. The tools are specific to different guest OSes such as Windows, Linux, Mac OS and can be used to launch the attacks at VM layer.

*SQLMap*: SQLmap is an open-source tool utilized in infiltration testing to distinguish and take advantage of SQL infusion defects. SQLmap mechanizes the most common way of identifying and taking advantage of SQL injection. An attacker can influence any site or web application that might have a SQL information base connected to it as MySQL, SQL Server, Oracle, and numerous others. SQLmap can help in tracking down this sensitive information.

*Xerosploit*: Xerosploit is a toolbox for penetration testing. It was released in 2016. It includes the ability to perform man in the middle attacks for testing purposes. It also includes a number of modules that enable efficient attacks, as well as DoS attacks and port scanning. It is compatible with Parrot OS 3.1, Ubuntu 16.04, and Kali Linux attack, port scanning, network mapping, HTML code injection, Javascript code injection, DNS spoofing, and Driftnet are some of its basic functions.

*hping3*: Hping3 [8] is a net penetration tool and can issue customized TCP/IP packets and create target responses similar, as how ping displays ICMP responses. Using the command line interface, hping3 can manage fragmentation as well as practically any packet size and content. It can also be used to test a variety of networking devices such as firewalls, routers, hubs, and so on. It can be used as a traceroute software for all supported protocols, as well as for firewalking, OS fingerprinting, and port scanning.

*Tor's hammer*: Tor's hammer [9] is a network assault tool capable of launching a successful DDoS attack. It debuted in 2014 and is written in Python. Because it is new and efficient, it has the potential to cause harm to unprotected web servers. It generates an enumerable number of connection requests to the OSI model's layer 7 (HTTP), flooding the network. This causes the web server's resources to be depleted, resulting in a DoS condition for any valid traffic.

*High Orbit Ion Canon (HOIC)*: An anonymous hackers[3] group originally introduced HOIC in 2012 during Operation Megaupload. It is a popular tool for launching DoS and DDoS assaults, which try to flood a victim's network with obsolete web traffic and bring a site or service nonfunctional. This assault tool was designed to be a replacement for the LOIC by enhancing its capabilities and integrating customizations. The HOIC can carry out tailored attacks that are difficult to address utilizing the HTTP protocol.

### 6.3.3 NETWORK ATTACKING TOOLS AT THE VMM LAYER

In this section, we have listed all the Network Attacking Tools at the VMM layer. All the VMMs (either KVM, Xen, VMware OS) in virtualization are under VM layer.

*HInjector*: HInjector [10] is a well-known tool among cloud security professionals and hackers that directly assaults the hypervisor layer's internals. It was released in 2014. It is a flexible framework that can inject hypercall assaults into a partially or fully para-virtualized guest virtual machine part of a Xen-based environment. The purpose of HInjector is to put the sensors of a standard VMI-based IDS to the test.

*Xensploit*: Xensploit [11] is a tool for performing MITM attacks during virtual machine live migration. It was introduced in 2008 as part of a study revealing the weaknesses and limits of current hypervisors. It operates during a live migration, by manipulating the VM's memory as it traverses the network. Xensploit is built on the fragroute framework. Its name is derived from the first HpyerVisor (Xen) to which it was applied, Xensploit is also capable of manipulating VMware migrations.

*SubVirt*: SubVirt [12] is a new type of malware in its class known as Virtual Machine Based Rootkits (VMBR). Current rootkits must choose between capabilities and secrecy. SubVirt demonstrates how hackers can use virtual-machine technology to circumvent the limitations of existing malware and rootkits. It was created with the idea of how hackers might set up a VMM beneath an OS and use that VMM to host arbitrarily defined malicious software. With this tool, the malicious VM can easily hide and spoof the virtual network.

*Canvas*: Immunity Inc. developed CANVAS [13] a commercial penetration testing tool. At Black Hat USA 2009, Cloud-burst, a CANVAS exploit, was illustrated. In 2008, Core Security Technologies discovered a vulnerability in VMware (CVE-2008-0923), which allowed VMEscape on VMware Workstation 6.0.2 and 5.5.4. It was demonstrated that the canvas tool can be used to make contact with the host OS, outside of the virtual machine in which it is running.

## 6.4 NETWORK SECURITY TOOLS

As enterprises' dependency on virtualization technology grows, so does the demand for more secure environments expands. In this section, numerous network security solutions in the virtualized environment are discussed as mentioned in Table 6.2. These tools are classified based on its target layer of the virtual system. All of the essential information, requirements, and system configuration for the security tools are discussed below.

### 6.4.1 NETWORK SECURITY TOOLS AT THE VM LAYER

*Snort 3*: Snort [24,25] is an open-source intrusion prevention system (IPS) that can analyze and log real-time traffic. Snort 3 is the most recent version, released in 2021. It safeguards users' networks against anomalous traffic, malware, spam, and scamming documents. Snort 3 includes many advanced features such as support for numerous packet forwarding threads, auto-detect services for port-less configuration, auto-generation of reference documentation, improved cross-platform assistance, and many more.

*IronWASP*: Iron Online Application Advanced Security Testing Platform (IronWASP) [Ironwasp] is a free tool used for detecting vulnerabilities in web applications. It was first released in 2012 and is written in Python and Ruby. It has a variety of features and plug-ins that skilled pen-testers can use. IronWASP scans for Cross-Site Scripting (XSS), SQL injection, Cross-Site Flashing, Open URL Redirection, Click-jacking, Sensitive Data Exposure, and other vulnerabilities.

*Invicti*: Invicti [15] is a scalable, automated, and integrated web vulnerability management tool. The Invicti platform, which is based on a cutting-edge web vulnerability scanner, applies unique Proof-Based Scanning technology to discover and validate vulnerabilities, clearly displaying results that are not false positives. Invicti is extremely effective as an independent solution as well as when integrated into the SDLC.

*Argus*: Argus [14] is a fixed-model Realtime Flow Analyzer that tracks and reports on the status and performance of every network activities encountered in a data network traffic stream. On a per-transaction basis, Argus provides a consistent data format for providing flow characteristics, including demand, loss, delay, connectivity, capacity, and jitter. It can monitor and report on TCP + UDP usage, IP connection, SNMP OIDS, programs, databases, and so on.

*Owasp ZAP*: Owasp ZAP [Zaproxy] is a free and open-source web scanner tool used to perform penetration tests. ZAP builds a proxy server and routes website traffic through it. The usage of auto scanners in ZAP aids in the detection of vulnerabilities on the website. It offers some really useful features like porced browsing, proxy server interception, automated scanner, conventional and AJAX web crawlers, passive scanning, WebSocket support, and Plug-n-Hack support.

### 6.4.2 NETWORK SECURITY TOOLS AT THE VMM LAYER

*LibVMtrace*: LibVMtrace [18] is a tool for analyzing Linux-based virtual machines. It allows to set up and insert software breakpoints for security analysis. The data logging layer allows you to monitor VM network activity. When certain network packets occur, LibVMtrace can extract information from the traffic or trigger memory analysis. It can also be used to create advanced monitoring tools.

*SolarWinds*: SolarWinds Virtualization Manager (VMAN) [Solarwinds] is a comprehensive solution for monitoring VMs. It is designed to aggregate a range of relevant observations into a single interface. VMAN can provide extensive insight into the health and performance of hypervisors such as Azure, Amazon EC2, Nutanix AHV, VMware vSphere, and Microsoft Hyper-V. VMAN can also be used to identify usage anomalies and troubleshoot problems. Captured metrics give historical comparisons for tracking resource usage trends (such as CPU spikes and lulls) and determining whether those trends can become concerns or not.

*V-Sight*: V-Sight [19] is a network analysis tool for virtual networks, formed on software-defined networking (SDN). There are issues produced by a lack of network monitoring that makes network optimization and crucial network controls impossible. V-Sight, a complete network monitoring tool for SDN-NV, was designed to address these issues. V-Sight has three approaches: (1) statistics virtualization: isolating statistics per VN; (2) transmission disaggregation: reducing transmission latency; and (3) pCollector: gathering to minimize control channel utilization.

*OpManager*: OpManager [Engine] offers VMware performance monitoring features. It can monitor VMware real-time and historical performance stats. Over 30 important reliabilities and performance monitoring are pre-configured with parameters. It provides its users to even build up auto-remediation measures using bespoke scripts, if it detects any vulnerable conditions. Monitor and analyze the performance of your VM and guest systems, avoid VM sprawl, and provide optimum resource allocation. OpManager is compatible with VMware, Hyper-V, and Xen systems.

*vNetTracer*: vNetTracer [26] is a virtualized network packet profiler that is both efficient and configurable. The vNetTracer uses the extended Berkeley Packet Filter (eBPF) to dynamically insert user-defined trace programs into a live virtualized network with no changes to the applications or network restarts. It allows efficient, flexible, and end-to-end network performance monitoring for virtualized network applications. vNetTracer also provides extensive performance monitoring metrics, it also supports customized network packet tracing, and can be configured to meet variety of needs.

In the fast and advanced growing era of virtualization, various security threats require immediate attention, which has led to the development of more effective security solutions. The chapter gives a comprehensive classification of diverse network attacks and security tools in virtual environment, which will direct some pathways for the future works [25]. Furthermore, the key tools have been identified and informative description is provided for each of them, based on their key features. The classification is done at both VMM and VM layer.

## 6.5 CASE STUDY

In this section, a case study is provided on XAI [27] based intrusion detection system for network analysis. A network attack data set (UNSW-NB 15 [28]) has been considered during analysis purposes along with various XAI machine learning (ML) algorithms. The algorithms used during analysis differentiate the network traffic between normal or attack. The analysis is performed on a physical machine having UBUNTU 20.04 OS, Intel Core i7 processor, 16 GB RAM and 512 GB SSD. Let us briefly explain various terminologies/concepts of XAI-ML algorithms and associated libraries considered during analysis.

## 6.6  EXPLAINABLE AI

AI is getting advanced nowadays and it is now becoming feasible to understand and backtrack the AI algorithms using XAI concepts and libraries. In case of "black box" analysis [29–31], it is difficult to interpret the results of ML algorithms and to explain how an algorithm produces a specific decision/outcome 2022 [32]. Explainable AI is a set of tools/frameworks which help us to better interpret the results/predictions made by ML models [27]. The fairness and transparency of predictions made by different algorithms can be better explained using XAI. In this chapter, a supervised ML algorithms, i.e., XGBoost [32] classifier, is employed as a case study to demonstrate the applications of XAI based tools.

*XGBoost classifier*: XGBoost [32] refers to "eXtreme gradient boosting" algorithm. XGBoost is an implementation of Gradient Boosted decision trees. The eXtreme gradient boosting aims to construct a valiant classifier from the number of weak classifiers, whereas in gradient boosting, every predictor has the responsibility to correct its predecessor's flaws.

*The advance approach using XGBoost, Scikit-Learn and XAI libraries*: After preparing the UNSW-NB15 data set, the XGBoost classifier is trained on it in this phase. The binary categorization of normal or attack, represented by 0 or 1, respectively, makes up the target feature. Using the cleaned-up UNSW-NB15 testing data set, the trained model is evaluated. The effectiveness of the model is assessed using an accuracy score. Some repositories are used as follows to describe how machine learning models are interpreted.

*SHapely Additive explanations (SHAP)*: SHAP is built on the idea of game theory, where each player's participation is significant. The goal is to use computation to simulate the contribution of each attribute to the forecast in order to explain the forecast of any variable x.

*Local inter pretable model-agnostic explanations (LIME)*: LIME is a tool that uses a local, interpretable model to estimate ML models and interpret each individual prediction.

## 6.7  RESULTS AND DISCUSSION

*XGBClassifier*: The training data set is used to create a XGB classification model for the binary behavior designating the class as attack or normal using the XGBClassifier. The model is evaluated on the relevant UNSW-NB15 data set, and it attained a performance accuracy of 89.92%, indicating that it is extraordinarily good at identifying either normal or attacking behavior, as shown in Table 6.3.

For substantial feature relevance, ten features are chosen. Using the Scikit-Learn package, a feature significance graph is generated. Feature importance can be understood from Figure 6.2, which is a reference. The source to destination time to live value, or sttl, is shown as the most significant feature in the classification prediction feature importance graph. In Figure 6.2, the relevance of characteristics declines as we move from top to bottom.

*SHAP Package*: In order to address the question of "how an algorithm arrived at a specific decision?," SHAP is considered. Individual attribute predictions made

**TABLE 6.3**

**XAI Results on UNSW-NB15 Dataset (XGBoost Classifier)**

| Class | Precision | Recall | F1-Score | Support |
|---|---|---|---|---|
| Normal | 77.00 | 98.00 | 86.00 | 56000 |
| Attack | 99.00 | 86.00 | 0.92 | 119341 |
| | | | | |
| Accuracy | | | 90.00 | 175341 |
| Macro avg. | 88.00 | 92.00 | 89.00 | 175341 |
| Weighted avg. | 92.00 | 90.00 | 90.00 | 175341 |

Overall accuracy: 89.9230642006148

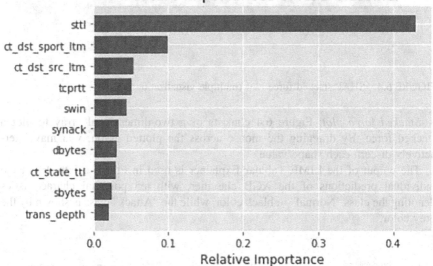

**FIGURE 6.2**  XGBoost feature importance.

using SHAP can be understood using the "Marginal Distribution" notion. Row-wise shape inspection is carried out using a force plot mechanism. A force plot displays each potential's role play from their participation in prediction in a single row and a rank.

The role play of each prospective attribute to class prediction is explained in Figure 6.3. The contribution is directly proportional to the block's width of the potential. The value that serves as a starting point for an individual's participation in an attribute is known as the base value. Attacking class is represented by a f(x) value closer to 1, while normal class is represented by a value closer to 0.

**FIGURE 6.3**   SHAP row-wise force plot (one visual).

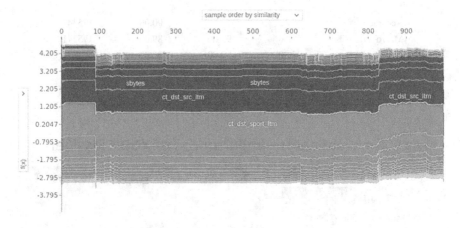

**FIGURE 6.4**   SHAP stacked force plot (multiple visualization).

*Stacked force plot*: Figure 6.4 consists of a two-dimensional array to plot a stacked force. By dragging the mouse across the plotted graph, you may interactively discern each shape value.

The output of the LIME Tabular Explainer is used in Figure 6.5 to depict the individual predictions of the XGB classifier, with ten potential characteristics denoting the class "Normal" in black color, while the "Attack" class is shown by the grey color.

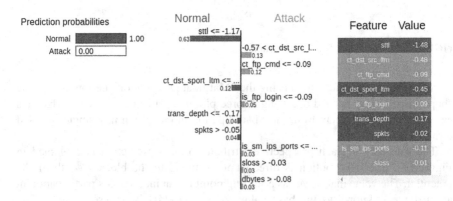

**FIGURE 6.5**   XGB classifier explanation for single classification.

## 6.8 CONCLUSION

Virtualization was introduced in the 20th century, and has been under research even in present. It is definitely the future of computing. It provides a platform to share important elements such as network bandwidth, memory usage, CPU cycles, and other computing resources. As virtualization provides many benefits that include improved workload mobility, increased performance, efficiency and availability of resources, and automated operations; it has become a dependency for new firms and also a favorite target for attackers to launch various attacks. A detailed classification about the various state-of-the-art malware attacks and security tools is provided along with their functionalities in this chapter. Such a listing is very important for researchers to know the latest secure solutions available in the domain. An abundant of data can be collected using these tools to prepare new generation security framework. A practical demonstration has also been provided for the better understanding of working a security framework that employs XAI and ML algorithms. The UNSW-NB15 data set has been used to train XGBoost classifier model, which predicts the behavior of network traffic. The more interesting factor is that accurate predictions made by different classifiers through LIME and SHAP libraries help in better understanding of whole ML framework. The XAI will bring a large number of possibilities in the field of cloud security to tackle the security challenges effectively in upcoming future.

## ACKNOWLEDGMENTS

The Science and Engineering Research Board, Department of Science and Technology (SERB-DST) provided funding for this study under Project File No. SPG/2021/002003. The authors would like to express their gratitude to SERB-DST for their intellectual generosity and research assistance.

## REFERENCES

[1] Finbold (2021). Revealed: 86% of hacked google cloud accounts used for illegal crypto mining. https://finbold.com/revealed-86-of-hacked-google-cloud-accounts-used-for-illegal-crypto-mining/.
[2] aws-data-breaches-of-2021/.
[3] Baror, S. O. and Venter, H. (2019). A taxonomy for cybercrime attack in the public cloud. In International Conference on Cyber Warfare and Security, pages 505–X. Academic Conferences International Limited.
[4] Wikipedia (2006). Virtual machine escape using canvas – wikipedia. https://en.wikipedia.org/wiki/Virtual_machine_escape. Accessed 4/6/2022.
[5] Ahmed, M., Pal, R., Hossain, M. M., Bikas, M. A. N., and Hasan, M. K. (2009). NIDS: A network based approach to intrusion detection and prevention. In 2009, International Association of Computer Science and Information Technology-Spring Conference, pages 141–144. IEEE.
[6] Bernardo Damele, A. G. M. S. (2006). sqlmap. https://sqlmap.org/.
[7] Chandel, R. (2018b). Xerosploit – a man-in-the-middle attack framework. https://www.hackingarticles.in/xerosploit-a-man-in-the-middle-attack-framework/.

[8] Chandel, R. (2018a). Hping – active network security tool. https://www.hackingarticles.in/xerosploit-a-man-in-the-middle-attack-framework/.

[9] Milenkoski, A., Payne, B. D., Antunes, N., Vieira, M., and Kounev, S. (2013). Hinjector: Injecting hypercall attacks for evaluating vmi-based intrusion detection systems. In Poster Reception at the 2013 Annual Computer Security Applications Conference (ACSAC 2013). Applied Computer Security Associates (ACSA).

[10] Mishra, P., Pilli, E. S., Varadharajan, V., and Tupakula, U. (2017). Out-VM monitoring for malicious network packet detection in cloud. In 2017, ISEA Asia Security and Privacy (ISEASP), pages 1–10.

[11] Openargus (April). openargus/argus. https://github.com/openargus/argus. April 1, 2022). Repetto, M. and Carrega, A. (2022). Monitoring network flows in containerized environments. In Cybersecurity of Digital Service Chains, pages 32–55. Springer.

[12] Manral, B., Somani, G., Choo, K.-K. R., Conti, M., and Gaur, M. S. (2019). A systematic survey on cloud forensics challenges, solutions, and future directions. *ACM Computing Surveys (CSUR)*, 52(6): 1–38.

[13] Yang, G., Jin, H., Kang, M., Moon, G. J., and Yoo, C. (2020). Network monitoring for SDN virtual networks. In IEEE INFOCOM 2020-IEEE Conference on Computer Communications, pages 1261–1270. IEEE.

[14] Singh, G., Goyal, S., and Agarwal, R. (2014). Intrusion detection using network monitoring tools. Available at SSRN 2426105.

[15] Invicti (2022). Web vulnerability scanner | invicti. https://www.invicti.com/web-vulnerability-scanner/.Ironwasp. Ironwasp – open source advanced web security testing platform. http://blog.ironwasp.org/.

[16] Kali. tls-prober. https://en.kali.tools/all/?tool=1433.

[17] King, S. T. and Chen, P. M. (2006). Subvirt: Implementing malware with virtual machines. In 2006 IEEE Symposium on Security and Privacy (S&P'06), page 14. IEEE.

[18] Techopedia (2021). What is network-based intrusion prevention system (nips)? – definition from techopedia.

[19] Zaproxy. Owasp zap. https://www.zaproxy.org/.

[20] Mazebolt (2018). Tor's hammer attack | perform DDoS attack using tors hammer | mazebolt knowledge base. https://kb.mazebolt.com/knowledgebase/tors-hammer-attack/.

[21] Solarwinds. Virtualization manager | solarwinds. https://www.solarwinds.com/virtualization-manager.

[22] Snort (2022). Snort-3-officially-released. https://blog.snort.org/2021/01/snort-3-officially-released.html#:~:text=Tuesday%2C%20January%2019%2C%202021.

[23] Moustafa, N. and Slay, J. (2015). UNSW-NB15: a comprehensive data set for network intrusion detection systems (UNSW-NB15 network data set). In 2015 military communications and information systems conference (MilCIS), pages 1–6. IEEE.

[24] Suo, K., Zhao, Y., Chen, W., and Rao, J. (2018). vnettracer: Efficient and programmable packet tracing in virtualized networks. In 2018, IEEE 38th International Conference on Distributed Computing Systems (ICDCS), pages 165–175.

[25] Taubmann, B. (2020). Improving Digital Forensics and Incident Analysis in Production Environments by Using Virtual Machine Introspection. PhD thesis, Universität Passau.

[26] Tcydenova, E., Kim, T. W., Lee, C., and Park, J. H. (2021). Detection of adversarial attacks in ai-based intrusion detection systems using explainable AI. Human-Centric Computing and Information Sciences, 11.

[27] https://www.techopedia.com/definition/4030/network-based-intrusion-prevention-system-nips.

[28] Oberheide, J., Cooke, E., and Jahanian, F. (2008). Empirical exploitation of live virtual machine migration. In Procedings of BlackHat DC convention, pages 1–6. Citeseer.

[29] Choi, S.-H. and Park, K.-W. (2022). Cloud-blackbox: Toward practical recording and tracking of VM swarms for multifaceted cloud inspection. Future Generation Computer Systems.

[30] Cloudflare. What is the high orbit ion cannon (HOIC)? I HOIC definition I cloudflare. https://www.cloudflare.com/learning/ddos/ddos-attack-tools/high-orbit-ion-cannon-hoic/.

[31] Engine, M. Manageengine opmanager free edition. https://www.manageengine.com/network-monitoring/free-edition.html.

[32] Bhattacharya, S., Maddikunta, P. K. R., Kaluri, R., Singh, S., Gadekallu, T. R., Alazab, M., and Tariq, U. (2020). A novel PCA-firefly based XGBoost classification model for intrusion detection in networks using GPU. *Electronics*, 9(2):219. Boulevard, S. (2021). Worst AWS data breaches of 2021 – security boulevard. https://securityboulevard.com/2021/12/worst-.

# Section B

Integration of Cloud Computing with Technologies like AI, ML, IoT, Mobile, and Big Data

# 7 Integration of the Cloud with Fog Computing to Secure Data Transmission between IoT and Cloud

*Shatakshi Kokate and Urmila Shrawankar*

## 7.1 INTRODUCTION

The Internet of Things (IoT) and end users are becoming more and more powerful across a range of industries, including engineering, logistics, medicine, and agriculture [1]. To make it easier to run applications, this technology connects commonplace items like sensors, actuators, and gadgets to the Internet. When data needs to be saved in the cloud, IoT device utilization and the resulting high volume and integrity of data transmission provide a significant challenge [2–5]. As a result, the risk posed by data security and confidentiality increases [6]. The IoT network is easily vulnerable to attacks from outside intruders or malicious agents who are prone to the security and corruption of data. IoT and cloud systems today face various difficulties, including network security issues and unwanted access [7]. Many IoT applications fail to work with cloud computing, thus it is useful to work with fog computing [8]. It is having a distributed approach, which ensures industrial IoT necessity. As the distance between IoT and the cloud is very long, vast data that is produced by IoT devices requires more time and cost when there is a need to transfer it to the cloud for further action. As operation on data is performed at the fog level, only consolidated data and requests that require more computational power will transfer to the cloud; thus, it is used to reduce the bandwidth and latency and increase the security [9–12]. It also reduces the amount of back-and-forth conversations in the IoT and cloud network. The majority of IoT applications use cloud computing and storage services [13]. In fog computing, devices are used on networks that are close to the consumers to carry out communication, storage, and computing tasks [14]. Processing data close to the local network rather than far away on the cloud improves the efficiency of many IoT applications which they are large scale in nature. Fog computing is typically situated on the local network and is close to the system's nodes [15]. In contrast, the cloud is accessible online from any location. Data analysis, processing, and filtering are all made easier

DOI: 10.1201/9781003341437-9

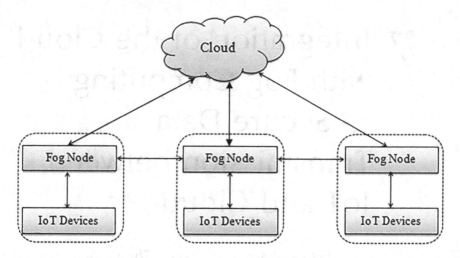

**FIGURE 7.1**   Fog-based IoT cloud system.

by fog computing, which also improves security for critical data [16]. Fog computing provides better privacy and security, uses less network bandwidth, and can tolerate tough environmental conditions in areas like tracks, automobiles, under the sea, factory floors, etc. This technology also offers superior environmental resistance. The data gathered by IoT devices is analyzed and aggregated by fog computing [17]. This layer receives enormous amounts of data from IoT devices, which are then dispersed to numerous devices connected in this layer [18].

Figure 7.1 shows fog computing based on IoT and cloud system. Fog computing is a type of computer architecture where a network of nodes continuously collects data from IoT devices. With less response times, these nodes process data in real time as it comes in. The nodes periodically transmit to the cloud analytical summary data. The data obtained from the numerous nodes are then analyzed by a cloud-based application with the aim of delivering insight that can be put into practice. It takes more than simply computer power to implement this architecture. High-speed connectivity between IoT and fog is important. The processing is done within a few milliseconds, which is the aim of using fog computing. For instance, a manufacturing floor IoT sensor may be able to take advantage of a connected connection. A different type of connectivity is necessary for resources that are mobile or isolated, such as autonomous vehicles. The security of data is achieved by using fog computing.

## 7.2   CHALLENGES IN CLOUD COMPUTING

Some challenges that are faced by using cloud computing are listed below:

1. *Network and communication*: An Internet-based computing concept, called cloud computing, uses the Internet. The Internet has many different types as well as topologies and varied network speeds. On the Internet, the data transmission path frequently varies due to dynamic communication paths.

Thus, numerous problems with the non-homogenous and loosely managed nature of the cloud-IoT architecture arise, including latencies and bandwidth restrictions that negatively impact QoS.

2. *Latency constraint*: One of the major problems with an Internet-based approach is network latency, which is brought on by communication delays and jittery delays. Network latency has a significant negative impact on any real-time application that allows for real-time interaction. Due to the cloud's distance from the event's origin, information communication is experiencing a significant amount of delay. It is ideal for data processing, and analysis to take place near the user in order to fulfill the demanding timing requirements of IoT-based applications.

3. *Network bandwidth*: The interconnected "things" generate data quickly. The high-speed transmission of such massive amounts of data through the continuum is bandwidth and network intensive, depleting resources. In many IoT scenarios, it may not be realistic to meet the requirement for very high bandwidth since the devices are connected to the cloud through a variety of network architectures with several hops and different network device data transmission rates.

4. *Servicing heterogeneous devices*: IoT is made up of diverse, sparsely re-sourced devices that connect using various protocols. These gadgets depend on the cloud to meet their computing needs. The fact that each of these devices needs high processing of allocated resources and the managing of direct communication with them makes it quite unrealistic and unaffordable for the cloud. For instance, data encryption and decryption are necessary for data transmission. These operations, which require complex algorithms and take a lot of resources and time, are carried out at both ends. To handle complex encryption and decryption approaches, the IoT node ends need frequent firmware upgrades from the cloud, which sounds incredibly impossible.

5. *Security Challenges*: IoT data must pass through numerous hops and intricate network structures because of the great distance between the source and the cloud, which renders it prone to security problems. Data becomes more prone to corruption and assault as it passes through network edges and many nodes. Additionally, third parties are used by cloud-based services for security and storage.

6. *Privacy*: With or without the concern of users, their data can be accessible to the host company. Service providers can also access the data stored in the cloud. They might delete information accidentally, on purpose, or even maliciously.

7. *Compliance*: In many areas, there exist laws governing data and hosting. The user may be forced to employ pricey deployment techniques in order to adhere to requirements.

## 7.3   INTRODUCTION TO FOG COMPUTING

Fog computing is close to the network where data is generated. All computations will now be done on to the local level than the remote level. Edge computing is referred to by Cisco as fog computing. An IT computing infrastructure, called cloud computing, allows for the hosting and low-cost operation of software services and applications. The cloud services presumptively process data remotely and are decentralized. However, modern cloud computing cannot fulfill the demands placed on IoT devices. Systems hosted in the cloud have low latency. In order to create IoT systems that are latency-sensitive, the researchers also explored alternative scenarios. Fog computing is one that can address issues of latency, security, and efficiency. Urgent processing requests are delivered to the fog. Less sensitive data is sent to the primary data centers, which are present on the cloud. Most data are stored in the cloud under typical circumstances; local storage is used when bandwidth conservation is a top concern. When the Internet connection isn't always reliable, fog computing can be helpful as well. On connected trains, for instance, fog computing can access locally stored information in locations where the Internet connection cannot be maintained. Additionally, it enables the implementation of data processing at the local network level, which is advantageous for time-sensitive activities and real-time data analytics. Fog computing offers various services that the cloud is offering near the origin of data. In many cases, the user wants a quick response such as in the case of a heart attack, this is possible only by using fog computing. Figure 7.2 shows the analysis between the two technologies viz. cloud and fog computing, which clearly

| Features | Cloud computing | Fog Computing |
|---|---|---|
| Distance | Far from the edge | Network close to the edge |
| Scalability | High, easy to scale | Scalable within network |
| Latency | High | Low |
| Data analysis | Less time-sensitive data processing, | Real-time, decides to process locally or send to cloud |
| Computing power | High | Limited |
| Interoperability | High | High |
| Capacity | Does not provide data reduction while sending | Fog Computing reduces the amount of data sent to cloud computing. |
| Response time | Low | High |
| Security | Less | High |
| Speed | Access speed is high depending on the VM connectivity. | High even more compared to Cloud Computing. |
| Data Integration | Multiple data sources can be integrated. | Multiple Data sources and devices can be integrated. |
| Mobility | Limited | High |
| Location Awareness | Partially Supported | Fully Supported |
| Number of Server Nodes | Few | Large |
| Geographical Distribution | Centralized. | Decentralized and distributed. |
| Location of service | Services provided within the internet. | Services provided at the edge of the local network. |
| Communication mode | IP network | Wireless communication: WLAN, Wi-Fi, 3G, 4G, ZigBee, etc. or wired communication (part of the IP networks) |
| Dependence on the quality of core network | Requires strong network core. | Can also work in Weak network core |

FIGURE 7.2   Chart showing analysis of cloud and fog computing.

shows that the introduction of fog computing is a better solution to overcome problems that the current IoT and cloud system is facing.

## 7.4   ADVANTAGES OF FOG COMPUTING

The following are the advantages of fog computing:

1. *Low latency*: As data processing is done at the fog network, it can help to increase the speeds of computing as well as decrease the latency.
2. *Better data control*: Third-party servers are not available on the local network as available in cloud computing. There is no third-party control over the user data. Fog computing manages a lot of data locally which is used to improve security.
3. *Flexible storage system*: Fog computing doesn't need constant access to the Internet. As data is stored locally, with or without the Internet, data can be accessible to the end users.
4. *Connecting centralized and decentralized storage*: Decentralized data storage is available in fog computing, whereas centralized storage is available in the cloud. Linking decentralized storage to centralized storage is done by using fog computing.
5. *Bandwidth conservation*: Only summarized information or information with greater computational resources will send to the cloud which saves bandwidth.
6. *Improved response time*: Processing of data is done near the source which improves the response time.

## 7.5   THREE-TIER ARCHITECTURE

The three-tier architecture using IoT, fog computing, and the cloud is as shown in Figure 7.3. Due to the fact that some cloud functionalities are active in fog nodes, it can offer services similar to those of a cloud server. It enables the resolution of latency issues and offers real-time data processing. The IoT layer is the bottom or lowest layer. Sensors and actuators from the IoT are positioned at this layer. The backend of the system receives and processes the data that all IoT devices in this tier send to it continuously.

Fog computing is present as an interface between the IoT layer and cloud. The n number of fog nodes makes up its structure. The cloud gateway connects all the components in the network. The fog nodes are having limited storage capacity as compared to the cloud. After analyzing the data, they communicate with the source devices by sending feedback.

Each fog node offers the following data services for IoT data:

- *Data filtering*: Removing noise and other unnecessary data to isolate the key data.
- *Segregation*: The same resources are shared by several IoT applications, where fog computing is useful to support a multi-tenancy paradigm.

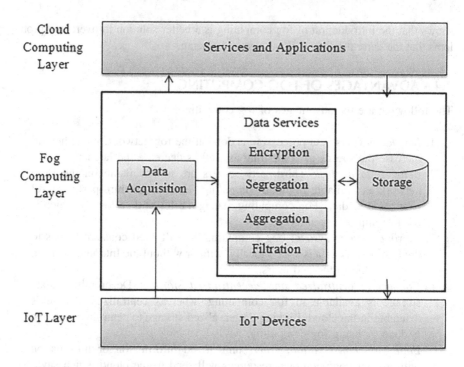

**FIGURE 7.3**   Three-tier architecture.

Segregating means clearly identifying and separating the data that are exclusive to each application.
- *Aggregation*: Collection of data from the applications which are similar to each other over a time period.
- *Data encryption*: The acquired data from the IoT is encrypted to ensure privacy and security requirements.
- *Caching*: Fog offers sufficient storage space, allowing data to be kept close to the user than the remote server.

The fog and cloud are interconnected to each other. The fog utilizes application tools available in the cloud. Data gathering and aggregation are done by the fog layer. The pertinent and important data is preprocessed and transmitted by the fog.

At the last layer, the data centers are crucial elements. As a result, system performance can be seen there. Data center has a wide range of capabilities for handling, storing, and offering other services.

## 7.6   APPLICATIONS OF A FOG-BASED CLOUD SYSTEM

In an IoT-cloud system, fog computing will be particularly beneficial for providing security, lowering latency, and increasing bandwidth in time sensitive application as shown in Figure 7.4.

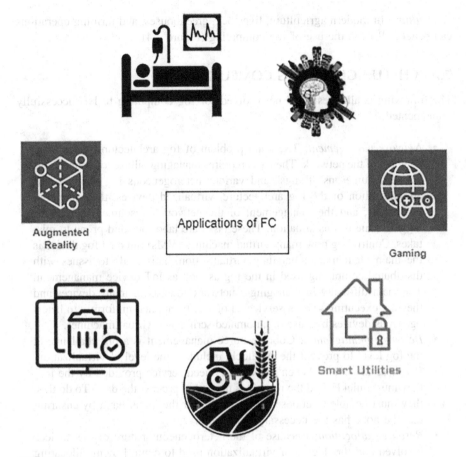

**FIGURE 7.4** Applications of fog-based cloud system.

*Augmented reality*: Real time overlaying of important information onto the physical world is possible with fog computing.

*Healthcare*: For healthcare, data must be delivered securely to the cloud, and data processing and response times must be very quick. Fog computing has a significant role to play in this situation.

*Smart utility services*: Telephone, water, power, etc. are utility services that can be handled smartly by using fog computing.

*Caching and processing*: Many sites that are having a lot of data sets need to be processing data quickly and require keeping it secure. Fog computing can be used on this website to process data locally, reducing latency, and maintaining security.

*Gaming*: These days, online multiplayer games with several players rely on real-time processing, where fog computing might be deployed.

*Decentralized smart building controls*: Fog computing is introduced to improve the security and efficiency of smart building systems.

*Agriculture*: In modern agriculture, livestock, greenhouses, and farming operations can benefit all from the use of fog computing (Figure 7.4).

## 7.7   CHALLENGES IN FOG COMPUTING

The following challenges must be resolved for fog computing to be successfully implemented.

- *Network management*: The main problem of fog architecture is the management of the network. The work requires managing billions of connections between numerous "things" and various heterogeneous fog devices. The administration of the fog architecture, virtualized devices, their interconnectedness, and the management of the network's resources present the biggest issue in this situation. These tasks are laborious and prone to mistakes. Controlling how many virtual machines (VMs) run on a fog device is the main challenge in handling virtualization. This leads to issues with distributed computing used in the fog as well as IoT device management. The main difficulty in managing a network consists of many devices and they are executing several services. Fog can be applied uniformly to heterogeneous devices because of automated scripts and virtual machines.
- *Resource management*: Good resource management is a big challenge at the fog level to prevent the deadlock, including the level of virtualization.
- *Resource discovery*: When IoT devices need service provided by the fog, they must quickly find the resources needed to process the data. To do this, they must be able to choose the best node for the job at hand by ensuring that the node has the necessary bandwidth.
- *Resource allocation*: Because of the heterogeneous nature of the devices involved and the degree of virtualization used to control them, allocating specific resources in the fog architecture is a complex problem. As a result, it is important to consider resource allocation because it can stop the entire system.
- *Task scheduling*: The task must be scheduled evenly among various VMs at the fog level to maximize the throughput with less conflict.
- *Job offloading*: When any of the fog nodes fails, their jobs are assigned to the fog node available in the network. Job offloading is another issue that must be addressed by fog computing for better performance.
- *Storage issues*: The fog is having limited storage capacity. There should be an efficient backup policy to handle the constant data streaming flow.

## 7.8   SUGGESTIONS TO OVERCOME FOG COMPUTING CHALLENGES

Suggestions to overcome the fog computing challenges are as follows:

- *Network management*: To manage the network, proper load balancing should be employed before sending data to the fog nodes.

- *Resource management*: Mutual exclusion techniques can be used to avoid deadlock while managing the resources among fog nodes.
- *Resource discovery*: By understanding the run time environment, IoT devices can choose the best node for the job at hand by ensuring that the node has the necessary bandwidth.
- *Resource allocation*: As the fog is having a heterogeneous nature of the devices, there should be a proper resource allocation technique. Dynamic resource allocation technique can be used to allocate the resources to the task submitted to fog nodes.
- *Task scheduling*: Efficient task scheduling algorithm must be used to schedule the tasks when they are submitted to the fog nodes.
- *Job offloading*: The job offloading issue can be addressed by identifying an idle fog node or one with less workload and assigning the job to that node.
- *Storage issues*: As fog nodes are having limited storage space and need to store vast data collected from various IoT devices, this problem can be addressed by using a data compression technique.

## 7.9  SUMMARY

According to the most recent projections, IoT devices are increasing daily and will continue to change the Internet. There is a huge amount of data produced by these gadgets. They are typically processed, stored, and analyzed via cloud computing. The distance between IoT and the cloud is very large, which is prone to delay, data corruption, and security. There should be a paradigm that will process the data at the local level rather than processing it far away in the cloud. Fog computing has become a viable option for providing small-scale services similar to the cloud near the network. This system is useful to reduce the network latency. Fog computing is useful for processing real time applications more quickly. Context-aware computing has been greatly facilitated by characteristics like mobility assistance, geographic distribution, and proximity awareness, which would not have been possible without the use of cloud computing. Even while load dispersion, support for heterogeneous devices, managing enormous amounts of data, and limitations on computing power and memory capacity present many problems for fog computing, its benefits are immeasurable. The other stage toward achieving cognitive IoT, in which the physical and digital worlds merge into one, would be fog computing.

## REFERENCES

1. P. Bellavista, J. Berrocal, A. Corradi, S. K. Das, L. Foschini, and A. Zanni (2019), "A Survey on Fog Computing for the Internet of Things," *Pervasive and Mobile Computing*, vol. 52, pp. 71–99. 10.1016/j.pmcj.2018.12.007.
2. Dhule and Shrawankar (2019), "Energy Efficient Green Consolidator for Cloud Data Centers," 2019 6th International Conference on Computing for Sustainable Global Development (INDIACom), New Delhi, India, pp. 405–409.
3. F. A. Kraemer, A. E. Braten, N. Tamkittikhun, and D. Palma (2017), "Fog Computing in Healthcare—A Review and Discussion," *IEEE Access*, vol. 5, pp. 9206–9222, doi: 10.1109/ACCESS.2017.2704100.

4. Ghutke and Shrawankar (2014), "Pros and Cons of Load Balancing Algorithms for Cloud Computing," *2014 International Conference on Information Systems and Computer Networks (ISCON)*, Mathura, India, 2014, pp. 123–127, 10.1109/ICISCON.2014.6965231.

5. H. Sabireen and V. Neelanarayanan (2021), "A Review on Fog Computing: Architecture, Fog with IoT, Algorithms and Research Challenges," *ICT Express*, vol. 7, no. 2, pp. 162–176, 10.1016/j.icte.2021.05.004.

6. J. Y. Lee and J. Lee (2021), "Current Research Trends in IoT Security: A Systematic Mapping Study," *Mobile Information System*, vol. 2021, 10.1155/2021/8847099.

7. L. Bittencourt et al. (2018), "The Internet of Things, Fog and Cloud Continuum: Integration and Challenges," *Internet of Things*, vol. 3–4, pp. 134–155, 10.1016/j.iot.2018.09.005.

8. A. A. Laghari, A. K. Jumani, and R. A. Laghari (2021), "Review and State of Art of Fog Computing," *Archives of Computational Methods in Engineering*, vol. 28, no. 5, pp. 3631–3643.

9. M. Mukherjee, L. Shu, and D. Wang (2018), "Survey of Fog Computing: Fundamental, Network Applications, and Research Challenges," *IEEE Communications Surveys & Tutorials*, vol. 20, no. 3, pp. 1826–1857, thirdquarter 2018, 10.1109/COMST.2018.2814571.

10. Neware and Shrawankar (2019), "Fog Computing Architecture, Applications, and Security Issues," vol. 3, no. 1, 10.4018/ijFC.2020010105.

11. P. Habibi, M. Farhoudi, S. Kazemian, S. Khorsandi, and A. Leon-Garcia (2020), "Fog Computing: A Comprehensive Architectural Survey," *IEEE Access*, vol. 8, pp. 69105–69133, 10.1109/ACCESS.2020.2983253.

12. Paul, H. Pinjari, W. H. Hong, H. C. Seo, and S. Rho (2018), "Fog Computing-Based IoT for Health Monitoring System," *Journal of Sensors*, vol. 2018, 10.1155/2018/1386470.

13. R. Rani, V. Kashyap, and M. Khurana (2020), "Role of IoT-Cloud Ecosystem in Smart Cities: Review and Challenges," *Materials Today: Proceedings*, vol. 49, 2020, pp. 2994–2998, 10.1016/j.matpr.2020.10.054.

14. S. Yi, Z. Hao, Z. Qin, and Q. Li (2015), "Fog Computing: Platform and Applications," 2015 Third IEEE Workshop on Hot Topics in Web Systems and Technologies (HotWeb), Washington, DC, USA, pp. 73–78, 10.1109/HotWeb.2015.22.

15. Sarhan, "Fog Computing as a Solution for IoT-Based Agricultural Applications," Smart Agricutural Services Using Deep Learning, Big Data, and IoT, no. January, pp. 46–68, 10.4018/978-1-7998-5003-8.ch003

16. U. Shrawankar and C. Shrawankar (2022), "Blockchain for Smart Systems: Computing Technologies and Applications: BlockCloud: Blockchain as a Cloud Service," Chapman and Hall/CRC.

17. Shrawankar, Dhule (2020), "Cloud Computing Technologies for Smart Agriculture and Healthcare: Virtualization Technology for Cloud-Based Services," Chapman and Hall/CRC.

18. T. T. Aung, A. M. Thaw, N. A. Zhukova, T. Man, and V. V. Chernokulsky (2021), "Data Processing Model for Mobile IoT Systems," *Procedia Computer Science*, vol. 186, pp. 235–241, 10.1016/j.procs.2021.04.143.

# 8 Cloud Services through a Blockchain to Enhance the Security

*Sonali Shinge and Urmila Shrawankar*

## 8.1 INTRODUCTION

Cloud computing is on-demand technology. The user can use cloud services via the internet to obtain technology services like computing power, databases as needed, etc. This is managed by a cloud service provider (CSP). For a monthly subscription fee or usage-based charges, the CSP makes these services available to users [1–21].

### 8.1.1 TAXONOMY OF CLOUD SERVICES

IaaS, PaaS, DaaS, and SaaS are the majority of cloud computing services. They are residing one after another like a stack; they are normally used as the cloud computing stack. By using these services, users can achieve their objectives. Figure 8.1 shows the taxonomy of cloud services. Figure 8.2 shows the cloud computing stack.

## 8.2 CLOUD SECURITY CHALLENGES

There are major security challenges that occur in cloud computing. They are listed as follows:

1. *Trust problem*: The main issue for everyone is trust between the user and service ends. Because the user at the receiving end never knows whether the service end is providing reliable data, the service ends are assured by a service level agreement (SLA) document.
2. *Authenticity problem*: Integrity is a way of determining whether or not information has been improperly modified. Cloud computing should be extremely secure. A cloud user must be genuine.
3. *Encryption problem*: In cloud computing, generally, encryption is used as a data securing mechanism. But the main disadvantage of encryption is that it requires high computational power.
4. *Key management problem*: In the cloud, to manage the well-organized use of the key is a big security problem. To store the encrypted key in the cloud is a very difficult procedure.

DOI: 10.1201/9781003341437-10

**FIGURE 8.1**   Services in cloud computing.

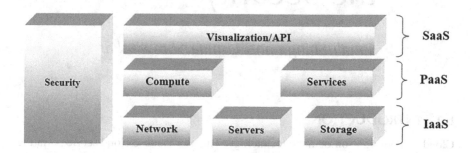

**FIGURE 8.2**   Stack of cloud computing.

5. *Privacy problem*: Analytic server's data or knowledge may be processed outside of the user's locations. As an outcome, data privacy must be protected.

To overcome the above-mentioned challenges, the cloud proposed a system by using blockchain technology.

## 8.3   BLOCKCHAIN TECHNOLOGY

Nowadays, blockchain is an emerging technology. In the blockchain, block is an immutable, which are used to log transactions. A blockchain is a collection of blocks like a linked list.

By using a blockchain mechanism, organizations can communicate data quickly and securely without sacrificing security. The transaction is not subject to the control of any one party.

### 8.3.1   CATEGORIES OF BLOCKCHAIN

Nowadays, four different blockchain networks exist: consortium, private, public, and hybrid blockchains.

#### 8.3.1.1   Public Blockchains

A public blockchain is available to all without any limitation. Every user can join through the Internet and can use this to send transactions; sign up as a validator. Such networks typically provide financial rewards to individuals that protect them using a various consensus algorithm. Bitcoin and Ethereum are examples of public blockchains.

### 8.3.1.2  Private Blockchains

A private blockchain is permission oriented. Without a network administrator's permission, a user cannot join the network. Those users and validators that have permission are allowed to use this network. Generally, Distributed Ledger Technology (DLT) is used in private blockchains to differentiate them from other peer-to-peer decentralized database applications.

### 8.3.1.3  Hybrid Blockchains

A combination of centralized and decentralized elements produces hybrid blockchains. Depending on which parts of centralization and decentralization is used, the exact operation of the chain may change.

### 8.3.1.4  Consortium Blockchain

A set of private blockchains is known as a consortium blockchain. Each blockchain is controlled by various foundations that have merged services to share data in order to improve current processes, transparency, etc.

### 8.3.2  FEATURES OF A BLOCKCHAIN

A blockchain has many features, which are listed as follows:

1. *Anonymity*: Every user has a unique address in the blockchain network, not a user ID. By using a public blockchain, user privacy is achieved.
2. *Cryptography*: Due to complex calculations and encryption blockchain, transactions are considered valid and reliable.
3. *Decentralization*: Each user in the blockchain structure has rights to access the complete distributed database. The network is controlled by using consensus algorithms rather than the central systems.
4. *Provenance*: Based on the fact that the blockchain record contains the source of every transaction.
5. *Immutability*: A transaction on a blockchain is immutable or cannot be deleted.
6. *Transparency*: This network is resistant to fraud. It will require more processing power to completely replace the network; this is very unlikely to happen.

### 8.3.3  STRUCTURE OF A BLOCKCHAIN

A collection of blocks is called a blockchain. Figure 8.3 shows the structure of a blockchain. The blockchain architecture has different components used. They are as follows:

1. *Node*: In blockchain architecture, a user or computer acts as a node.
2. *Transaction*: It is the smallest element, which may contain records, information, etc. A transaction is a primary function in the blockchain system.

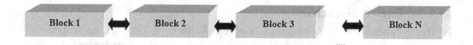

**FIGURE 8.3**   A blockchain structure.

3. *Block*: A data structure that maintains a collection of transactions that are discrete to whole network nodes is known as block.
4. *Chain*: A particular order of created blocks is known as a chain.
5. *Miners*: It is the block verification process. After completion of this process, anything can be added in the blockchain structure.
6. *Consensus (consensus protocol)*: It is a set of procedures and guidelines for operating blockchains.

In the blockchain, for creation of a block, any new record or transaction is used. The authorization of every transaction is confirmed by signing a digital signature. Verification of each block must be done before adding that to the network.

## 8.4   BLOCKCHAIN AS A SERVICE (BAAS)

The cloud-based service has been designed to overcome the above-mentioned challenges that occur in the cloud. The various algorithms and techniques have been used to design the blockchain as a service on the cloud. The planned system architecture, shown in Figure 8.4, if for developing BaaS and the various steps included. This is as follows:

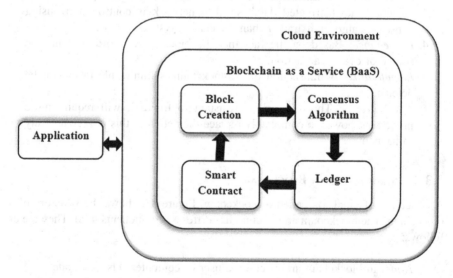

**FIGURE 8.4**   System architecture of Blockchain as a Service.

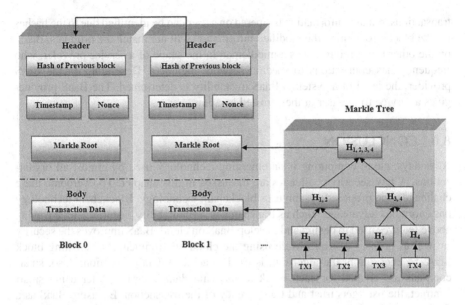

**FIGURE 8.5** Block structure.

1. *Block creation*:When users want to connect to the cloud environment, they will always send a request through the CSP. At the beginning, user contents are used as an input to create the block. For creation of block, SHA256 encryption algorithm is used. Figure 8.5 shows the block structure in the blockchain.
2. *Consensus algorithm*: After creation of a block, use the hybrid consensus algorithm. It validates the created block. Consensus algorithm is used for providing network security. A Proof of Work (PoW) or Proof of Stake (PoS) algorithm is used to stop unauthorized users from confirming fraudulent transactions.
3. *Ledger creation*: In this step, ledgers are created for these blocks. The distributed ledger keeps track of all communication between network users. Blockchain technology has Markle trees as a part store summary of all transaction in block. This tree helps to verify the data integrity.
4. *Creation of smart contract*: In blockchain, smart contracts are computer programs or protocols for automated transactions. It has executes at desired conditions. An Application Logic Contract (ALC) type of smart contract is created. In the smart contract, the user has to add the digital signature, so that the user trust and transparency could be maintained. Also, data integrity is achieved.

## 8.5  BLOCKCHAIN AS A SERVICE CHALLENGES

The transaction history on a blockchain is immutable, meaning it can never be changed without causing the chain to break. Each user's file structure stores blockchain transactions, but any information tampered on a user can be identified due to the hashes for the blocks containing the modified information will not match the originals. BaaS, on the other hand, reintroduces a middleman in the shape of a service provider, who frequently has connections to specific network members. Depending on the BaaS provider, the level of a system's BaaS trustability is determined. The BaaS provider gives a service to the user at their trusted location.

## 8.6  CONCLUSION

Nowadays, cloud computing is an emerging technology used by almost all organizations. A few security challenges are discussed in this chapter. To overcome these challenges, the proposed system uses blockchain technology. Blockchain technology has enormous advantages such as transparency, immutability, security, etc. By using above features used to design and develop BaaS on cloud. BaaS improves the security as well as privacy of users while using the cloud environment. For creating block SHA256 encryption, the algorithm is used to achieve data encryption. Also, smart contracts are created for each block to maintain data integrity. After using smart contract, the user gets trust and transparency of the transaction. By using BaaS as a SaaS in the cloud, the security as well as privacy of data has improved.

## REFERENCES

[1] E. Bellini, P. Ceravolo, and E. Damiani. (2019). Blockchain-based e-Vote-as-a-Service. *IEEE 12th International Conference on Cloud Computing (CLOUD)*, doi: 10.1109/CLOUD.2019.00085

[2] G. Kuldeep and Q. Zhang. (2022). Multi-class privacy-preserving cloud computing based on compressive sensing for IoT. *Journal of Information Security and Applications*, doi: 10.1016/j.jisa.2022

[3] H. Han. (2021). Research on adaptive relationship between trust and privacy in cloud service. *IEEE Access*. pp. 43214–43227, doi: 10.1109/ACCESS.2021.3054634

[4] J. Bernal Bernabe, J. L. Canovas, J. L. Hernandez-Ramos, R. Torres Moreno, and A. Skarmeta. (2019). Privacy-preserving solutions for blockchain: Review and challenges. *IEEE Access*. pp. 164908–164940, doi: 10.1109/ACCESS.2019.2950872

[5] J. Lauder and S. Sajal. (2022). Jaxium: A trusted social network with maximum privacy. *IEEE International Conference on Electro Information Technology (eIT)*. pp. 389–392, doi: 10.1109/eIT53891.2022.9814062

[6] A. Kesarwani and P. M. Khilar. (2022). Development of trust-based access control models using fuzzy logic in cloud computing. *Journal of King Saud University – Computer and Information Sciences*. pp. 1958–1967.

[7] R. Krishnamurthi. (2021). A brief analysis of blockchain algorithms and its challenges. *Research Anthology on Blockchain Technology in Business, Healthcare, Education, and Government*. IGI Global, doi: 10.4018/978-1-7998-5351-0.ch002

[8] Kunz, A. Schneider, and C. Banse. (2020). Privacy smells: Detecting privacy problems in cloud architectures. *IEEE 19th International Conference on Trust, Security and Privacy in Computing and Communications (TrustCom)*. pp. 1324–1331, doi: 10.1109/TrustCom50675.2020.00178

[9] M. J. Priya and G. Yamuna. (2022). Privacy preserving data security model for cloud computing technology. *International Conference on Smart Technologies and*

Systems for Next Generation Computing (ICSTSN). pp. 1–5, doi: 10.1109/ICSTSN53084.2022.9761350

[10] M. Mohammed and F. A. Omara. (2020). A framework for trust management in cloud computing environment. *International Conference on Innovative Trends in Communication and Computer Engineering (ITCE)*. pp. 7–13, doi: 10.1109/ITCE48509.2020.9047791

[11] A. Mondal, S. Paul, R. T. Goswami, and S. Nath. (2020). Cloud computing security issues & challenges: A review. *International Conference on Computer Communication and Informatics (ICCCI)*. pp. 1–5, doi: 10.1109/ICCCI48352.2020.9104155

[12] P. Solainayagi, G. O. Jijina, K. Sujatha, N. Kanimozhi, N. Kanya, and S. Sendilvelan. (2022). *Trust discovery and information retrieval using artificial intelligence tools from multiple conflicting sources of web cloud computing and e-commerce users. Artificial Intelligence and Machine Learning for EDGE Computing*, Academic Press. pp. 103–119.

[13] S. Mittal, P. Jindal, and K. R. Ramkumar. (2021). Data privacy and system security for banking on clouds using homomorphic encryption. *2nd International Conference for Emerging Technology (INCET)*. pp. 1–6.

[14] S. Pavithra, S. Ramya, and S. Prathibha. (2019). A survey on cloud security issues and blockchain. *International Conference on Computing and Communications Technologies (ICCCT)*. pp. 136–140, doi: 10.1109/ICCCT2.2019.8824891

[15] S. V. Shinge and U. Shrawankar. (2023). An efficient technique for improving trust and privacy in Blockchain as a Service (BaaS). Accepted for publication in *IEEE International Conference (SCEECS 2023)* will be held on 18–19 February 2023.

[16] U. Shrawankar and C. Shrawankar. (2022). *BlockCloud: Blockchain as a cloud service. Blockchain for smart systems: Computing technologies and applications*, Chapman and Hall/CRC, doi: 10.1201/9781003203933

[17] U. Shrawankar and C. Dhule. (2021). *Cloud computing technologies for smart agriculture and healthcare: Virtualization technology for cloud-based services*, Chapman and Hall/CRC.

[18] W. Li, J. Wu, J. Cao, and N. Chen. (2021). Blockchain-based trust management in cloud computing systems: A taxonomy, review and future directions. *Journal of Cloud Computing: Advances, Systems and Applications*, doi: 10.1186/s13677-021-00247-5

[19] W. Ma, T. Zhou, J. Qin, X. Xiang, Y. Tan, and Z. Cai. (2022). A privacy-preserving content-based image retrieval method based on deep learning in cloud computing, *Expert Systems with Applications*, doi: 10.1016/j.eswa.2022

[20] W. Wang, Y. Jin, and B. Cao. (2022). An efficient and privacy-preserving range query over encrypted cloud data. *19th Annual International Conference on Privacy, Security & Trust (PST)*. pp. 1–10.

[21] W.-Y. Tsai, T.-C. Chou, J.-L. Chen, Y.-W. Ma, and C.-J. Huang. (2020). Blockchain as a platform for secure cloud computing services. *ICACT2020 February 16~19*.

# 9 Analyzing and Evaluating IoT and Cloud Platforms for Smart Cities

*Jatin Madan and Suman Madan*

## 9.1 INTRODUCTION

The term "smart city" is a relatively new concept whose dispersion has been quickly expanding somewhat recently. There are many definitions for the term "smart city," and we can say a smart city could be characterized as "high tech innovations, like energy production, logistic, information communication technologies (ICTs), and so on in a well-defined geographical area, cooperate together to give benefits to the people of society in terms of atmosphere quality, growth of intelligence, consideration and support, prosperity; it is addressed by an obvious pool of subjects, prepared to communicate the rules, and methodology for the local government and improvement" [1,2]. Smart cities work with the help of IoT. In an IoT climate, gadgets can be totaled by their topographical position and additionally surveyed by applying dissecting frameworks. IoT devices work with the help of sensors. Sensor administrations are used for getting together explicit information about certain continuous activities such as observing every cyclist, vehicle, parking area, and so on. There has been a ton of administration space for applications, which uses an IoT foundation to improve on tasks in air and commotion contamination control, development of vehicles, management frameworks, and so on. From time to time, the smart city idea has been blamed for being too "technology centric" from the very first endeavors of its practical implementations, driven mainly by the own agenda of these technological organizations, while lacking any consideration in regard to the district and the citizen's necessities. Subsequently, this has driven to a summed-up need for a more feasible approach [3,4].

The smart city is much smarter now than it was ever before because of the present development of digital innovations. Smart urban areas have a variety of technologies applied by a few applications, like cameras in a checking framework, sensors in a transportation framework, etc. Moreover, use of individual portable hardware can be spread. Smart cities are benefited through "big data" and the interconnected devices that the permitted cities give rights to acquire information that's never been available before. A well-designed data analytics blueprint gives the officials of these cities the potential to access and anatomize an enormous amount of data and simply glean meaningful, actionable insights. The smart city

DOI: 10.1201/9781003341437-11

Urban Greenery
Occupation
Quality of Air
Smart Energy Applications
Legitimacy and Defence
Digitization
Quality of Water
Tourism
Smart Governance
Smart Mobility
Smart Waste Mangement

**FIGURE 9.1** Key areas to be focused on in a smart city.

system has an adaptable structure, so its applications and design can be adapted by any city, no matter what its size is. Detection of traffic rules and regulations violations and a video surveillance of city is provided by automatic video content through analysis applications. Smart city technologies can provide cities with forecast analytics to identify those areas that need repair work before there can be any infrastructure failure. This will prevent any complications that can occur later in the future. Smart technologies, such as intelligent traffic signals, improve the flow of traffic, and alleviate traffic jams during peak travel times. A smart parking management system allows a city to earn additional revenue [5]. Thus, through the initiation of innovation in IoT, smart cities can work on various parts of their urban management, as shown in Figure 9.1, such as public lighting, mobility in urban areas, public transportation, e-administration, security, safety, and monitoring the environment. The adaptation of IoT technologies in a city will embark on a new and improved era for our world; it will allow us to control, observe, and manage all the resources available, like land, electric power, water, citizens, and so on in a manner which could guarantee a better future for all of us.

M. Sheik Dawood et al. (2018) stated that the various important real-life applications of IoT play vital roles in the daily life of human beings and this IoT field is emerging on daily basis. He explained that this evolving networking concept will have an impact on every aspect of our lives, from automated homes to smart health and the environment, all of which will be monitored by embedding intelligence into the electrical devices that surround us. As technology advances, the application's capabilities never become limited [6].

László Gere (2019) stated the meaning of IoT and what it does and what its role is in our life. He had stated that to make smart cities, first we must become smart. We should upgrade the technology not for selfish reasons but for creating a healthy and livable environment in and around the cities [7].

Antar Abdul-Qawy et al. (2015) stated how the Internet is a crucial part of our life and in the near future, the number of Internet-connected things will be larger than the number of people. The objects that surround environments will be connected to the Internet in some way. These things are intelligent, computing, sensing, remote monitoring, and control devices that are effortlessly connected to the Internet [8].

## 9.2    INTERNET OF THINGS

The Internet of Things (IoT) is a worldwide network of physical devices like voice assistants, wearable fitness trackers, IoT healthcare applications, and smart cars connected to the Internet. The "Things" in the Internet of Things are the devices that have the ability to capture and transmit data over a network or the Internet without the need for manual intervention. These devices are equipped with sensors and further information transfer mechanisms. The devices are typically combined with means of association to manage and/or processing units. Internet of Things or IoT theory suggests that "the inanimate apparatus will be able to speak." It provides everybody with high transparency in nearly each and every field of activity [9,10].

### 9.2.1    IoT- AND CLOUD-BASED SMART APPLICATIONS

Curiosity is the sole trait that distinguishes humans from other living creatures. We humans are inquisitive and ask a lot of questions, which leads to improvement in any field that relates or affects our lives in some manner [11,12]. IoT, often known as the fourth industrial revolution, has a wide range of applications and has the potential to revolutionize sectors. Some of these applications are as follows.

#### 9.2.1.1    Self-Driving Delivery Car

In Houston, Domino's is testing self-driving auto delivery of pizza. Domino's is continuing to improve the delivery experience by teaming up with Nuro, a robotics firm, to become the first quick-service restaurant in the United States to offer autonomous pizza delivery. Customers who place a prepaid order from a participating Domino's location can have their pizza delivered by Nuro's R2 robot – the first entirely self-driving, occupant-less on-road vehicle to receive regulatory approval from the U.S. Department of Transportation. Customers can also use the GPS on the order confirmation page to track the robot. It works as:

    Step 1. Opt in Nuro's R2 delivery
    Step 2. Domino's will text you an access pin. Meet the self-driving robot at your Curb.
    Step 3. Enter the pin and grab your order.

#### 9.2.1.2    Dash Shopping Cart

Amazon is introducing smart grocery carts called Dash Carts that allow customers to skip the checkout line. This service will be offered at Amazon's new grocery store in the Los Angeles area, which will launch later this year. Dash Carts feature cameras, sensors, and a smart display built in. They keep track of a shopper's order automatically.

   To utilize a Dash Cart, shoppers must have an Amazon account and a smartphone. When customers enter the Amazon grocery store, they use the Amazon app to scan the cart's QR code, which registers them in the cart and connects to their Amazon account. Dash Carts are an extension of Amazon's cashier-less technology. By allowing customers to grab and go, the company intends to improve the shopping experience.

The cart contains a built-in scale for products like fresh produce. A display on the front of the cart updates the total price as shoppers add and remove goods. When customers are ready to depart, they can use the Dash Cart lane in the store. Amazon will charge the credit card associated with the Amazon account and send a copy of the receipt to the email address provided.

### 9.2.1.3 NE-1 Helmet

NE-1 helmet is the world's first powered air purifying respirator, designed for use by anyone, anywhere. With N95 filtration, this evolved facemask has launched a crowdfunding campaign on IndieGoGo.

With built-in features like Bluetooth audio and speakers, a neoprene neck seal, powered air filtration technology, and an anti-fog, anti-glare face shield to smile safely, the NE-1 helmet solves the daily problems of COVID-19.

### 9.2.1.4 Polar Seal Heated Tops

At the press of a button, you can get instant heat, choose from three different warming levels, and activate two separate or combined heating zones. It is now possible to feel warm in the cold and all around you, and it is simple to use. Polar seal heated tops, composed of flexible and lightweight material, have been tested in rigorous Alpine circumstances. These are breathable and water resistant, making them ideal for sports like cycling, skiing, and hiking before heading out into nature. Tops made of polar seals can be worn alone or under heavier outer garments. They're also excellent for unwinding and keeping warm on cold days. It will keep you warm for up to eight hours on a single charge and is available in a variety of colors and sizes for both men and women.

### 9.2.1.5 JetBot 90 Al+

Object recognition technology is used to identify and classify things as well as determine the optimal cleaning paths. Lidar sensors for location detection and 3D sensors to distinguish even the smallest barriers allow it to clean close to stuff like toys while staying away from fragile goods like vaz's. It also has a built-in camera, so you can keep an eye on your pets while it cleans your house.

### 9.2.1.6 Cancer Detecting Pills

Google is working on a medication that detects cancer and heart attacks. They're making a special kind of ordinary capsule that needs to be taken like other medicines, but it's so sophisticatedly made that it will include very little magnetic nanoparticles. This one swallowed by a human would start working by joining into the flow of the blood in the human body and in return would transmit certain signals in advance before the cancer develops. It would also be beneficial in the case of heart and kidney issues. Nanoparticles, which can be read by wearing wristbands sensor units, may easily read this shift in human behavior.

### 9.2.1.7  Solara-50 Drone

Drons Titan aerospace, a company that builds solar-powered drones that can fly nonstop for years, was pulled in by the IT giant. Titan aerospace has announced the world's first solar-powered drone/unmanned aircraft, as well as the world's first solar-powered atmospheric satellites with a mission range of over 4 million kilometers. This drone can perform most of the functions of an orbital satellite, such as weather monitoring and earth imaging, but at a lower cost. When the sun rises, the solar panel covering the craft's surface stores enough energy to allow them to ascend to a position of 20 kilometers above sea level and fly aloft continuously for five years without having to descend and refuel. Solara only weighs 160 kilograms and can carry a payload of 32 kilograms, and it can travel at speed of up to 104 kilometers per hour (64 miles per hour).

### 9.2.1.8  Smart Mirrors

Smart mirrors are a great example of an IoT application. These mirrors may be used to show temperature, news, weather, calendars, and clocks, among other things. They can also be used to take ideal selfies with the help of built-in camera. It can also be equipped with speakers to play music, as well as be used to browse the Internet, make phone calls, and collaborate with other gadgets.

It can be turned into a security system to detect human presence when no one is at home. When someone enters the room, a sensor will identify the person's movement as he passes by the mirror and take the image, which will be saved in the drop box. Smart mirror system can also be used as a security system because it notifies the owner by updating the captured image in the drop box.

### 9.2.1.9  Smart Doors

It is mostly used to intelligently control human entry and exit. When you pass by, the doors open and close automatically. This door can also be controlled remotely. By using a certain app on your smartphone, you might unlock the door for a friend. You will be notified as soon as they leave. The owner has complete control over who has access to the door. In a scenario where the door is accessed by a person who has been blacklisted, a notification will be triggered immediately and an alert regarding the same will be sent to the administrator via the GSM module [13].

To enhance the system's usability and efficiency, we can utilize a real-time voice assistant. In the unfortunate scenario of a power outage or data loss, we can have the system connect to a separate cloud service which also ensures database privacy.

### 9.2.1.10  Smart Alarm Clock

There are many different types of alarm clocks, but this one is self-setting. This smart alarm clock checks your Google calendar for appointments before setting the alarm and considers the weather to alter your awake time automatically.

In order to determine whether a person is sleeping enough, we can place a sensor below his mattress or pillow which can be connected to a smart alarm clock. The alarm sound of traditional alarm clocks can be quite irritating at times. However, with a smart alarm clock, you may customize the alarm tone to your liking. It may also turn on the LED lights, which will keep you energized throughout the day.

## 9.2.2   INDIAN GOVERNMENT'S IoT POLICY

A pivotal role in making the vision of 100 smart cities a reality is played by the private sector, which has also been acknowledged by the Minister of Urban Development. He stated that private investments are critical to the development and realization of smart cities. Aside from drawing in interest in regions like energy, physical foundation, financial freedoms, and so forth, the Indian government believes that the agreement to build 100 smart cities throughout the nation could provoke an enormous and quick advancement of IoT in the country [3]. The Department of Electronics and Information Technology (DeiTY) brought forward a document highlighting the IoT policies. Recognizing the requirement for a policy structure that acts like a pillar to the private sector companies, i.e., support them, especially those working in the IoT and M2M space. The DeiTY created a draught IoT policy paper for people working in the IoT and M2M area, in particular that revolves around the following aims:

- Establishing an IoT industry within India worth of US$ 15 billion by the year 2020. It is expected that India would conquer 5–6% of IoT industry worldwide.
- To attempt limit improvement (human and technology) for IoT explicit ranges of abilities for homegrown and worldwide business sectors.
- To embrace research and improvement for all the helping advancements.
- To foster IoT items explicit to Indian requirements in every single imaginable space.

The government intends to establish demonstration centers to develop domain-specific IoT strategies, such as telematics and supply chain, smart cities, smart grid, supply chain, hospitals, automotive, connected homes, agriculture, industrial monitoring, green buildings, safety and security, wildlife and forest, natural disasters, and so on [14]. The DeiTY would also provide INR 125 crores in 50% funding (PPP mode) for five projects that will be implemented over the next three years in the following areas.

- Smart supply chain and logistics
- Smart safety
- Smart agriculture
- Smart health care (remote)
- Smart waste management
- Smart environment
- Smart city
- Smart water

### 9.2.2.1   Bringing in Existing Programs in Accordance with the Smart City Agenda

Between 2007 and 2011, India noticed a CAGR of 26% in hi-tech exports with exports increasing by US$ 13 billion, reaching US$ 21 billion from US$ 8 billion in 2007.

This trend continued despite industry associations highlighting concerns regarding administrative boundaries, moderate recuperation in worldwide business sectors, and absence of foundation. This recommends that India has the basic abilities to respond to the call of planning, assembling, and selling savvy city advancements. "Make in India" campaign has been launched by Indian government in order to increase supply-side advantages for manufacturing. This new national program, proposed by India's prime minister, has the agenda of facilitating investment, protect intellectual property, focus on enriching and upskilling while promoting innovation and building an efficient manufacturing infrastructure.

### 9.2.2.2 Making an Empowering System for the Assembling of M2M Technologies

Smart city features are citizen-friendly, and the MoUD has distinguished web-empowered stages and IT capabilities to work with citizen commitment. With a gained impetus on the necessity of smart cities, digital, spatial, and GIS maps will become a necessity to be developed on a constantly improved and updated Open Data Platform. An access to an open dataset like this would enable us to define administrative applications along with innovative instruments as examined in the past. This will probably affect the telecom, gadgets, and IT areas, especially up-lifting the interest for handheld gadgets.

In fact, it is anticipated that smartphone demand would exceed 2,700 million by 2014 and will rise at a compounded annual growth rate of 15% to exceed 6,100 million by 2020.

IEEE 802.15, which is for wireless personal area networks, is the most important standard for smart cities. This standard is made up of several components, including Bluetooth, coexistence, interoperability, high-rate WPAN, low-rate WPAN, mesh networking, body area networks, visible light communication, peer-aware communication, key management protocol, layer 2 routing, and wireless next-generation standing committee.

### 9.2.2.3 National Optical Fiber Network (NOFN)

The Indian government is working on NOFN, a project that is estimated to cost INR 20,000 crores (US\$ 4 billion) and would deliver the broadband connection to over two lakh (2,00,000) gram panchayats all over India. This project will leap India forward in its ability to provide e-services/e-applications all over India. By 2016, the NOFN intends to be able to assemble around 7 lakh kilometers of optical fiber network so that we can connect all the "panchayats" of villages with the high-speed Internet services. E-commerce, e-entertainment, and a slew of other services will boom as digital infrastructure spreads across the country.

### 9.2.2.4 National Knowledge Network (NKN)

The government of India is also insisting on the continuation of National Knowledge Network (NKN), whose agenda is to build high-quality universities with the required research facilities along with a group of highly skilled individuals. The NKN is made up of an ultra-high-speed CORE and a distribution layer running at suitable speeds. The network supports virtual networks and dedicated networks along with overlay networks. At Indian educational establishments, the highest connectivity speed is now 1 GBPS through NKN; still, the government aims to expand it to 10 GBPS, so as to reach international connectivity standards. The NKN also has another agenda to serve as a platform where they can provide distance education successfully with real-time interactions between students and teachers, so as to improve educational access while overcoming factors such as infrastructure and location.

### 9.2.3 ARCHITECTURE

Some researchers have envisioned a dream for smart city development. It is suggested as per the usual guidelines to develop smart cities in a three-layer architecture design that constitutes the application layer, the perception layer, and the network layer. Perception layer, which is the primary interface is responsible for collecting the data from various sources like cameras and GPS. The second layer, which is the network layer, deals with communicating information sourced by Layer 1 to the data storage center. Application layer, the third layer, contains applications which analyze and process large amounts of data stored and gathered by the second layer [15].

In addition to three basic layers suggested by authors, we conceptualized the layers in four divisions, as shown in Figure 9.2. The primary layer is the perception layer which is categorized as sensing layer in the below architecture. The second layer is further divided into two layers: the network layer and the data processing layer. The application layer is categorized as application layer only. There are basically four important layers when we are working with IoT, and we can begin with the bottom-up approach.

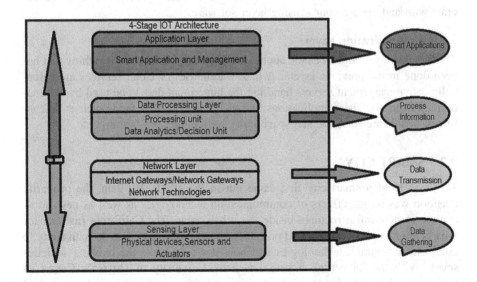

**FIGURE 9.2**   Four-stage IOT architecture.

### 9.2.3.1  Sensing Layer

In the first layer, we have the sensing layer. The sensing layer is where you actually have your actuators, you have your sensors, and all kinds of entities that can actually do something; for example, you have a gas leakage detector, you might have a light sensor, or you might have a camera that can pick up motion or can have a temperature-sensing entity, etc. These sensors or entities process data and emit data over network. Network layer: to make these sensors talk to other layers of the task, there is one more important layer, which is the second layer.

### 9.2.3.2  Network Layer

To make these sensors talk to other layers of the task, there is one more important layer, which is the second layer/network layer. This layer basically contains Internet/network gateways and data acquisition systems (DAS). DAS collects and aggregates data and then converts analogue data gathered from the sensors and digitizes it. Gateways are special devices that connect our sensor network with the cloud. In order to implement virus prevention and filtering, along with special decision-making abilities based on the input data and other data management services, we utilize advanced gateways.

This layer basically helps to connect the third layer or data processing layer to the sensing layer.

### 9.2.3.3  Data Processing Layer

The heart of an IoT device lies in the third layer, the data processing layer, as it collects data from sensing devices, analyzes it, and pre-processes it before uploading it to a data center. At the data center, various applications, i.e., business applications, analyze, monitor, and manage the data. To plan further actions, this data processing layer can also troubleshoot your sensing layer, as well as collaborate with and update your sensing layer software.

### 9.2.3.4  Application Layer

The topmost layer, known as the application layer, makes use of everything that has been done in the previous layers. A data warehouses or cloud services are essentially data management servers handling the huge input data to be used by the end-user applications. These applications find their use in various fields such as defense forces, healthcare services, aerospace units, agriculture and farming, etc.

## 9.3  SMART CITY

The concept of a smart city first came out in the 1990s. By then, the primarily attention was on the effects of communication technologies as well as new information on new infrastructures inside the urban areas. The California Institute for Smart Communities concentrated primarily on how they can come up with a city to establish information technologies and how it would make the existing societies smart. With this in action, a year later, the University of Ottawa's Centre of Governance began to condemn smart cities as being excessively revolving around technologies. Recently, researchers reached out to the smart cities in existence to step forward and define the true meaning of being a "smart" city. The terms "smart city" and "digital city" or "intelligent city" are used interchangeably. These differences are classified into three groups: technology, people, and community.

Arranging the smart city environment treats the utilization of technology as an essential component, just as to consider human and social capital aspects. These days, there are enormous numbers of smart city deployments, which are all dependent on the custom frameworks and solutions; however, this might not be the case for different cities all throughout the planet and sometimes just a subset of the different aspects should be taken in account [16,17].

In the accompanying, the fundamental obstructions, current difficulties, and issues recognized for the smart city are summed up in Figure 9.3. More exhaustively, we distinguished that these challenges can be partitioned inside four fundamental measurements, as displayed in the following figure: citizens, mobility, governance, and environment.

The national ranking system, iCityRank, targets at providing a measure of the advances made by various Italian districts (such as Parma) toward the goal of

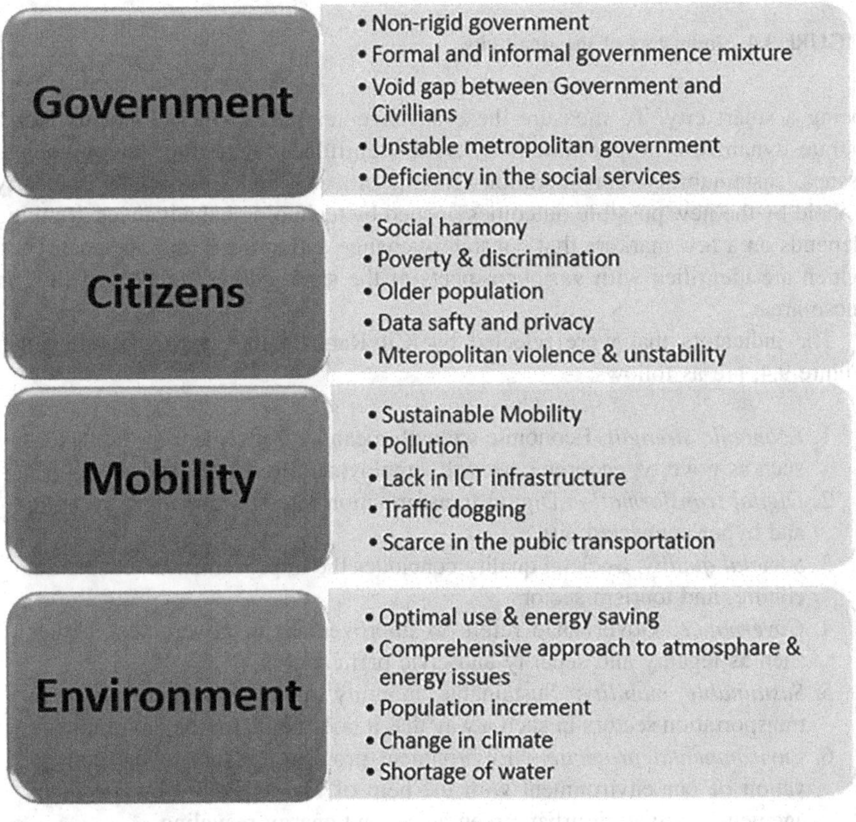

**Government**
- Non-rigid government
- Formal and informal governmence mixture
- Void gap between Government and Civillians
- Unstable metropolitan government
- Deficiency in the social services

**Citizens**
- Social harmony
- Poverty & discrimination
- Older population
- Data safty and privacy
- Mteropolitan violence & unstability

**Mobility**
- Sustainable Mobility
- Pollution
- Lack in ICT infrastructure
- Traffic dogging
- Scarce in the pubic transportation

**Environment**
- Optimal use & energy saving
- Comprehensive approach to atmosphare & energy issues
- Population increment
- Change in climate
- Shortage of water

**FIGURE 9.3** Smart city challenges.

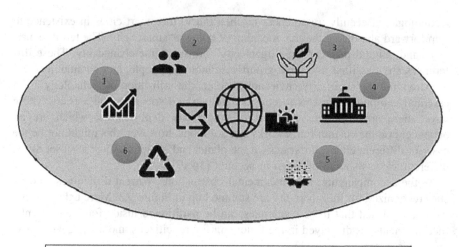

1. Economic Strength 2. Societal Quality     3. Protecting Environment

4. Governance          5. Digital Transformation   6. Sustainable Mobility

**FIGURE 9.4**   Indicators of the smart city.

being a smart city. To measure these advancements, legit measurements incorporate dynamism, proper functionality, thoughtfulness regarding environmental issues, sustainability, considerations for the citizens, and so on. This is clearly upheld by the new possible outcomes opened by technological advances. Ranking depends on a few markers that constantly change and are re-examined each year, which are identified with various aspects of the standards of "quality of life" in these areas.

The indicators that were selected by iCityRank in the year 2019, shown in Figure 9.4, are as follows:

1. *Economic strength*: Economic strength means improvement in the factors such as poverty, economic growth, employment, research, and work.
2. *Digital transformation*:Digital transformation refers to making a synergic and hyper-connected city.
3. *Societal quality*: Societal quality concludes the improvement in education, culture, and tourism sectors.
4. *Governance*: Governance refers to improvement in government bodies such as legality and security and civic participation.
5. *Sustainable mobility*: Sustainable mobility refers to improvement in transportation sectors in such a way that it does not harm the environment.
6. *Environmental protection*: Environment protection refers to the conservation of our environment with the help of factors such as waste management, cultivating urban green areas, and energy recycling.

As cities and capitals grow more dense, it becomes crucial that every subsystem works together as a single unit with intelligent computing being applied to every subsystem. Researchers who believe in this integrated view emphasize the significance of the organic composition of different subsystems (education sector, transportation sector, infrastructures, hospitals, energy, public safety and security) of a city into one whole united system to build up smart cities. Thus, we can sum up the required possible attributes for the smart city development as smart residents, smart living, smart administration, smart transportation, smart economics, and smart infrastructure.

After literature study, we defined a structure, as given in Figure 9.5, that a smart city is made up of three components: institutions, technology, and citizens. Given

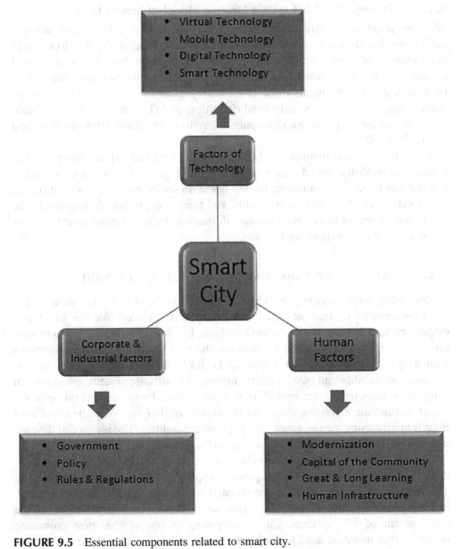

**FIGURE 9.5** Essential components related to smart city.

the relationship between these variables, the city can be identified as "smart" if the human capital is completely utilized and it invests heavily in an IT framework to drive sustainable growth and raise living standards through an active governing body (institutional factor).

### 9.3.1 ROLE OF IoT IN THE CONSTRUCTION OF A SMART CITY

The operators of a smart city breadth and scale are advancements in ICT and data-sharing innovation. This quick development has led to the emergence of construction of smart cities since the beginning of IoT. All the difficulties and challenges faced in the development are discussed as well.

#### 9.3.1.1 Emergence of IoT with a Diverse Model of Sensor Data

With the accelerating advancements in cloud and sensor technologies, storage, and processing ability, and diminished cost of sensor creation, the development in deployments of sensor applications has expanded throughout the most recent couple of years. In contrast to a smart city, IoT came into existence fundamentally from the advancements made in technologies and not because of clients' or applications' needs. The widely used definition of IoT is that "Using any path/network and any service, we can connect anytime, anyplace, with anything and anyone" [18–20].

Regardless of their distinctions, both the smart cities and IoT are going hand in hand to accomplish a shared goal, as summed up in Figure 9.6. It ought to be noticed that the way toward implementing models based on sensor data in terms of attributes of a location, observed objectives, status, and time is unpredictable because of the assortment of sensor platforms, location information, technical requirements, sensor processes, and observation mechanisms.

### 9.3.2 ROLE OF CLOUD COMPUTING IN SMART CITY DEVELOPMENT

As computing requirements grow, cloud computing is the obvious new paradigm in the advancement of Internet-based computing and services. As the smart IoT devices expand beyond the cloud environment, IoT can improve the performance, efficiency, and throughput. Smart cities are the next generation of establishments with a special attention to an improved IT infrastructure, with a focus on environmental stability and sustainability, improved healthcare system, urban system authorities, knowledge, and upskilling of human capital with a focus on network-driven development. Within the cloud infrastructure, IoT will reap the benefits of improved efficiency, performance, and payload capabilities. The issues that develop in a dynamic, shared environment are the IoT's main focus.

The IoT is a large category that includes a variety of flexible and unconventional devices with constrained storage, power supply, and performance capabilities. These limitations, which include complicated issues like compatibility, efficiency, full functionality, and availability, serve as a barrier and impediment to the development of IoT systems. Cloud computing is one of the most promising strategies that might be used in conjunction with IoT to get over these constraints.

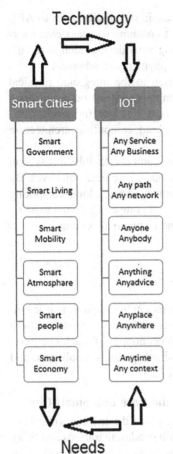

FIGURE 9.6  Connection and relationship among smart city and IoT.

The cloud offers shared resources (network, storage, computers, and software) that stand out for their accessibility, affordability, and aesthetic appeal. The applications for communication, processing, and storage on a cloud-based IoT platform for smart cities are described in this study. These platforms can rely on cloud services to source, transfer, analyze, process, and save data, even in complex scenarios due to cloud's scalable and reliable architecture.

ICT services can now be provided as a carrier thanks to cloud computing, which is the next stage in the development of Internet-based computing. Cloud computing allows for the connection of computer resources, infrastructure (such as servers and storage), systems, business processes, and other essential resources [21]. With the rise of cloud computing, it has become simpler to create flexible business models that let companies consume resources as their operations expand. Instead of requiring a drawn-out provisioning process, cloud computing enables instant access to cloud delivery, unlike companies that offer traditional web-based services (such web hosting). In cloud computing, each provisioning and withdrawal of resources can happen again [22–24].

Applications and resource records can communicate in the cloud thanks to APIs (application programming interfaces), which also let consumers access cloud services. Payment options include invoicing and rating providers, which offer the assistance needed to use the rating aid and to make payments in advance.

*Monitoring and assessing performance*: In addition to the integrated physical computing system and its methodologies, cloud computing infrastructure offers a carrier management environment for monitoring and assessing performance.

*Security*: To protect sensitive information, the cloud computing architecture allows secure operations.

*Cloud computing offers two benefits*: (1) cost savings and (2) flexible, timely, and necessary access to computer resources as needed to achieve corporate objectives. By transforming capital expenditures (CapEx) into operating costs, cloud computing promises to save costs. This is due to the fact that cloud computing favors existing management and enables more flexible scheduling and resource allocation.

### 9.3.3 Issues and Challenges

#### 9.3.3.1 Data Privacy

One of the key issues in data privacy of an IoT-driven environment is that it employs geo-location, geo-tagging services, and monitors human decisions, while a smart city enables new horizons such as knowledge economies. To achieve maximum citizen buy-in, the government must urge business partners, coalitions, and developers to approach this issue as a top priority [22,23].

#### 9.3.3.2 Implanting Ecological Sustainability at the Core of a Smart City

While guaranteeing well-being and security is basic, given the trillion-dollar venture needed to fulfill the developing need for metropolitan administrations and bring existing Indian urban areas up to worldwide norms, it is likewise basic to join practical improvement standards into brilliant city arranging and execution. Including fiber-optic network provisions into the design phase of infrastructure such as open spaces, buildings, roads, and pipeline networks may significantly cut costs, energy consumption, and greenhouse emissions. Other sectors where sustainability principles apply include waste management, water, and transportation. Encouraging companies to use measures like embodied energy, life-cycle analysis, and carbon footprinting can assist cities in making better decisions.

#### 9.3.3.3 Emphasizing on Promoting Advancing Energy-Saving Smart Technology

There is no doubt that IoT and machine-to-machine (M2M) technologies will minimize environmental externalities by optimizing resource usage. Nonetheless, for all the stakeholders, it is critical to understand that the ICT industry has a significant footprint in terms of production, electricity consumption, and e-waste creation. With the rise of linked technologies, the worldwide ICT industry is expected to generate over 1,100 million tons of $CO_2$ by 2020, up from 1.3% in 2007 to around 2% in 2020. As a result, it's critical to combine a drive for smart city manufacturing with a "green manufacturing strategy."

## 9.4 OPPORTUNITIES MADE BY A SMART CITY INITIATIVE

### 9.4.1 INCLINATION IN THE EMPLOYMENT

Indian government initiatives like "Digital India," "Make in India," and "100 Smart Cities," recruiting portals predict that 9.5 lakh new jobs would be created in 2015, with the IT and ITeS industries emerging as key employers. The Indian government believes that smart city initiatives would result in a 10–15% increase in employment over the long term. The FFC (The Forum for Future Cities) predicted that GIFT (Gujarat International Finance Tec-City), an intelligent city, may generate up to 1 million jobs in Gujarat for both qualified and unskilled workers. Aside from IT, electronics, and telecommunications, the energy industry, notably solar, is projected to provide considerable job growth, based on the previous government's aim of solar energy of 20 GW by 2022. In 2013, the Ministry of New and Renewable Energy projected that the solar sector produced 50,000 direct jobs between the years 2010 and 2013.

### 9.4.2 ECONOMIC OPPORTUNITY EMERGENCE

Smart cities are seen as a catalyst for economic growth and job creation all over the world. For instance, an estimation by the UK Department for Business, Innovation and Skills (BIS) found that there is a global market for smart solutions in five distinct industries – waste, transportation, electric-energy, water, and assisted living – to be worth US $400 billion by 2020, with 10% of that already existing in the mature economy of the United Kingdom. Using a broader definition that covers smart buildings, urban planning, and cybersecurity, among other technologies, Markets & Markets predicted the industry to be worth US $1 trillion by 2016. In India, industry groups predict that M2M services would see enormous growth to satisfy the demands produced by the government's INR 7,000 crore "Smart Cities" project.

## 9.5 CONCLUSION

IoT enables cities and states to be connected and manage multiple sectors spanning a multitude of services in a centralized fashion. From smart lighting and dash shopping carts to waste management and self-driving cars – a typical smart city contains a diverse plethora of IoT models. One attribute shared by all these models is their outcomes. Applying these IoT solutions to these cities is like a sure shot investment that leads to reduced cost for energy, safer and secured cities, an efficient usage of our limited natural resources, and overall, a healthier and eco-friendly environment. In order to completely reap these benefits of a smart city, we would need to adopt a well-defined and consistent yet iterative approach to achieve a scalable, functional, and adaptable smart city architecture. A well-planned architecture as such will aid us in reducing the further developmental and maintenance costs improving the turnaround time for developing more future ready intelligent establishments, with a future scope for expansion. To reach the objective of smart city, only together with the civilians and the service providers, we can identify all the challenges and the goals, and find the optimal tools to meet those needs to build a smart city. As László Gere wrote in his paper, "The creation of smart cities starts with smart people, not with smart technology."

## REFERENCES

[1] Monzon, A. (2015) Smart Cities Concept and Challenges: Bases for the Assessment of Smart City Projects. International Conference on Smart Cities and Green ICT Systems Lisbon, Portugal, May 20–22, 2015; pp. 1–11. DOI: 10.1007/978-3-319-27753-0_2

[2] Gopal, K. (2014) Bootstrapping India's Smart Growth – Foundation for Future Cities. http://www.futurecities.org/images/media/pdf/Karunagopal-smartcitiesgrowth-indiafuturarc.pdf

[3] Government of India report. (2015) Smart Cities India – Smart Solutions for a Better Tomorrow. http://www.smartcitiesindia.com/pdf/SCI-Conference-ExhibitionsBrochure-2015.pdf

[4] Laroiya, C., Bhatia, M. K., Madan, S., Komalavalli, C. (2023) IoT and Blockchain-Based Method for Device Identity Verification. In: Gupta, D., Khanna, A., Bhattacharyya, S., Hassanien, A. E., Anand, S., Jaiswal, A. (eds.) *International Conference on Innovative Computing and Communications. Lecture Notes in Networks and Systems*, vol. 473. Springer: Singapore. DOI: 10.1007/978-981-19-2821-5_23

[5] Sheik Dawood, M. (2018) Review on Applications of Internet of Things(IoT). https://www.researchgate.net/publication/329672903_Review_on_Applications_of_Internet_of_Things_IoT

[6] Su, K., Li, J., Hongbo, F. (2011) Smart City and the Applications. International Conference on Electronics, Communications and Control, Ningbo, China, IEEE. DOI: 10.1109/ICECC.2011.6066743

[7] Gere, L. (2019) Smart Cities: What Does It Mean and How Can We Get There. In *Focus: Smart Homes Cities Nations*, pp. 34–37. https://www.academia.edu/49170749/Smart_Cities_What_Does_It_Mean_and_How_Can_We_Get_There

[8] Abdul-Qawy, A., Mangesh, E., Tadisetty, S. (2015) The Internet of Things (IoT): An Overview. https://www.semanticscholar.org/paper/The-Internet-of-Things-(-IoT-)-%3A-An-Overview-Antar-Abdul-Qawy-Pramod/be9948d8ad53873c5e07d0b26d824ccedc460aac

[9] Gazis, V., Görtz, M., Huber, M. (2015) A Survey of Technologies for the Internet of things. 2015 International Wireless Communications and Mobile Computing Conference, pp. 1090–1095.

[10] Hammi, B., Khatoun, R., Zeadally, S., Fayad, A., Khoukhi, L. (2018) IoT Technologies for Smart Cities. *IET Networks*, 7(1), 1–13. DOI: 10.1049/iet-net.2017.0163

[11] Al-Ani, K. W., Abdalkafor, A. S., Nassar, A. M. (2019) Smart City Applications: A Survey. In Proceedings of 9th International Conference on Information Systems and Technologies, Cairo, Egypt, ACM, New York, USA. DOI: 10.1145/3361570.3361616

[12] Madan, J., Madan, S. (2022) Intelligent and Personalized Factoid Question and Answer System. 2022 10th International Conference on Reliability, Infocom Technologies and Optimization (Trends and Future Directions) (ICRITO), Noida, India, pp. 1–7. DOI: 10.1109/ICRITO56286.2022.9964818

[13] Priyanka, R., Dhanalakshmi, D., Kalaivani, S. (2019) Automated Door System

Using Face Recognition by Machine Learning. *International Journal of Engineering Applied Sciences and Technology*, 4(6), 205–208, ISSN No. 2455-2143. https://www.ijeast.com/papers/205-208,Tesma406,IJEAST.pdf

[14] Ullah, A. (2016) Prospects of Smart Cities Development in India through Public Private Partnership. *International Journal of Research in Advent Technology*, 4(1). Available at SSRN: https://ssrn.com/abstract=2711066

[15] Alawadhi, S., Aldama-Nalda, A., Chourabi, H., Gil-Garcia, J. R., Leung, S. (2012) Building Understanding of Smart City Initiatives. In: Scholl, H. J., Janssen, M., Wimmer, M. A., Moe, C. E., Flak, L. S. (eds) *Electronic Government. Lecture Notes in Computer Science*, vol. 7443. Springer: Berlin, Heidelberg. DOI: 10.1007/978-3-642-33489-4_4

[16] Harrison, C., Eckman, B., Hamilton, R., Hartswick, P., Kalagnanam, J., Paraszczak, J., Williams, P. (2010) Foundations for Smarter Cities. *IBM Journal of Research and Development*, 54(4), 1–16. DOI: 10.1147/jrd.2010.2048257

[17] Dameri, R. (2013) Searching for Smart City Definition: A Comprehensive Proposal. *International Journal of Computers & Technology*, 11(5), 2544–2551. DOI: 10.242 97/ijct.v11i5.1142

[18] Nam, T., Pardo, T. A. (2011) Conceptualizing Smart City with Dimensions of Technology, People, and Institutions. International Digital Government Research Conference on Digital Government Innovation in Challenging Times - Dg.o '11. DOI: 10.1145/2037556.2037602

[19] Hollands, R. G. (2008) Will the Real Smart City Please Stand Up?, *City*, 12(3), 303–320. DOI: 10.1080/13604810802479126

[20] Albino, V., Berardi, U., Dangelico, R. M. (2015) Smart Cities: Definitions, Dimensions, Performance, and Initiatives. *Journal of Urban Technology*, 22(1), 3–21. DOI: 10.1 080/10630732.2014.942092

[21] Madan, S., Goswami, P. (2019). K-DDD Measure and Map-Reduce Based Anonymity Model for Secured Privacy Preservation Big Data Publishing. *IJUFKS*, 27(2), 177–199. DOI: 10.1142/S0218488519500089

[22] Roy, S., Sarddar, D. (2016). The Role of Cloud of Things in Smart Cities. *International Journal of Computer Science and Security*, 14, 683–698.

[23] Madan, S., Bhardwaj, K., Gupta, S. (Aug 2021) Critical Analysis of Big Data Privacy Preservation Techniques and Challenges. In: International Conference on Innovative Computing and Communications: Proceedings of ICICC 2021, volume 3, vol. 1394. Springer Nature, p. 267.

[24] Madan, S. (2021) Privacy-Preserved Access Control in E-Health Cloud-Based System. In *Disruptive Technologies for Society 5.0*. CRC Press: Boca Raton, FL, pp. 145–162.

# 10 Development in IoT and Cloud Computing Using Artificial Intelligence

*Mamata Rath, Niva Tripathy,*
*Subhranshu Sekhar Tripathy, Vandana Sharma,*
*and Mahendra Kumar Garanayak*

## 10.1 INTRODUCTION

The most pre-overwhelming innovation for which everybody expects can change the world, the potential of artificial intelligence (AI) is becoming more and more clear as it can address concerns like space exploration, overcoming psychological oppression, and even creating craftsmanship. There are still many significant hurdles facing this dynamic advancement in AI, but they must be overcome before its full potential can be realized [1]. Meeting those challenges is frequently seen as the most pressing task facing the specialized industry right now. Swarm intelligence (SI) is a key idea in AI. Many see meeting those difficulties as an assignment of the most extreme need for the specialized business at this moment. One of the major contributions of AI is in SI, which is an AI method based around the investigation of aggregate conduct in decentralized, self-sorted-out frameworks. SI is regularly made up of a populace of basic specialists. Instances of SI in conditiosn are subterranean insect provinces, feathered creature rushing, creature crowding, and so on [2].

Many specialists in the domain of AI, explorers, and foundations focus on the issue that people don't experience comfortableness when they can't understand how the reason works since AI is a "black box," according to this concern. For instance, calculations utilized by banks are chiefly direct maths and it's really simple to clarify the way from the contribution to the yield "I denied your home loan application since, you don't have a vocation, or whatever." With multi-layer neural systems that the normal human doesn't see, we're now making expectations dependent on things that individuals don't comprehend and that is going to make individuals awkward. Although this revolt is bound to appear as online networking battling and blacklists, than crushing machines and torching get together plants, it's an obstacle that could crash endeavors to drive progress [3]. The understanding here is giving individuals a chance to see that this innovation works. Actually, there's an incredible chance to improve things by having progressively exact forecasts with

DOI: 10.1201/9781003341437-12

approximation analysis and prescriptions. People must be made aware of to comprehend and acknowledge those suggestions [4].

## 10.2 LITERATURE STUDY

Over the past two decades, AI has advanced significantly, influencing practically every aspect of life. Due to the dearth of fundamentally strong professionals up until recently, this is a notable challenge. Scientific authors have discussed and attempted to understand simulated intelligence in the depths of academic IT research labs [5–10]. The specifics of the technical approaches and topic matters employed by numerous authors are described in Tables 10.1 and 10.2 in order to do a thorough research and review of related applications.

When combined with AI, emerging ideas like virtual-reality and IoT edge devices like elegant specs (smart glass) ensure being utilized as aids that incorporate human (or human-like) insider knowledge [22,23]. Table 10.3 displays various concepts discussed by researchers in the domain of IoT and CC.

Another innovative application of AI integrated with IoT is presented here. Challenges related with creating investigation activities at the edge of Industrial Internet of Things (IIoT) organizes where information is being produced much of the timeand includes creating examination arrangements from the ground up [24,25]. Figure 10.1 represents confluence of AI in CC and IoT environment.

**TABLE 10.1**

**List of Technical Approaches by Other Contributors in a Similar Field (Part 1) [1,3,4,6,11–14]**

| Ref. | Literature | Year | Research Theme with Approach / Concept |
|---|---|---|---|
| [1] | Y. Cheng et al. | 2019 | Intelligent Animal Care Management and architecture using IoT and AI |
| [3] | P. Kiss et al. | 2018 | IoT applications on 5G Edge |
| [4] | P. Mendki et al. | 2018 | Docker container based analytics at IoT edge video and analytics use case |
| [6] | E. Oyekanlu et al. | 2018 | Osmatic computing approach to use deep learning at IIoT (Industrial IoT ) |
| [11] | C. V.Krishna et al. | 2018 | AI methods for data science and data analytics |
| [15] | M. Al-Rakhami et al. | 2018 | Cost efficient edge intelligence framework using docker containers |
| [17] | H. Jeong et al. | 2017 | Cloud based machine learning for IoT devices with privacy and security |
| [18] | T. Lee et al. | 2018 | Cloud computing architecture for context aware IoT services |

**TABLE 10.2**

**List of Technical Approaches by Other Contributors in a Similar Field (Part 2) [14–21]**

| Ref. | Literature | Year | Research Theme with Approach / Concept |
|------|-----------|------|----------------------------------------|
| [18] | T. Lee et al. | 2018 | Cloud computing architecture for context aware IoT services |
| [19] | Y. Son et al. | 2018 | Cloud of Things based on linked data |
| [20] | M.Y. Wang et al. | 2017 | IoT Surveillance system for fall detection |
| [21] | N. Kumar et al. | 2018 | Water quality monitoring system using IoT and Machine learning |
| [22] | J. Wu et al. | 2018 | Local area service based on IoT and Cloud intellect switch |
| [23] | G. Peralta et al. | 2017 | Fog computing based efficient IoT scheme for Industry 4.0 |
| [24] | T. Muhammed et al. | 2018 | Personalized ubiquitous cloud and edge supported health care system for smart cities |
| [25] | T. Yamakami et al. | 2018 | Edge based Artificial Engine with edge cloud co-ordination |

**TABLE 10.3**

**Various Concepts Discussed by Researchers in the Domain of IoT and CC**

| |
|---|
| ❖ [I-O-T, Health Observance System, Fog Computing, health-care] |
| ❖ [e-health, I-O-T, fog computing, cloud computing] |
| ❖ [Fog computing, Cloud computing, Wearable devices, I-O-T sensors, Health care systems, Data Analytics] |
| ❖ [fog computing, I-O-T, health-care, mobility, migration, fog positioning] |
| ❖ [Internet of Things, Fog Computing, Advance Encryption Standard] |
| ❖ [Fog computing, Task Placement, Internet of Things(I-O-T), Network Resource Optimization, Response Time, Energy consumption Optimization] |
| ❖ [Internet of Things, I-O-T, e-health, Quality of Service, Fog Computing, Cloud Computing, Performance Analysis] |
| ❖ [FOG computing, CCN, E-health, I-O-T] |
| ❖ [Internet of Everything, Health care, Smart Gateway, Sensor Network, Heart Rate, Blood glucose, SPO2, Fog Computing] |
| ❖ [Bayesian belief network (BBN), fog computing, Internet of Things (I-O-T), temporal health index (THI), temporal mining] |
| [Personal health record, Blockchain, fog computing, Internet of Things, distributed systems, health informatics] |

| Artificial Intelligence | |
|---|---|
| Cloud Computing | |
| Blockchain & IoT | |
| Serverless computing | Fault Tolerance |
| Deep Learning | Fog Computing |
| Big Data Analytics | Quantum Computing |
| SDN (Software Defined Network) | Application Design |
| Security & Privacy | BitCoin Currency |
| Resource Management | Quality of Service in WSN |
| Software Engineering | Energy Management |

**FIGURE 10.1** Applications of AI, cloud technology, blockchain, and IoT.

## 10.3 SIGNIFICANCE OF ARTIFICIAL INTELLIGENCE IN NEW TECHNOLOGIES

Figure 10.2 shows different cloud services in smart city applications. According to AI logic firm deep intuition, each new piece of malware will often have code that is almost identical to previous iterations, but between 2% and 10% of the records will vary from emphasis to cycle. Their learning technique can predict which recordings are malware with exceptional accuracy and has no trouble with the 2–10% variants. Individual protection using AI and machine learning is demonstrating that technology can be used to spot items that human screeners might overlook during security checks at airports, arenas, sporting events, and other public places.

*AI in financial trading*: There are a lot of financial applications of AI in different areas, which are depicted in Figure 10.3.

*AI in healthcare sector*: In the following healthcare sectors, AI and IoT have huge applications.

- Accurate cancer diagnosis
- Customer service chatbots
- Virtual health assistants
- Treatment of rare diseases
- Targeted treatments
- Automation of redundant healthcare tasks
- Management of medical records
- Reduction of the dosage error
- Robot assisted surgery
- Automated Image diagnosis

| SMART GRID | SMART HOSPITAL | SMART MOBILITY | SMART ENERGY |
|---|---|---|---|
| SMART INFRASTRUCTURE | SMART TRAFFIC OPTIMIZATION | SMART HEALTHCARE USING MACHINE LEARNING | SMART HOME AUTOMATION |

**FIGURE 10.2** Different cloud services in a smart city [26].

- Stock market prediction
- Sales forecasting
- Trading
- Personalized banking
- Process automation
- Risk management
- Anti fraud system
- Credit card & loan distribution

**FIGURE 10.3**   Financial applications of AI in different areas.

- Personalized websites
- Personalized content
- Personalized messaging
- Product recommendation
- Personalized ad targeting
- Personalized AI-powered chatbots
- Better customer sentiment analysis
- AI-enabled avatars, robots and greeters

**FIGURE 10.4**   Personalized applications of AI.

Participation of AI lies in different fields of human society such as security systems, financial trading, healthcare, personalization, marketing, fraud identification, search engine, and natural language processing (NLP).

*AI in personalization*: Sometimes you might have experienced the situation when you browse an item in an online store but decide not to buy it, and then you observe ongoing online discounts for that exact item for a while thereafter. Various personalized applications of AI are depicted in Figure 10.4.

There are experts who, despite the fact that not formally prepared or basically utilized as information pros, create down-to-earth competency at working with information and investigation, for the most part to propel their work in their very own specific field. Another challenge is the move toward giving stages and instruments that empower AI-driven work "as-an administration." Instead of structuring everything starting with no outside help, associations are progressively ready to take instant arrangements and just module their own information collecting the outcomes which overlooking the specialized activities going on "at the back end." Application areas of AI include spacecraft design, entertainment, vehicular communication, games, driving less vehicles, language processing, robotics, and stock market monitoring. Examples of these applications are as follows:

- Autonomous planning and development of tasks aboard a spacecraft
- Defeating Gary Kasparov in a chess match

- Navigation a driver-less car
- Considering language understanding
- Robotic facilitate in surgery
- Monitoring buy and sell in the stock bazaar to see if insider trading is going on

Approximately a couple of years back there was a hypothetical part of AI that had been around in principle for quite a while, yet after continuous advancement of many dispersed preparing systems, the kinds of AI began to start in vivified usage in relationship with advances; for example, IoT, CC, robotics, SI, and WoT greatly affect society.

## 10.4  ASSORTMENT OF AI WITH DIVERSE TECHNOLOGIES

AI has the power of integrating with versatile technology and enabling a machine/system/platform that performs actions that express the nature of human aptitude such as showing wisdom, power of analysis, decision-making, and self-correction comparable to human beings. AI is being comprehensively used in many fields and the lives of people have improved with the use of this versatile technology. In recent times, the application of AI in the areas of machine learning, CC, and IoT have drastically changed the performance in multiple sectors such as business, healthcare, robotics, data analytics, and many more.

## 10.5  ASSOCIATED APPLICATIONS OF AI WITH MACHINE LEARNING

Figure 10.5 shows the association of AI with machine learning.

Figure 10.6 demonstrates various applications of machine learning in different imperative fields. Geographic data analysis and prediction is a very important application of machine learning. Machine learning is associated with different fields such as business intelligence, personal assistants, IoT, robotics, and CC. In the machine learning approach of re-enforcement learning, computer programs correspond with some lively situations in which they have a particular objective. Man-made intelligence focuses on creating a framework that works like the human

Dynamic Websites and forecasting

Tailored Recommendations for Customers

Personalized Email and Message in Marketing

Nvidia adds generative AI suite to Omniverse platform

AI platform based medical company screen babies' eyes

Data Mining and Information analytics with AI predictions

Nvidia and Intel Collaboration on energy efficient AI server

The chances of Microsoft using ChatGPT to challenge Google

**FIGURE 10.5**  Applications of AI with ML.

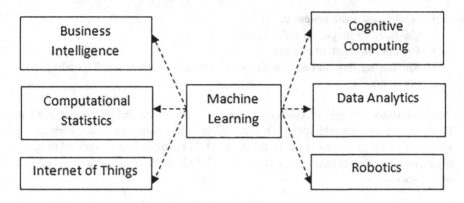

**FIGURE 10.6**   Machine learning submissions in various substantial fields.

cerebrum. Because of a few reasons, AI can be connected to some specific application zone. Chess has been one of the successfully connected AI regions to a field of practice.

## 10.6   GROUPING OF AI WITH THE INTERNET OF THINGS

These days, the most recent innovative headways have changed the incorporated CC model, experiencing edge and IoT, which are nearer to end clients. Specifically, current CC programming models manage the ongoing development of the IoT wonder since smart gadgets are ending up increasingly unavoidable, groundbreaking, and cheap [27–34]. There are many researches developed using various issues when IoT was combined with heterogeneous technologies such as Challenges in Cloud applications [28], Social challenges in IoT [29], IoT in retail [30], Autonomous system using iOT [31], Challenges when applied in Social systems [32] and security in E-Health [33]. Difficulties faced by AI applications in IoT environments are as follows.

### 10.6.1   COMPATIBILITY

The IoT is a gathering of numerous parts and frameworks that are on a very basic level distinctive in existence.

### 10.6.2   COMPLEXITY

The IoT is an entangled framework with many moving parts and nonstop stream of information, making it an exceptionally convoluted biological system.

### 10.6.3   PRIVACY/SECURITY/SAFETY (PSS)

PSS is dependably an issue with each new innovation or idea. How far AI can help without trading off PSS? One of the new answers for such an issue is utilizing blockchain technology.

## 10.6.4 ETHICAL AND LAWFUL ISSUES

It's another world for some organizations without any points of reference, an untested area with new laws and cases rising quickly [35–39]. There are proper ethics in IoT [35] which are mentioned in the vision document of IoT implemenattion [36]. There are serious ethical problems associated with Oject based IoT [37] and IoT in military [38].

## 10.6.5 ARTIFICIAL STUPIDITY

Back to the basic idea of garbage in garbage out (GIGO), AI still needs "preparing" to comprehend human responses/feelings the choice will bode well.

There are many functionalities in the sensor layer of the IoT platform. The facilities offered by the IoT make it conceivable to build up various applications dependent on it, of which just a couple of uses are as of now conveyed. In the accompanying subsections, a portion of the imperative precedent uses of IoT are quickly talked about [40–42]. Information centric networing using IoT [40] has been implemented correctly with positive performance and Security in IoT and related issues have been identified [41]. Figure 10.1 presents the sensor layer planning, which comprises of sensor networks and sensor devices. Different types of communication signals are propagated here, such as RFID, photo-electric signals, infrared, GPS, analog, digital, and electro-mechanical. These signals are managed by Wi-Fi networks such as Zigbee, Ethernet, Bluetooth, UWB, and WIRED.

## 10.7 CLOUD COMPUTING AND BIG DATA APPLICATIONS

Cloud services offered by CC are virtual machines, load balancing in network traffic, web server management, virtual desktop, communication facilities, and run-time execution [26]. There are basic characteristics of cloud computing that makes it so strong in current technology and when it gets associated with AI to implement the services dynamically, then the service facility gets optimized and managed properly. With the gigantic customer measure and huge applications attempting to profit by the cloud administration, it makes it a difficult assignment for the edge cloud server farms to work in a power sparing mode.

Basic concerns in CC are related to the performance, reliable service, and service level agreement (SLA). There is no standard for application programs interface (API) and further it is a combination of representational state transfer (SOAP) and Simple Object Access Protocol (REST). Accessibility of the network connection among the equipment and the programming server can go anyplace from a mechanical system, to home appliances, to electronic sensors, to vehicles, customer and business programming frameworks, or even a structure or foundation [43–45]. Anomaly detection of IoT devices has been surveyed in [43] with special focus on IoT embedded business systems with possible opportunities [44] that helps a lot in the growth of the industry. The IoT universe gives unlimited conceivable outcomes to purchasers just as for organizations. However, exploiting this development requires a perception of the web benefits that move it. Organizations hoping to exploit this pattern must look to master engineers to appropriately actualize and program APIs with the proper web administration to get to conventions not to bargain execution, security, or information respectability. The interim network and connection between the divergent programming frameworks is basically made conceivable by the conventions SOAP and REST that are utilized to access web administrations. They work with arrangements, for example, XML (eXtensible Markup Language) and JSON (JavaScript Object Notation) separately to trade information [43]. With the prevalence of cloud computing, gigantic data from different terminal gadgets is transmitted to cloud servers, which results in the nearby coordination of big data with CC. Big data empowers individuals to use cloud computing to manage disseminated inquiries crosswise over multi-data sets and convenient return results. Cloud computing gives a major structure to asset the board, which can coordinate with a lot of appropriated stockpiling and handling advances to address the difficulties emerging from big data.

## 10.8  CONCLUSION

The basic objective of this research piece was to put a spotlight on the real utilizations of joining AI with other related advanced technologies, like IoT and CC, which are being utilized in different business, production, software, scientific, and research units today. Secondly, its goal was to show significant strategies used by AI and future use cases for technologists who need to get a layout of a future vision that is needed for how artificial realization may be encouraged and comprehended to the intelligence associated with gadgets in the coming time. This chapter has been composed in view of the research purpose of experts or officials, scientists, students, and researchers.

## REFERENCES

1. Y. Cheng, "A Development Architecture for the Intelligent Animal Care and Management System Based on the Internet of Things and Artificial Intelligence," *2019 International Conference on Artificial Intelligence in Information and Communication (ICAIIC)*, Okinawa, Japan, 2019, pp. 078–081. 10.1109/ICAIIC.2019. 8669015
2. S. Shekhar, "Dynamic Data Driven Cloud Systems for Cloud-Hosted CPS," *2016 IEEE International Conference on Cloud Engineering Workshop (IC2EW)*, Berlin, 2016, pp. 195–197. 10.1109/IC2EW.2016.38
3. P. Kiss, A. Reale, C. J. Ferrari, and Z. Istenes, "Deployment of IoT Applications on 5G Edge," *2018 IEEE International Conference on Future IoT Technologies (Future IoT)*, Eger, 2018, pp. 1–9. 10.1109/FIOT.2018.8325595
4. P. Mendki, "Docker Container Based Analytics at IoT Edge Video Analytics Usecase," *2018 3rd International Conference on Internet of Things: Smart Innovation and Usages (IoT-SIU)*, Bhimtal, 2018, pp. 1–4. 10.1109/IoT-SIU.2018.8519852
5. L. Carnevale, A. Celesti, A. Galletta, S. Dustdar, and M. Villari, "From the Cloud to Edge and IoT: A Smart Orchestration Architecture for Enabling Osmotic Computing," *2018 32nd International Conference on Advanced Information Networking and Applications Workshops (WAINA)*, Krakow, 2018, pp. 419–424. 10.1109/WAINA.2018.00122

6. E. Oyekanlu, "Distributed Osmotic Computing Approach to Implementation of Explainable Predictive Deep Learning at Industrial IoT Network Edges with Real-Time Adaptive Wavelet Graphs," *2018 IEEE First International Conference on Artificial Intelligence and Knowledge Engineering (AIKE)*, Laguna Hills, CA, 2018, pp. 179–188. 10.1109/AIKE.2018.00042

7. S. Chen et al., "Keynote speech: The usage of cloud computing in China Regional Healthcare," *2011 IEEE International Conference on Cloud Computing and Intelligence Systems*, Beijing, 2011, pp. i–v. 10.1109/CCIS.2011.6045151

8. S. Shekhar and A. Gokhale, "Poster Abstract: Enabling IoT Applications via Dynamic Cloud-Edge Resource Management," *2017 IEEE/ACM Second International Conference on Internet-of-Things Design and Implementation (IoTDI)*, Pittsburgh, PA, 2017, pp. 331–332.

9. J. Wan, J. Yang, Z. Wang, and Q. Hua, "Artificial Intelligence for Cloud-Assisted Smart Factory," *IEEE Access*, vol. 6, pp. 55419–55430, 2018. 10.1109/ACCESS.2018.2871724

10. M. Shen, B. Ma, L. Zhu, X. Du, and K. Xu, "Secure Phrase Search for Intelligent Processing of Encrypted Data in Cloud-Based IoT," *IEEE Internet of Things Journal*. 10.1109/JIOT.2018.2871607

11. C. V. Krishna, H. R. Rohit, and Mohana, "A Review of Artificial Intelligence Methods for Data Science and Data Analytics: Applications and Research Challenges," *2018 2nd International Conference on I-SMAC (IoT in Social, Mobile, Analytics and Cloud) (I-SMAC)I-SMAC (IoT in Social, Mobile, Analytics and Cloud) (I-SMAC), 2018 2nd International Conference on*, Palladam, India, 2018, pp. 591–594. 10.1109/I-SMAC.2018.8653670

12. M. Al-Rakhami, M. Alsahli, M. M. Hassan, A. Alamri, A. Guerrieri, and G. Fortino, "Cost Efficient Edge Intelligence Framework Using Docker Containers," *2018 IEEE 16th Intl Conf on Dependable, Autonomic and Secure Computing, 16th Intl Conf on Pervasive Intelligence and Computing, 4th Intl Conf on Big Data Intelligence and Computing and Cyber Science and Technology Congress (DASC/PiCom/DataCom/CyberSciTech)*, Athens, 2018, pp. 800–807. 10.1109/DASC/PiCom/DataCom/CyberSciTec.2018.00138

13. H. Jeong, H. Lee, and S. Moon, "Work-in-Progress: Cloud-Based Machine Learning for IoT Devices with Better Privacy," *2017 International Conference on Embedded Software (EMSOFT)*, Seoul, 2017, pp. 1–2. 10.1145/3125503.3125626

14. T. Lee, B. M. Lee, and W. Noh, "Hierarchical Cloud Computing Architecture for Context-Aware IoT Services," *IEEE Transactions on Consumer Electronics*, vol. 64, no. 2, pp. 222–230, May 2018. 10.1109/TCE.2018.2844724

15. Y. Son and K. Lee, "Cloud of Things Based on Linked Data," *2018 International Conference on Information Networking (ICOIN)*, Chiang Mai, 2018, pp. 447–449. 10.1109/ICOIN.2018.8343157

16. C. C.-H. Hsu, M. Y.-C. Wang, H. C. H. Shen, R. H.-C. Chiang, and C. H. P. Wen, "Fall Care+: An IoT Surveillance System for Fall Detection," *2017 International Conference on Applied System Innovation (ICASI)*, Sapporo, 2017, pp. 921–922. 10.1109/ICASI.2017.7988590

17. N. Kumar Koditala and P. Shekar Pandey, "Water Quality Monitoring System Using IoT and Machine Learning," *2018 International Conference on Research in Intelligent and Computing in Engineering (RICE)*, San Salvador, 2018, pp. 1–5. 10.1109/RICE.2018.8509050

18. J. Wu and M. Jian, "Smart Local Area Services Based on IOT Identification with Adaptive Cloud Intelligent Switch," *2018 IEEE International Conference on Applied System Invention (ICASI)*, Chiba, 2018, pp. 554–557. 10.1109/ICASI.2018.8394312

19. G. Peralta, M. Iglesias-Urkia, M. Barcelo, R. Gomez, A. Moran, and J. Bilbao, "Fog Computing Based Efficient IoT Scheme for the Industry 4.0," *2017 IEEE*

*International Workshop of Electronics, Control, Measurement, Signals and their Application to Mechatronics (ECMSM)*, Donostia-San Sebastian, 2017, pp. 1–6. 10.1109/ECMSM.2017.7945879

20. T. Muhammed, R. Mehmood, A. Albeshri, and I. Katib, "UbeHealth: A Personalized Ubiquitous Cloud and Edge-Enabled Networked Healthcare System for Smart Cities," *IEEE Access*, vol. 6, pp. 32258–32285, 2018. 10.1109/ACCESS.2018.284 6609

21. T. Yamakami, "An Experimental Implementation of an Edge-Based AI Engine with Edge-Cloud Coordination," *2018 18th International Symposium on Communications and Information Technologies (ISCIT)*, Bangkok, 2018, pp. 442–446. 10.1109/ ISCIT.2018.8587931

22. Y. Yang, L. Wu, and S. Yang, "The Structure of Intelligent Grid Based on Cloud Computing and Risk Analysis," *2012 4th International Conference on Intelligent Human-Machine Systems and Cybernetics*, Nanchang, Jiangxi, 2012, pp. 123–126. 10.1109/IHMSC.2012.126

23. K. E. Skouby and P. Lynggaard, "Smart Home and Smart City Solutions Enabled by 5G, IoT, AAI and CoT Services," *2014 International Conference on Contemporary Computing and Informatics (IC3I)*, Mysore, 2014, pp. 874–878. 10.1109/IC3I.2014. 7019822

24. B. Power and J. Weinman, "Revenue Growth Is the Primary Benefit of the Cloud," *IEEE Cloud Computing*, vol. 5, no. 4, pp. 89–94, Jul./Aug. 2018. 10.1109/MCC.201 8.043221018

25. X. Yu, F. Sun, and X. Cheng, "Intelligent Urban Traffic Management System Based on Cloud Computing and Internet of Things," *2012 International Conference on Computer Science and Service System*, Nanjing, 2012, pp. 269–2172. 10.1109/ CSSS.2012.539

26. https://iotdesignpro.com/articles/iot-and-cloud-computing [Last accessed on 23/01/ 2023]

27. E. P. Yadav, E. A. Mittal, and D. H. Yadav, "IoT: Challenges and Issues in Indian Perspective," *2018 3rd International Conference on Internet of Things: Smart Innovation and Usages (IoT-SIU)*, Bhimtal, 2018, pp. 1–5. 10.1109/IoT-SIU.2018. 8519869

28. A. R. Biswas and R. Giaffreda, "IoT and Cloud Convergence: Opportunities and Challenges," *2014 IEEE World Forum on Internet of Things (WF-IoT)*, Seoul, 2014, pp. 375–376. 10.1109/WF-IoT.2014.6803194

29. K. Routh and T. Pal, "A Survey on Technological, Business and Societal Aspects of Internet of Things by Q3, 2017," *2018 3rd International Conference on Internet of Things: Smart Innovation and Usages (IoT-SIU)*, Bhimtal, 2018, pp. 1–4. 10.1109/ IoT-SIU.2018.8519898

30. N. N. Dlamini and K. Johnston, "The Use, Benefits and Challenges of Using the Internet of Things (IoT) in Retail Businesses: A Literature Review," *2016 International Conference on Advances in Computing and Communication Engineering (ICACCE)*, Durban, 2016, pp. 430–436. 10.1109/ICACCE.2016.8073787

31. S. Park, N. Crespi, H. Park, and S. Kim, "IoT Routing Architecture with Autonomous Systems of Things," *2014 IEEE World Forum on Internet of Things (WF-IoT)*, Seoul, 2014, pp. 442–445. 10.1109/WF-IoT.2014.6803207

32. A. Garg, "A Lucid IoT Challenge to Sustainable Society," *2018 Second International Conference on Inventive Communication and Computational Technologies (ICICCT)*, Coimbatore, 2018, pp. 1529–1533. 10.1109/ICICCT.2018.8473188

33. R. Giaffreda, L. Capra, and F. Antonelli, "A Pragmatic Approach to Solving IoT Interoperability and Security Problems in an eHealth Context," *2016 IEEE 3rd World*

Forum on Internet of Things (WF-IoT), Reston, VA, 2016, pp. 547–552. 10.1109/ WF-IoT.2016.7845452

34. S. Rhee, "Catalyzing the Internet of Things and Smart Cities: Global City Teams Challenge," *2016 1st International Workshop on Science of Smart City Operations and Platforms Engineering (SCOPE) in Partnership with Global City Teams Challenge (GCTC) (SCOPE-GCTC)*, Vienna, 2016, pp. 1–4.

35. A. AboBakr and M. A. Azer, "IoT Ethics Challenges and Legal Issues," *2017 12th International Conference on Computer Engineering and Systems (ICCES)*, Cairo, 2017, pp. 233–237.

36. S. Chen, H. Xu, D. Liu, B. Hu, and H. Wang, "A Vision of IoT: Applications, Challenges, and Opportunities With China Perspective," *IEEE Internet of Things Journal*, vol. 1, no. 4, pp. 349–359, Aug. 2014. 10.1109/JIOT.2014.2337336

37. J. A. Colley and A. Crabtree, "Object Based Media, the IoT and Databox," *Living in the Internet of Things: Cybersecurity of the IoT – 2018*, London, 2018, pp. 1–6. 10. 1049/cp.2018.0034

38. B. Jalaian, T. Gregory, N. Suri, S. Russell, L. Sadler, and M. Lee, "Evaluating LoRaWAN-Based IoT Devices for the Tactical Military Environment," *2018 IEEE 4th World Forum on Internet of Things (WF-IoT)*, Singapore, 2018, pp. 124–128.

39. N. Shahid and S. Aneja, "Internet of Things: Vision, Application Areas and Research Challenges," *2017 International Conference on I-SMAC (IoT in Social, Mobile, Analytics and Cloud) (I-SMAC)*, Palladam, 2017, pp. 583–587. 10.1109/I-SMAC. 2017.8058246

40. J. Hong, "Challenges of Name Resolution Service for Information Centric Networking toward IoT," *2016 International Conference on Information and Communication Technology Convergence (ICTC)*, Jeju, 2016, pp. 1085–1087.

41. M. Frustaci, P. Pace, G. Aloi, and G. Fortino, "Evaluating Critical Security Issues of the IoT World: Present and Future Challenges," *IEEE Internet of Things Journal*, vol. 5, no. 4, pp. 2483–2495, Aug. 2018.

42. R. J. Mangialardo and J. C. Duarte, "Integrating Static and Dynamic Malware Analysis Using Machine Learning," *IEEE Latin America Transactions*, vol. 13, no. 9, pp. 3080–3087, 2015.

43. R. Alharthi, M. Zohdy, and H. Ming, "AD-IoT: Anomaly Detection of IoT Cyberattacks in Smart City Using Machine Learning," *2019 IEEE 9th Annual Computing and Communication Workshop and Conference (CCWC)*, Las Vegas, NV, USA, 2019, pp. 0305–0310. 10.1109/CCWC.2019.8666450

44. S. Singh and N. Singh, "Internet of Things (IoT): Security Challenges, Business Opportunities & Reference Architecture for E-commerce," *2015 International Conference on Green Computing and Internet of Things (ICGCIoT)*, Noida, 2015, pp. 1577–1581.

45. M. M. E. Mahmoud, J. J. P. C. Rodrigues, K. Saleem, J. Al-Muhtadi, N. Kumar, and V. Korotaev, "Towards Energy-Aware Fog-Enabled Cloud of Things for Healthcare," *Computers & Electrical Engineering*, vol. 67, 2018, pp. 58–69, 2018. ISSN 0045-7906, 10.1016/ j.compeleceng. 2018.02.047

# 11 Integrating Big Data and Cloud Computing

*Ankit Singhal, Jatin Madan, and Suman Madan*

## 11.1 INTRODUCTION

There has been an increase in the amount of data stored and processed over the last few years, especially in the areas of finance, science, and government. The ability to create large data-supporting systems and host them using cloud computing has been demonstrated to be practical. Rather than storing and processing data, big data is stored and processed by the cloud. For big data systems to succeed, availability, fault tolerance, and scalability are essential. Big data analytics plays a key role in determining correlations, patterns, and trends in big data for business and scientific areas. Figure 11.1 shows the importnt benefits of integrating cloud computing with big data. Utilizing these two technologies is crucial because they may increase corporate competitiveness and give research the means to compile and evaluate information obtained from experiments such as the ones at the Large Hadron Collider.

Big data approaches relate to methods for analyzing, systematically retrieving data from, or interacting with data collections that are too large or intricate for traditional data-processing application software. As its name suggests, big data is just a term for extremely large datasets. Using 4Vs, the usual data qualities may be stated. Cloud computing refers to the on-demand usage of computer memory space, primarily processing power and data storage. Users who utilize cloud computing frequently have access to, use, edit, and alter their work while working with others. Cloud computing allows users to work whenever convenient, and big data offers knowledge and information [1,2].

There are three vital features that determine big data: a large amount of data, data that cannot be categorized into conventional relational databases, and rapid generation, collection, and processing of the data. The development of data mining and storage technology permits the preservation of an expanding volume of data, as shown by a shift in the type of data that organizations hold [3]. It is astounding how quickly new data is produced. Because of this growth pace, it is becoming increasingly difficult for academics and practitioners to develop suitable cloud computing services for workloads requiring intense data processing and updating [4]. As a result, cloud computing – one of the most important developments in modern ICT and service for commercial applications – has developed into a formidable architecture for extensive and complex computing.

DOI: 10.1201/9781003341437-13

**FIGURE 11.1** Cloud computing with big data.

As part of the analytics process, characteristics are analyzed, cloud storage is managed, huge amounts of data are analyzed, and conclusions can be drawn. Therefore, data security is among the most critical aspects nowadays. Security is crucial when dealing with huge amounts of data since it contains private information, code words, and passwords that, if hacked, might have disastrous effects. Therefore, security is crucial when thinking about large data and cloud computing. Different methods, including node verification, encoding, authentication protocols, honeypot nodes, etc., can be used to accomplish security. Several issues may arise throughout the system's deployment, including information storage, efficiency, confidentiality, computation, conveyance, representation, structure, connection, reliability, etc. Big data and cloud computing have applications in various industries, including management and finance.

Handling enormous amounts of data is one of the main issues with cloud computing. Databases are either immediately visible or available to users as a component of the infrastructure or are concealed behind service interfaces. This is completely sovereign of the entity shared in the cloud [5]. In other words, data must be split up and replicated throughout many Internet data centers. The top search engines of Google and Amazon have built new data centers to host cloud computing applications. As society becomes more instrumented, enormous volumes of data are being stored. Analytics tools that work with unstructured and structured data are crucial because they enable businesses to learn from the vast volumes of data that are freely accessible online and their own privately collected data. Big data is the popular phrase used to describe this concept. Social media, the IoT (Internet of Things), and multimedia have increased the amount of data that enterprises regularly capture, resulting in a massive flow of data in both organized and unstructured formats.

The primary advantages of cloud computing are parallel processing, data security, virtualized resources, and connections across data services. Cloud computing lowers the cost and places fewer restrictions on automation and digitalization for certain processes and businesses. It also offers minimal infrastructure, efficient management, and user access. Due to the advantages, many apps have been created that utilize various cloud platforms, dramatically increasing the quantity of data that these programs produce and use [5]. Initial users of big data in cloud computing include professionals who used Hadoop clusters in relatively variable and scalable computing environments offered by suppliers like IBM, Amazon, and Microsoft.

Organizations are capturing more and more information from numerous portable devices and multimedia, and this data volume has virtually doubled annually. This massive amount of data creation may be divided into structured and unstructured data, which are difficult to put into conventional relational databases. Pre-processing is needed for this huge data to turn the raw information into a presentable data collection that can be analyzed. These data are used for research and decision-making across many scientific disciplines, including healthcare, finance, engineering, and e-commerce. Big data can now be stored and mined, thanks to data science, storage, and cloud computing developments.

Through the use of the cloud, parallel computing, versatility, portability, data integrity, resource virtualization, and interaction with data storage have all grown. The expense of creating massive data centers and investing in hardware, buildings, utilities, and other infrastructure has been avoided thanks to cloud computing. Big data applications can scale up and down as needed to accommodate changing workloads, thanks partly to the flexibility of cloud infrastructure. With the help of cloud virtualization, it is possible to spawn numerous computers at once on a virtual platform made up of storage and server operating systems. This offers a method for resource sharing and hardware separation to improve data access, administration, analysis, and computing.

## 11.2 BIG DATA

We currently live in a data-driven world. The only thing we can see is data. Therefore, how data is stored and processed is crucial. To be precise, what is big data? *Big data* is the term used to describe information that cannot be processed or stored with current technology. Traditional database technology only allows for storing, processing, or analyzing small amounts of data. Big data has an elusive character and requires a variety of techniques to transform the data into fresh insights. The phrase "big data" is still relatively new in the IT sector and commercial firms. However, several researchers and consumers have used the term "big data" in earlier publications [1]. There are several active theories of big data nowadays. "Big data" refers to enormous and challenging data to handle, store, and analyze using conventional databases. A scalable infrastructure is needed to store, manipulate, and analyze them effectively. The massive volume of data created originates from a variety of sources, including social media posts, traffic signs, utility meters, consumer wearables like fit meters, point-of-sale terminals, and consumer wearables like electronic medical records [1]. In order to extract hidden information from this complicated, transforming diverse data into insightful knowledge, competitive advantage, and better judgement, many technologies are integrated. Big data is a collection of methods and tools that use innovative integration approaches to glean valuable insights from sizable, complicated, and massively scaled datasets.

## 11.2.1  BIG DATA ANALYTICS

Big data in the cloud refers to extraordinarily big datasets that might number in the petabytes and hundreds of terabytes, making it very difficult to work with them using a traditional local computer-based database management system. The ideal choice is to use the cloud since growing storage, displaying data, managing, and recording becomes very time- and money-consuming tasks [4]. The term "big data analytics" refers to the complex procedure of sorting through massive amounts of data in order to find information that can help organizations make educated decisions about their operations, such as correlations, trends, insights, competitive analysis, and consumer preferences. Organizations can use analytics tools and methodologies to assess datasets and get fresh insights. Business intelligence (BI) analytics provide essential insights into how firms function and operate. Advanced analytics, which includes components like statistical algorithms, what-if analysis, and predictive models driven by the computing system, is a subset of big data analytics.

Data scientists, analysts, analytics experts, statisticians, and other analytics specialists are gathering, processing, cleaning, and analyzing increasing amounts of structured data records and different types of data that conventional BI and analytics tools don't use.

The four phases of the big data analytics procedure, shown in figure 11.2, are summarized as follows .

1. Information is gathered by data professionals from a number of sources. Semi-structured and unstructured data are frequently blended. Despite the fact that every firm uses distinct data streams, some frequent sources include:
   - Social media content
   - Internet clickstream data
   - Cloud apps
   - Web server logs
   - Text from customer emails, and survey results
   - Mobile applications
2. Data generation and processing. Data professionals must correctly segment, categorize, and arrange data for analytical queries once it has been gathered and stored in a warehouse or data lake. Processing and treating data carefully improves the effectiveness of analytical operations.

**FIGURE 11.2**  Big data analytics phases.

3. To enhance its quality, the data is cleaned. Data cleaning professionals use automated technologies or quality management software to filter the data. They clean up the data, arrange it, and look for any formatting or duplication issues.

4. After being collected, cleaned up, and processed, the data are then examined using analytics software. There are tools for:

   • Predictive analytics, which develops models to anticipate future situations, events, trends, and consumer behavior.

   • Machine learning, which use a variety of techniques to analyze enormous volumes of data.

   • Emerging technologies include tools for statistical analysis and text mining, standard business intelligence applications, artificial intelligence (AI), data visualization tools, and deep learning, a more advanced kind of machine learning.

## 11.2.2 BIG DATA CLASSIFICATION

1. *Analysis type*: If real-time or batch processing is used to analyze the data. Banks utilize real-time analysis to spot fraud, but batch processing may be used for strategic business decisions.

2. *Processing technique*: Business needs dictate whether a reporting, predictive, or ad hoc methodology should be employed.

3. *Data frequency*: It controls the amount of data consumed and the rate at which it arrives. Both time series-based data and continuous data, such as real-time feeds, are possible.

4. *Data type*: The data may be real time, transactional, or historical.

5. *Data format*: Relational databases may store structured data, such as transactions. NoSQL data stores may be used to store both unstructured and semi-structured data. The types of data storage used to collect and organize them are determined by their formats [6].

6. *Data source*: This identifies the data source, such as social media, a machine, or a human.

7. *Data consumers*: A list of every user and program that uses the processed data.

Big data is categorized according to its source, format, data store, frequency, processing technique, and forms of analysis, as shown in Figure 11.3.

## 11.3 CLOUD COMPUTING

Cloud computing enables faster innovation, adaptive resources, intense computation, cost savings, and parallel data processing by providing online access to computer resources such as storage, servers, databases, software, networking, analytics, and intelligence [1]. Enterprises may concentrate on their core operations by separating processing, storage, and networking devices to workloads as required and giving them access to a multitude of prebuilt services. On-premises and cloud

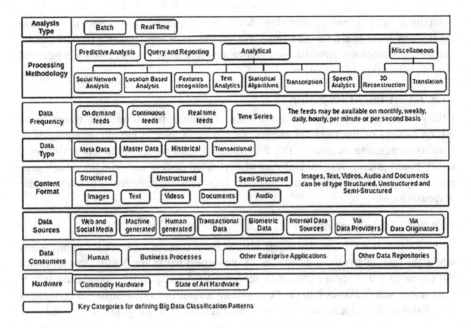

| Analysis Type | Batch | Real Time | | | | | | | |
|---|---|---|---|---|---|---|---|---|---|
| Processing Methodology | Predictive Analysis | Query and Reporting | | Analytical | | | | | Miscellaneous |
| | Social Network Analysis | Location Based Analysis | Features recognition | Text Analytics | Statistical Algorithms | Transcription | Speech Analytics | 3D Reconstruction | Translation |
| Data Frequency | On demand feeds | Continuous feeds | Real time feeds | Time Series | The feeds may be available on monthly, weekly, daily, hourly, per minute or per second basis | | | | |
| Data Type | Meta Data | Master Data | Historical | Transactional | | | | | |
| Content Format | Structured | | Unstructured | | Semi-Structured | Images, Text, Videos, Audio and Documents can be of type Structured, Unstructured and Semi-Structured | | | |
| | Images | Text | Videos | Documents | Audio | | | | |
| Data Sources | Web and Social Media | Machine generated | Human generated | Transactional Data | Biometric Data | Internal Data Sources | Via Data Providers | Via Data Originators | |
| Data Consumers | Human | Business Processes | | Other Enterprise Applications | | Other Data Repositories | | | |
| Hardware | Commodity Hardware | State of Art Hardware | | | | | | | |

Key Categories for defining Big Data Classification Patterns

**FIGURE 11.3** Big data classification.

services are different, as seen in Figure 11.3. It displays each computational layer's services and their variations.

## 11.3.1 DEFINITION

The word "cloud" is mostly used in marketing and used to denote a wide range of disparate concepts in various situations. However, a typical definition of cloud computing is when resources, such as CPUs and storage devices, are offered as standard utilities that users may lease and release instantly through the Internet [2,7]. Traditional cloud computing service providers include infrastructure providers and service providers. The advent of cloud computing has profoundly impacted the IT industry in recent years. To benefit from this new paradigm, businesses are attempting to modify their business strategies. Major search engines like Microsoft, Amazon, and Google are pushing to deliver more robust, dependable, and economical cloud platforms.

## 11.3.2 CLOUD COMPUTING TECHNOLOGIES

Cloud computing is frequently contrasted with the following technologies.

### 11.3.2.1 Grid Computing

It organizes labored resources to achieve a single computational goal and illustrates distributed computing. Scientific applications, which are frequently computationally intensive, were first responsible for the emergence of grid computing [8]. Both grid computing and cloud computing leverage dispersed resources to achieve application-level goals. Cloud computing, on the other hand, takes a step further by employing numerous virtualization techniques to enable resource interchange and flexible allocation of resources.

### 11.3.2.2 Utility Computing

Utility computing reproduces on-demand resource provision and usage-based billing instead of flat rates for clients. One way to look at cloud computing is as a utility computing awareness [8]. For financial reasons, it completely embraces a utility-based pricing system. Utilizing utility-based pricing and on-demand resource provisioning, service providers may see increases in resource utilization while decreasing costs.

### 11.3.2.3 Virtualization

Virtualization is a process that offers virtualized resources for complex applications while abstracting away the intricacies of real-world hardware. Virtual machines are the common name for a virtualized server. Cloud computing's foundation is virtualization, which allows it to pool computing resources from a cluster of computers and dynamically allocate or reassign virtual resources to programs as needed.

### 11.3.2.4 Autonomic Computing

Autonomic computing refers to the development of computer systems with the capacity for self-management, i.e., acting on local and global discoveries without human involvement. The basic objective of autonomous computing is to exceed the computational overhead of present computer systems. Although cloud computing has certain autonomous features, such as autonomous resource scheduling, its primary purpose is to reduce associated costs rather than simplify operations. In conclusion, cloud computing uses virtualization technology to realize the concept of offering computer resources as a service. Despite having definite similarities to grid computing and autonomous computing, they vary in various aspects. As a result, it provides valuable advantages and presents special problems to satisfy its demands [8,9].

## 11.3.3 Types of Clouds

When developing an enterprise solution in a cloud environment, there are several possibilities to consider. As an illustration, even though some network operators may prioritize enhancing security and high dependability, others may be more concerned with lowering operation costs. In addition, there are several kinds of clouds, each with advantages and disadvantages (Figure 11.4).

### 11.3.3.1 Public Clouds

Public clouds are those where communication firms offer their resources as services to the common people. In addition to requiring no initial infrastructure investment and transferring risk to infrastructure providers, they offer several other important benefits to service providers [2]. However, they are only practical in specific corporate situations since they require exact data control, security protocols, and network.

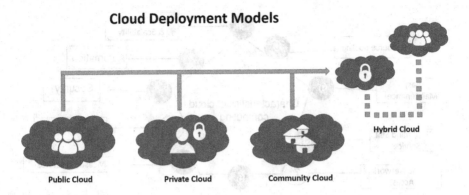

**FIGURE 11.4** Types of clouds.

### 11.3.3.2 Private Clouds

Private clouds, often known as internal clouds, are intended for usage just by one particular entity. It could be created and maintained by the company itself or by external contractors [2]. With a private cloud, you have the maximum control over performance, reliability, and security. However, they are sometimes accused of lacking qualities like no up-front capital expenses and being comparable to regular corporate server farms.

### 11.3.3.3 Hybrid Clouds

A hybrid cloud is one in which some of the service infrastructures are moved to private clouds, and some are moved to public clouds. Compared to both public and private clouds, hybrid clouds provide greater flexibility. In addition, comparatively speaking to public clouds, they offer secure control and protection over application data [2]. The disadvantage of establishing a hybrid cloud is that it necessitates carefully determining the appropriate ratio between private and public cloud components.

### 11.3.3.4 Virtual Private Cloud

Virtual private cloud (VPC) is another approach to overcoming the drawbacks of both public and private clouds. In essence, a VPC is a platform that rises above infrastructure. Thanks to this adaptive resource distribution capability, service providers have a great deal of autonomy in controlling their own operating expenses and resource use. For instance, a supplier of IaaS may achieve a significant amount of server consolidation while cutting costs and enhancing resource utilization, such as power and cooling use, by utilizing virtual machine migration technology.

### 11.3.4 CLOUD COMPUTING CHARACTERISTICS

The following are some key elements of cloud computing that set it apart from traditional service computing (Figure 11.5).

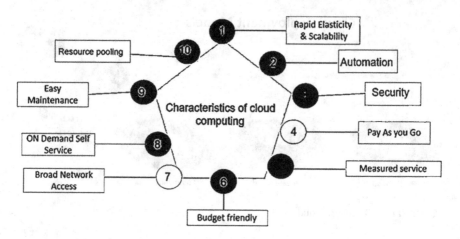

**FIGURE 11.5**   Characteristics of cloud computing.

### 11.3.4.1  Multitenancy

Many companies' services are co-located in a cloud environment in the same data center. The infrastructure and service providers are responsible for the performance and administration of these services. As a result of the tiered structure of the cloud, work can be divided logically as each layer's owner must concentrate on the particular purposes related to that layer. Nevertheless, multitenancy also makes it more difficult to comprehend and control the relationships between multiple stakeholders [10].

### 11.3.4.2  Shared Resource Pooling

The infrastructure provider makes a pool of computing resources accessible that may be dynamically distributed among several resource consumers. To get the most out of their services, a service provider may effortlessly keep onto their geodiversity.

### 11.3.4.3  Service Oriented

Cloud computing allows for the acquisition of a service-driven operating paradigm. As a result, it places a high emphasis on service management. The service level agreements (SLAs) that each PaaS, IaaS, or SaaS operator in a cloud computing system negotiates with its clients govern the services they deliver. As a result, every provider should make preserving SLA a top priority [10,11].

### 11.3.4.4  Dynamic Resource Provisioning

The capability of cloud computing to swiftly acquire and discharge computer resources is one of its most crucial features [12]. In contrast to the conventional strategy, which delivers resources as determined by high demand, dynamic resource provisioning allows service providers to purchase resources based on the entire requirement, which can significantly reduce operational costs during periods of high demand.

### 11.3.4.5  Self-Organizing

Since on-demand resources can be allocated or de-allocated, service providers can control resource consumption according to their demands. Service providers can react fast to sudden changes in customer demand because of high agility in automated resource management.

### 11.3.4.6  Utility-Based Pricing

Cloud computing employs a pay-per-use pricing model and uses utility-based pricing. One service to the other may have a different pricing structure. An IaaS provider may, for instance, provide a virtual machine to a SaaS provider hourly. On the other hand, according to the number of people it serves, a SaaS provider that offers on-demand customer relationship management (CRM) might charge its clients [10]. Utility-based pricing reduces service running costs by requiring pay-per-use from users. However, it also makes it more difficult to manage running costs. In this scenario, businesses like VKernel offer tools to assist cloud clients in understanding, researching, and reducing the unnecessary costs associated with resource utilization [11].

### 11.3.4.7  Geo-Distribution and Ubiquitous Network Access

The Internet serves as a network for transmitting services to clouds, which are frequently accessible through it. A laptop, personal digital assistant (PDA), mobile phone, or other Internet-connected devices may all access cloud services. In order to attain maximum connection speeds and localization, an increasing number of today's clouds are composed of data centers dispersed across numerous sites close to public clouds [10,13]. The main difference is that a VPC has an impact on VPN technology, which gives service providers the ability to design their architecture and security protocols, like firewall rules and regulations.

Virtual private clouds are more comprehensive architectures since they virtualize servers, applications, and hidden communication networks. Due to the virtualized network layer, VPC provides a smooth transition from a proprietary service architecture to a cloud-based infrastructure in advance for most businesses [11,13,14]. The business context will determine which cloud model is ideal for most service providers. For instance, scientific applications that require a lot of processing may be effectively implemented on public clouds. It is possible that some cloud kinds will be more well liked than others.

## 11.4  BIG DATA AND CLOUD CORRELATION

The notions of big data and cloud computing are intertwined. Big data is mostly about extracting value, whereas cloud computing focuses on scalable, adaptable, pay-per-use, and on-demand self-service models. Cloud computing gives big data analysis the required processing, storage, and flexible on-demand networked system resources [12]. However, huge data necessitates extensive on-demand processing power and scattered storage. Big data enables experts to do distributed searches over enormous datasets leveraging affordable computers and promptly delivering findings [3]. Another form of distributed data analysis technology, Hadoop, takes advantage of the cloud computing platform. Cloud computing also provides dispersed computation for adaptation and extension in order to meet the demands of increased data accumulation via virtual machines.

Due to the increased need for contextually analyzed data from all the stored data, analytical platforms were developed to fulfill user expectations, especially those of big data-driven organizations. A cluster that processes large datasets using a concurrent distributed algorithm from a distributed fault-resistant database. Data visualization's primary goal is to let decision-makers view analytical results graphically using various graphs. Big data uses distributed storage technology instead of local storage connected to an electronic device since it is based on cloud computing [15]. As a result, telecoms firms like Microsoft, Google, and Amazon now offer big data platforms that enable cost-effective data collection as well as the application of analytics to produce anticipatory and linguistic experiences (Figure 11.6).

Various companies and user terminals are present in the cloud computing environment. It covers multiple types of gear and software and subscription-based or pay-per-use services provided both online and in real time. In real-time big data techniques, data is gathered, analyzed, and stored in the cloud. Cloud computing offers on-demand resources and services for continuous data management. In big data analytics, there are three main approaches: Software as a Service (SaaS), Infrastructure as a Service (IaaS), and Platform as a Service (PaaS). Recently, clients have had access to analytics in the cloud and as a service [7,10,16]. Through the cloud, Analytics as a Service (AaaS) provides data analytics capabilities via subscription and processes for an instant and dynamic approach to combining data in structured, semi-structured, and unstructured formats, converting them and analyzing them.

An important aspect of virtualization is creating a software representation of a virtual server, operating system, network resources, and storage. It does this by establishing a virtual workspace on an already-running server where needed apps may operate without affecting any of the other services offered to other users by the host or server platform. It is a method that enables sharing an actual individual

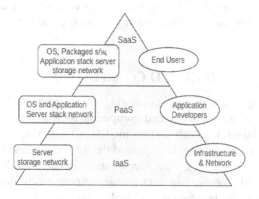

**FIGURE 11.6**  Cloud computing approaches.

example of a resource or program across several clients and businesses. To do this, it gives a physical storage device a logical name and, upon request, provides a reference to the device. In order to operate on separate virtual systems that are located on a physical host, several workloads that are now running on various physical servers can be combined via virtualization [15]. The data center's complexity, capital, and administrative expenditures are reduced by limiting the hardware requirements. This lowers and optimizes resource consumption and energy usage compared to the multi-node system. Workloads may be transferred to various physical servers for maintenance on hardware or software or in the event of an unplanned outage, thanks to the flexibility and mobility of virtual machines. In terms of asset usage, cost, and data warehousing, virtualized big data solutions like Hadoop outperform traditional infrastructure [15,17]. A wide variety of data sources is included in virtual data, facilitating data access from diverse contexts. For speedier data processing, it permits fast data sharing throughout the network.

One of the crucial components of big data is the security and privacy of personal information. Since data is processed and stored using services and infrastructure other parties provide, keeping it private and secure can be challenging. Big data poses more privacy and security risks the larger its volume, diversity, and integrity. In many respects, mobile health has transformed how healthcare is delivered. People can now manage their style of living, health, and fitness, as well as their diagnostic and drug references, thanks to various mobile health applications. Since everything is sent over mobile Internet, data privacy may be seriously threatened if the network is not properly protected or is open for intrusion. To foster user confidence and ensure that personal data is protected, a plethora of new legislation, data protection regulations, rules, safeguards, industry standards, and contractual agreements must be honored by service providers and customers. It must be protected from malicious hackers and kept in a secure state by cloud service providers; big data in the cloud needs to be secured.

An illustration of cloud computing's relationship with big data is shown in Figure 11.7. The input consists of large amounts of organized, unstructured, or semi-structured data that have been obtained from a variety of data sources, including cell phones and other smart devices. Before being put into Hadoop or another data repository, this enormous volume of data must first be cleansed. The saved data is then processed again utilizing cloud computing methodologies and tools in order to deliver services. All of the operations needed to alter input data are included in the processing steps. After data is processed for evaluation and presentation, the value obtained is eventually shown through output.

The Internet of Things (IoT) enables both cloud computing and big data. The maintenance of data in data storage is permitted by cloud providers, who also permit data transmission via the Internet or leased lines. The huge amount of data saved in the cloud is then filtered and analyzed using cloud computing tools and methodologies. The data can go down this path, be stored there, and then be processed. A single platform for big data and IoT is provided by cloud computing. As shown in Figure 11.8, the IoT is the data's source, and big data is its analytical and technological platform [1].

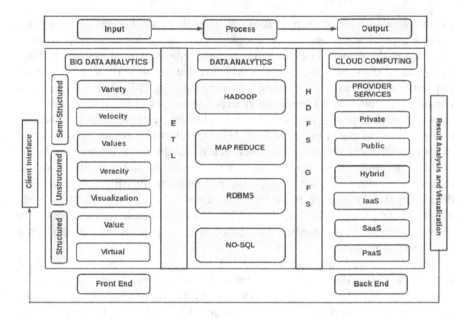

**FIGURE 11.7**   Cloud computing and big data.

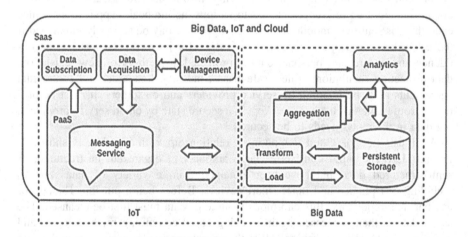

**FIGURE 11.8**   Overview of IoT, cloud computing, and big data processing.

## 11.5   CLOUD AND BIG DATA (CASE STUDIES)

Scalability, fault tolerance, and availability are required to store and process large amounts of data. Cloud computing, through hardware virtualization, provides all of these. Large data and cloud computing are thus complementary ideas since big data is made available, scalable, and fault-tolerant by the cloud.

Businesses see big data as a significant economic opportunity. As a result, several new organizations, including Hortonworks, Cloudera, Teradata, and many more, have started to focus on offering DbaaS (Database as a Service) or BdaaS (Big Data as a Service). In addition, customers may access big data on demand through companies like Google, IBM, Amazon, and Microsoft. How large data is effectively used in cloud contexts can be understood with the following examples.

## 11.5.1 NOKIA MOBILE COMPANY

Nokia was one of the first firms to see the benefits of utilizing big data in cloud systems. Communication using Nokia mobile phones is common. Nokia collects massive volumes of data from smartphones on a petabyte scale to completely understand user interactions and improve customer happiness with its phones. In order to enhance corporate decision-making processes and fully understand user involvement, to store the daily petabyte of unstructured data gathered from functional mobile phones, log files, services, and other sources, the company developed a Hadoop data warehouse as an ecosystem. Nokia was able to handle and analyze enormous amounts of data, get greater insights into how users interact with the system and do complex computations, such as "Which functionality should they work on next?" and "Where did they appear to lose themselves?" They have also developed a broad range of applications due to it, including three-dimensional digital maps with modeling techniques that account for speed categories, current road speed, elevations, daily traffic models, global video feeds, ongoing events, and more.

A few years ago, the business employed several Database management system (DBMS) to meet the needs of every application. After understanding about the advantages, the company decided to convert to Hadoop-based tools, merging data from other domains and using analytics algorithms to gain precise insights into its clientele. In comparison to conventional Relational DBMS (RDBMS), Hadoop's storage costs are lower per terabyte.

The most well-known open-source technologies in the Apache Hadoop stack are combined into a single, integrated package by CDH (Cloudera Distributed Hadoop), offering an excellent chance for deploying Hadoop setups and shifting IT and technical issues to the vendor's specialized teams. Cloudera, for instance, provided Nokia with a Hadoop environment that matched its requirements quickly through BDaaS. Hadoop greatly assisted Nokia, particularly CDH, in meeting their demands.

## 11.5.2 REDBUS

India's RedBus is an online travel service for purchasing bus tickets. RedBus chose to use Google's data processing and analytical technology to boost customer sales and manage the ticket reservation system. Its datasets are readily expandable to 2 terabytes. The software would need to analyze inventory and booking information from hundreds of bus companies operating over 10,000 routes. The business also wanted to avoid establishing and maintaining a complicated internal infrastructure. RedBus first contemplated using internal Hadoop server clusters to handle data. However, they soon realized that setting up such a system would require too much time and that the infrastructure would need to be maintained by specialist IT teams. RedBus could quickly handle enormous volumes of reservation and inventory data thanks to Google BigQuery. Applications that run on several servers continually send information about bookings, seat availability, and client searches to a central data-gathering system. This enormous amount of data is then uploaded to BigQuery, which executes complicated queries and responds to numerous analytical questions in a matter of seconds, such as:

- The number of times customers attempted to find a seat but were unsuccessful because of bus overload.
- Check for drops in reservations.
- Identify server issues quickly by analyzing data about server activities.

RedBus was able to address issues quickly, reduce missed revenue, and enhance customer support thanks to the whole infrastructure. Business benefits came from RedBus's shift to big data. Google BigQuery provided RedBus with real-time data analysis infrastructure at 20% of the expense of operating a sophisticated Hadoop system.

### 11.5.3 TWEET MINING IN CLOUD

Cloud computing was utilized by Noordhuis et al. to collect and analyze tweets. All calculations were carried out using Amazon cloud infrastructure. A webpage ranking model was employed following the crawling of tweets. To specify the significance of a webpage, Google utilizes page ranking. For example, the site-ranking mechanism generally believes that if Webpage A connects to Webpage B, the creator of Webpage A will see Webpage B as crucial. Thus, the frequency of in-edges serves as a proxy for the significance of a certain page. As a result, the number of inbound links to a page enhances its relevance.

Examples from Nokia, RedBus, and Tweet Mining in Cloud demonstrate how firms may acquire a competitive edge by embracing big data. Additionally, BDaaS offered by big data suppliers enables businesses to concentrate on their primary business requirements while leaving the technological intricacies to big data providers.

## 11.6 BIG DATA ISSUES

Even though big data is a field that is constantly evolving and has some unresolved issues, there are still many challenges with large amounts of data. This unit briefly explains some of the difficulties that big data and cloud computing have yet to address.

A physical cost-ineffectiveness arises from maintaining all data due to the rapid growth in data volume. Consequently, businesses must be able to develop rules that specify the life cycle and expiry info of data. They should also specify who has access to client data and for what purposes. Security and privacy issues are growing as data transfers to the cloud and are the focus of extensive study. "Big data heterogeneity" is a subject that is presently being researched since DBMSs frequently deal with a large amount of data from many sources (variety) [2,4]. Disaster recovery, the ease of uploading data to the cloud, and Exaflop computation are among the topics being investigated right now.

## 11.6.1 SECURITY

Big data security and cloud computing are important and ongoing research areas. This problem becomes a concern when businesses consider putting data on the cloud [18]. It might be difficult to define issues like who actually owns the data, where it is located, who has access to it, and what type of rights those individuals have. Businesses should be aware of and inquire about the following issues when working with cloud service providers.

### 11.6.1.1 Who Has Access to and Is the Actual Owner of the Data?

Clients of the cloud service provider pay a fee and submit their data to the cloud. What is the real ownership of the data between the two participants? Furthermore, is the client's data usable by the provider? What user access is required for it, and for what objectives it may be used? Finally, can the data be used by the cloud provider?

In reality, data clusters must be accessible to IT teams that preserve the client's data. Allowing restricted access to data would serve the client's best interests by limiting access to the data and ensuring only those with proper authorization could make use of it for legitimate purposes.

### 11.6.1.2 Where Is the Data?

For the customer's benefit, it is important to agree on the placement of the data because sensitive information that is lawful in one nation may be prohibited in the other, which might result in legal action being taken against the client.

To fully comprehend their respective responsibilities and the policies outlined in the SLAs that govern the organization's data, it is essential to thoroughly examine the agreements (SLAs) that underpin these issues. Usually, this needs to be carefully negotiated.

## 11.6.2 PRIVACY

Several privacy issues are brought up by data harvesting by using various analytical techniques to mine information. Due to the global dissemination and replication of information, it isn't easy to guarantee data security and safeguard privacy. Analytics frequently harvest customers' private data, including their health records, energy usage, online activity, grocery store purchases, etc. The attention this information receives prompts worries about profiling, prejudice, exclusion, and inability to control [18,19].

Privacy and data protection regulations are based on data reduction, purpose limitation, and individual control over information. But it's only sometimes obvious that limiting information gathering is a sensible method to protect privacy [20]. Today, the privacy measures used while processing activities depend on user agreement and the information people knowingly supply. Moreover, as computers hold large volumes of sensitive data daily, privacy is certainly a problem that must be improved.

### 11.6.3 HETEROGENEITY

Big data involves large amounts of data and a wide range of speeds (data arrives at various rates based on its primary utilization rate and network latency). The latter can understand vast and varied volumes of data from several independent sources [18]. Because retaining data from various sources may be advantageous for both research and industry, variety is seen as one of the "fundamental features of big data analysis."

Big data DBMS receives data from multiple sources in various forms and at varying rates. This is because various data collectors favor their conceptual frameworks or security procedures for data capture and multiple applications' inherent characteristics lead to different data representations. Big data systems must work challenging to handle the diverse data range and varying velocity rates. New file formats are being developed with no regulations, making this work more difficult [21]. However, providing a uniform and common approach to expressing and investigating complicated and changing connections from this data is currently challenging.

### 11.6.4 DATA GOVERNANCE

Regarding hardware pricing, storage is affordable, and its price will likely continue to decrease. A big data DBMS does, however, also consider additional costs like infrastructure upkeep, electricity, and software licenses. The total cost of ownership is the sum of all these charges, and it is seven times higher than the expenses connected with acquiring the hardware [21].

It is a broad phrase that describes policies to regulate data accessibility across its life cycle and applies to businesses with large databases. It is a problem that needs careful handling. Government policies will likely not be implemented if they are not enforced [19]. However, there are upper bounds to the benefits that data governance may provide since going too far in the opposite direction with stronger data control might be detrimental.

### 11.6.5 DISASTER RECOVERY

Data loss will undoubtedly lead to value loss because data is indeed a very significant business. Data losses must be kept to a minimum in the event of an emergency or dangerous disaster, such as an earthquake, a flood, or a fire. In order to meet this need, data must be readily accessible with little loss and downtime in the event of an incident. Even though this is a crucial topic, there have yet to be many investigations.

It's critical to have the ability to react quickly to dangerous occurrences since losing data might cost you money. Cloud DBMSs with huge amounts of data may require disaster recovery strategies in order to maintain fault tolerance and continuous availability [18,19,21].

## 11.6.6 OTHER PROBLEMS

Furthermore, big data platforms, cloud computing, and cloud computing, in general, raise other concerns. The following sections cover data transfer to the cloud, Exaflop computing, which is now a key concern, are discussed in the sections that follow:

1. Since uploading data to the cloud is relatively sluggish, businesses frequently prefer physically shipping hard disks to the data centers. However, there are more practical and secure methods to upload data to the cloud. Although efforts have been made over the years to enhance and develop effective data posting strategies to reduce upload times and offer safe means to transmit data out to the cloud, this procedure still needs to be revised [22].

2. Because the current systems hardly ever handle data surges automatically, elasticity and scalability in cloud computing, especially for massive data management systems, is an issue that needs additional investigation. Automatic scaling systems demonstrate that most techniques are proactive or reactive and study scalability from a performance perspective [7,20,23,24]. As a result, scalability is generally initiated individually rather than automatically. There are several factors that will determine if a system will be scalable, including security, workload balancing, and redundancy. Furthermore, load equalization and histogram construction are the foundations of the present data rebalancing techniques. The latter makes sure that each server receives a balanced load.

3. Today's supercomputers and clouds can handle petabyte-sized information. However, exabyte-sized datasets still raise many problems since they require a lot of speed and capacity to transport and analyze across a network. The problem may still need to be solved by cloud computing, which is regarded to be slower than supercomputers due to its latency and bandwidth constraints [20]. The most promising answer is high-performance computing (HPC), although this has a very high yearly cost. There are also several issues with developing Exaflop HPCs, particularly regarding effective power usage. In this case, GPU-based solutions predominate over CPU-based ones.

## 11.7  HADOOP TOOLS AND TECHNIQUES

Numerous tools and approaches are used by big data applications to process and analyze the data. A few of these are shown in Table 11.1 [25,26].

## 11.8  ADVANTAGES

Integrating cloud computing with big data has several benefits. First, because big data deals with a lot of data, it requires a lot of speed and variability, which increases the need for several servers. These numerous servers run in parallel to

**TABLE 11.1**

**Hadoop Tools and Techniques**

| Tools and Techniques | Description | Developed by | Written in |
|---|---|---|---|
| Ambari | UI for cluster administration on the web | Hortonworks | Java |
| Casandra | Column-oriented NoSQL | Facebook | Java |
| HCatalog | Data in HDFS is seen in a relational table | Apache | Java |
| HDFS | Massive data storage that is redundant and reliable | Google | Java |
| Mahout | A collection of algorithms for machine learning | Apache | Java |
| Hive | HiveQL, a language akin to SQL | Facebook | Java |
| Kafka | Data integration via a decentralized publication messenger service | LinkedIn | Scala |
| Flume | Data that is semi- or unstructured can be imported or exported into HDFS, ingesting data into HDFS tool | Apache | Java |
| HBase | Column-oriented NoSQL | Google's BigTable | Java |
| Map Reduce | Distributed data processing architecture | Google | Java |
| Oozie | Define the group of tasks together with their timing and execution order | Apache | Java |
| Pig | A system for running script languages pig Latin | Yahoo | Java |
| Sentry | Data storage on an Apache Hadoop cluster that has been authorized based on roles | Cloudera | Java |
| Map Reduce | Java API | Google | Java |
| Spark | Parallelism of data based on streams | Berkeley | Scala |

handle the tremendous needs of large data. Second, cloud computing makes use of a large number of servers, and resource allocation is currently conceivable. They are thereby producing large amounts of data on the various cloud multi-servers. By effectively allocating the resources that the cloud environment makes available, they are improving the effectiveness of big data analysis. Third, both will out-perform by utilizing a cloud infrastructure as a large data storage solution [27]. Cloud services can manage massive volumes of data simultaneously, based on distant multi-servers. With the help of cutting-edge analytics methods, this func-tionality allows big data to handle massive amounts of data. Finally, combining cloud computing and big data will result in cost savings.

Big data demands server and volume clusters to handle the volume of data. Cloud computing services will operate as the base for all of them instead of con-structing new big data servers and volumes, allowing for better versatility while still removing the major expenditures on big data devices and servers [27]. Additionally, employing cloud computing speeds up the provisioning of massive data since deploying servers in the cloud is so simple and practical. As a result, the cloud infrastructure can expand to meet large data processing requirements. Given that the quantity of the data gradually shrinks over time, big data demands this swift provisioning. Cloud computing typically works in conjunction with big data to provide a simple, on-demand, distributed computing platform with little overhead [27,28]. Additionally, it allows multi-tenancy, increases automation, and strengthens the environment. Big data enables businesses to investigate new market prospects and helps end consumers to view the data.

Another important advantage of big data is data analytics, which enables users to customize the information or connect to and interact with real-time websites. The two's confluence also makes large data resources easier to control, track, and report. Additionally, this integration enables a decrease in complication and a boost in efficiency. Cloud-based methods are the ideal models for implementing big data due to all of these advantages.

## 11.9 APPLICATIONS

In these big data applications, data acquisition is the first step in the conceptual framework of predictive manufacturing. Here, many forms of sensory data, including controller data, voltage, current, and auditory information, may be obtained.

When sensory data is combined with historical data, big data in manufacturing is created. The input is the big data produced as a result of the combination, as mentioned above. Computer clusters, web interfaces, and a parallel distributed computing system are merged in cloud computing. Software solutions for big data come with various tools and alternatives that let a person map the entire data field throughout the business and assess the internal dangers they face. One of the most important advantages of big data is that it guarantees data security. This ensures that potentially sensitive information processing complies with legal standards and makes it easier to spot information that needs to be adequately secured [27,28].

Predictive analytics and big data together provide a problem for many sectors. The combination examines all four possible areas: evaluate the risks on huge portfolios; implement high-value marketing campaigns; enhance overdue collections; and detect, stop, and re-evaluate financial fraud.

Big data may be used by businesses to create whole new business models, improve current ones, and even create new goods and services. Big data analytics may be utilized to achieve these advantages in various industries, including fraud detection, risk management, performance quality, and supply chain intelligence. In addition, big data analytics will be helpful in risk management for industries including investing, retail banking, and insurance. For example, big data analytics may help in investment selection by analyzing the likelihood of returns versus the possibility of losses, which is an important aspect of the financial sector [28]. Furthermore, big data from both within and outside the company may be reviewed in order to assess risk exposures fully and dynamically.

Detecting and preventing fraud is possible using big data analytics, particularly in the public sector, banking, and insurance sectors. Although analytics is still often utilized in automatic fraud detection, more and more businesses and industries are turning to big data to advance their infrastructure [2]. Big data may be used to correlate digital data from numerous public and private sources and speed up analyses.

Some of the industries that can profit from big data analytics include manufacturing, retail, the federal government, healthcare, communication, and banking.

## 11.10  RESEARCH CHALLENGES

Big data and cloud technologies integrate quite effectively, as was covered in Section 11.5. However, these two technologies present certain difficulties even if their alliance has been created.

The current problems with cloud computing and big data are summarized in Table 11.2. The first column covers today's issues, and the last one discusses today's fixes, and the following columns highlight the advantages and disadvantages of each strategy [29].

**TABLE 11.2**
**Research Challenges**

| Issues | Advantages | Disadvantages | Existent Solutions |
|---|---|---|---|
| Privacy | Offers an acceptable level of privacy or absolves the user of accountability | It was proved that demonstrable reverse engineering techniques could be used to de-identify most individuals | De-identification and user approval |
| Heterogeneity | The most common data types are hidden | Keeping track of such a diverse sample of information and speeds is difficult | Being able to handle various data coming in at different velocities is one of the traits of big data systems |
| Data governance | The handling of data should be specified – identify data access rules. Role elaboration | – Determining the data life cycle is difficult – Implementing data management principles too strictly may have unintended consequences | Data governance documents |
| Data uploading | Physically sending the data to the cloud provider is quicker than uploading data, but it is much more unsecure | – It is risky to physically transmit data to the cloud provider since the journey may harm HDDs – Data transfer over the network needs time and might be unsafe without security | – Deliver hard drives to the cloud service provider – Publish data online |
| Scalability | Scalability allows the system to grow on demand | Scalability is usually time consuming and has a lot of static components. As a result, numerous big data systems need to be adaptable to dynamic data | Cloud stack's three tiers, each offers scalability. There is horizontal (sharding) and vertical scalability at the platform level. |

**TABLE 11.2** *(Continued)*
**Research Challenges**

| Issues | Advantages | Disadvantages | Existent Solutions |
|---|---|---|---|
| Elasticity | Because of its elastic nature, the system can handle data peaks | The majority of load fluctuation evaluations are done manually rather than automatically | Several elasticity strategies exist, including live migration, replication, and resizing |
| Disaster recovery | Specify the data recovery locations and procedures | Usually, data can only be protected from one location | Recovery plans |
| High data processing (exabyte datasets) | Though HPCs are less expensive than cloud computing, they are thought to be considerably better at handling exabyte-sized files | HPCs are quite expensive, and it might be challenging to keep up with their annual cost. On the other side, it is thought that the cloud cannot handle the demands for such massive databases | – Cloud computing<br>– HPCs |
| Security | Data is encrypted | Querying encrypted data is time-consuming | Based on SLAs and data encryption |

## 11.11 CONCLUSION

Big data analysis is spurred by the rapid expansion of cloud-based apps created using virtualization technology. As for this consequence, cloud computing offers assets for big data processing and analysis as a service model. According to the author, the infrastructure for cloud computing can serve as a useful platform to handle the data storage needed to conduct big data analysis. A new paradigm for computer infrastructure allocation and a huge data processing approach is connected to cloud computing.

Big data systems are strong tools that help businesses and scientists gain insights from data, but certain worries require more research. For example, putting more effort into creating security measures and standardizing data formats is necessary. Scalability, which is often human rather than automatic in commercial solutions, is another essential component of big data. To solve this issue, further study must be conducted. The Hadoop technology and its key elements, Map Reduce and HDFS, as well as some sound design principles that may stimulate further research, are covered in this paper, coupled with an overview of applications of big data in cloud computing as well as the issues involved with data storage, transformation, and processing. Furthermore, it provides a basic overview of big data in cloud platforms, stressing its benefits and illustrating how well these technologies support one another while detailing the challenges they confront.

## REFERENCES

1. Malik, V. & Singh, S. (2019). Cloud, Big Data & IoT: Risk Management. 2019 International Conference on Machine Learning, Big Data, Cloud and Parallel Computing (COMITCon), pp. 258–262. 10.1109/COMITCon.2019.8862445
2. Madan, S. (2021). Privacy-Preserved Access Control in E-Health Cloud-Based System. *Disruptive Technologies for Society 5.0*. CRC Press: Boca Raton, FL, 2021; pp. 145–162.
3. Aburawi, Y. & Albaour, A. (2021). Big Data: Review Paper. *International Journal of Advance Research and Innovative Ideas In Education*. 7, 2021.
4. Goswami, P. & Madan, S. (2017). A Survey on Big Data & Privacy Preserving Publishing techniques. *Advances in Computational Sciences and Technology*. 10, 395–408.
5. Sether, A. (2016). Cloud Computing Benefits. 10.13140/RG.2.1.1776.0880
6. Madan, S., Bhardwaj, K., & Gupta, S. (2022). Critical Analysis of Big Data Privacy Preservation Techniques and Challenges. International Conference on Innovative Computing and Communications: Proceedings of ICICC 2021, volume 3, vol. 1394. Springer Nature, p. 267.
7. El-Seoud, S., El-Sofany, H., Abdelfattah, M., & Mohamed, R. (2017). Big Data and Cloud Computing: Trends and Challenges. *International Journal of Interactive Mobile Technologies (iJIM)*. 11, 34. 10.3991/ijim.v11i2.6561
8. Banger, N., Pallavi, K., & Shetty, Mrs (2022). A Review Paper on Cloud Computing Architecture, Types, Advantages and Disadvantages. *International Journal of Advanced Research in Science, Communication and Technology*. 14–22. 10.48175/IJARSCT-3144
9. (2022). An Approach to Cloud Computing. *International Journal of Advanced Research in Science, Communication and Technology*. 578–580. 10.48175/IJARSCT-5724
10. Rashid, A. & Chaturvedi, A. (2019). Cloud Computing Characteristics and Services: A Brief Review. *International Journal of Computer Sciences and Engineering*. 7, 421–426. 10.26438/ijcse/v7i2.421426
11. Sheth, Mrs, Bhosale, S., Kadam, H. 2021. Research Paper on Cloud Computing. *Contemporary Research in India*. 87–92. https://www.researchgate.net/publi-cation/3524 77780
12. Gautam, A. (2022). Cloud Computing: A Review Paper. *International Journal for Research in Applied Science and Engineering Technology*. 10.3233-3236.10.22214/ ijraset.2022.44588
13. Madan, Suman (2021). Privacy-Preserved Access Control in E-Health Cloud-Based System. *In Disruptive Technologies for Society 5.0; CRC Press: Boca Raton, USA*, 2021145–162.
14. Lamba, Dr, Mishra, S., & Rastogi, S. (2022). A Review Paper on Cloud Computing. *International Journal of Research Publication and Reviews*. 1893–1895. 10.55248/ gengpi.2022.3.3.7
15. Sadiku, M., Shadare, A., Musa, S., Akujuobi, C., & Perry, R. (2016). Data Visualization. *International Journal of Engineering Research and Advanced Technology (IJERAT)*. 12, 2454–6135.
16. Farrag, M. & Nasr, M. (2017). A Survey of Cloud Computing Approaches, Business Opportunities, Risk Analysis and Solving Approaches. *International Journal of Advanced Networking and Applications (IJANA)*. 9, 3382–3386.
17. Goswami, P. & Madan, S. (2022). Utilizing Deep Belief Network for Ensuring Privacy-Preserved Access Control of Data. *Lecture Notes in Networks and Systems*. Singapore: Springer, vol. 394, 2022.

18. Madan, S. & Goswami, P. (2021). Adaptive Privacy Preservation Approach for Big Data Publishing in Cloud Using K-Anonymization. *Recent Advances in Computer Science and Communications.* 14(8), 2678–2688. Oct. 2021.

19. Alabdullah, B., Beloff, N., & White, M. (2018). Rise of Big Data – Issues and Challenges" *2018 21st Saudi Computer Society National Computer Conference (NCC), Riyadh, Saudi Arabia*2018. 1–6. 10.1109/NCG.2018.8593166

20. Madan, S. & Goswami, P. (2021, August). A Technique for Securing Big Data Using K-Anonymization with a Hybrid Optimization Algorithm. *International Journal of Operations Research and Information Systems.* 12(4), 1–21.

21. Rawat, R. & Yadav, R. (2021). Big Data: Big Data Analysis, Issues and Challenges and Technologies. *IOP Conference Series: Materials Science and Engineering.* 1022, 012014. 10.1088/1757-899X/1022/1/012014

22. Jagani, N., Jagani, P., & Shah, S. (2021). Big Data in Cloud Computing: A Literature Review. *International Journal of Engineering Applied Sciences and Technology.* 5. 10.33564/IJEAST.2021.v05i11.029

23. Madan, S. & Goswami, P. (2021). A technique for securing big data using k-anonymization with a hybrid optimization algorithm. *International Journal of Operations Research and Information Systems.* 12(4), 1–21. 10.4018/IJORIS.202 0070102

24. Madan, S., &Goswami, P. & (2021). Adaptive privacy preservation approach for big data publishing in cloud using k -anonymization. 10.2174/266625581399920063 0114256

25. Han, J., Haihong, E., Le, G., & Du, J. (2011, October). Survey on NoSQL database. In *Pervasive Computing and Applications (ICPCA), 2011 6th International Conference on* (pp. 363–366). IEEE.

26. Zhang, L. C. Wu, Z. Li, C. Guo, M. Chen and F. C. M. Lau, et al. (2013). Moving Big Data to the Cloud. INFOCOM, 2013 Proceedings IEEE, pp. 405–409.10.1109/ INFCOM.2013.6566804

27. Madan, S. & Goswami, P. (2020). A Privacy Preservation Model for Big Data in Map-Reduced Framework Based on K-anonymization and Swarm-Based Algorithms. *IJIEI.* 8(1), 38–53.

28. Zulkarnain, N. & Anshari, M. (2017). Big Data: Concept, Applications, & Challenges. Proceedings of 2016 International Conference on Information Management and Technology, ICIMTech 2016, November, 307–310. 10.1109/ICIMTech.2016.7930350

29. Neves, P. C., Schmerl, B., Bernardino, J., & Cámara, J. (2016, October). Big Data in Cloud Computing: Features and Issues – ACME. *The Acme Project.* Retrieved from https://acme.able.cs.cmu.edu/pubs/uploads/pdf/IoTBD_2016_10.pdf

# 12 Machine Learning–Enabled Security Parameter Selection to Identify Attacks on the Cloud and Host

*Ravi Shanker, Prateek Agrawal, and Vishu Madaan*

## 12.1 INTRODUCTION

The attacker follows a clear and efficient set of steps to sign in and learn about the system, such as what protocols are used and what systems are available on the organization. When the organization's list of systems is identified, the attacker starts to extract information about each discovered resource to make a list of its weaknesses, running applications, and open ports [1]. After finding and marking the problem, the attacker's attempt to access the target system through remotely triggering the attack or accessing locally. Once the attackers have the user's log-in information, they will use client root (U2R) attacks to try to get into the system. After getting permission from the super client, the attacker stops the attack by taking or changing secret information. On the other hand, important information, changing pages, or adding secondary passages as a stepping-stone for future attacks [2,3]. The attacker can do anything he wants at this point. In the last few decades, many gadgets, some of which work and some of which don't, have been made to protect against digital attacks [4]. Host-based Intrusion Detection System (IDS) collects and breaks down information about the attacked system itself, while organization recognition collects and looks at information packets during the transmission process or by packer inspection before the attack gets to the end system [5]. Installing the network IDS as a second line of defense behind the firewall is the best approach to protect the organization from the attacker. Its goal is to recognize the interruptions caused by many hosts. Even though every PC should have an essential host system installed, it works for U2R disclosure. Also for R2L

DOI: 10.1201/9781003341437-14

attacks, but the costs of activity and support are high [6,7]. Both the host and the organization have different places from which they can keep an eye out, which makes it easier to spot different attacks.

Various attack detection techniques are discussed in Section 12.2. Section 12.3 addresses the various types of supervised and unsupervised AI methods used in IDS research. Section 12.4 examines feature selection approaches. In Section 12.5, we talk about the available data sets and tools. The performance parameters that were used to test how well the research can be conducted and implemented are discussed in Section 12.6. The current issues with IDS and what could be done to fix them is illustrated in Section 12.7. Section 12.8 discusses the conclusion and the direction of future research. The chapter ends with the references. The entire chapter is related with the approaches that can be generally applied for identification of intrusion attacks in cloud environment as well as on the individual host system.

## 12.2 DETECTION TECHNIQUES AND CLOUD SECURITY APPROACH

Users are worried about data security because they don't know where their data are stored. Users store their personal and sensitive information at the server's data center to make it easier to store and process. Cloud security is mostly set up with three layers: the cloud layer, the network layer, and the host end, which is where the user's virtual machines and containers are. The cloud management access and control are the most important part of cloud security. This is where effective intrusion detection techniques must be used in the best way possible. One example is that a patient stores their health record on the cloud service provider's (CSP) data center. The patient should only share his information with people he trusts, since any change to the information could put his life at risk.

There are some things that need to be done to improve security in a cloud environment.

- *Cloud service provider*: Data had to be stored at the data center in an encrypted form.
- *Access control*: For semi-trusted CSPs to be able to control who can see user data, they need a good way to control access.
- *Identity validation*: Weak usernames and passwords can't prove who the real user is because they're easy to guess.
- *Trustworthy user*: Figure out who can be trusted and wants to get to the data.
- *Log-based systems*: Service providers are required to keep good logs in order to protect data.
- *Trust*: A good way to figure out how trustworthy the CSP and third party are.
- *Fraud control*: The right way to share information.

With the technology we have now, when a data owner saves their data on a server, the data owner has to be online to give the data requester permission to access the data. In the cloud environment, a hacker could get unauthorized access or do a denial-of-service (DoS) attack. Intrusion detection depends on being able to tell the difference between normal and abnormal behavior of the traffic [8,9]. There are two different ways to deal with this problem, and some IDS use a mix of the two.

### 12.2.1 ANOMALY DETECTION

The method for detecting anomalies strives to replicate normal behavior. This method examines customer behavior over time and develops a model that consistently addresses the customer's actual (typical) behavior. Circumstances that greatly vary from this paradigm are viewed as suspicious. A worm may infect, for instance, a detachable public web worker that attempts to connect with a huge number of addresses. Irregularity detection generates alarms for any out-of-the-ordinary behavior; hence, it is commonly used to identify zero-day attacks. The peculiarity location model's task is to characterize examples of typical client behavior and to manage variations in typical client behavior. A further disadvantage of a method for detecting anomalies is that it produces numerous false positives. This is due to their incapacity to adapt and evolve with time [10,11].

## 12.3  MACHINE LEARNING

AI emerged from human reasoning and computer learning theory, where constructs models from tested data sources and made decisions or predictions based on the information [12]. The intrusion detection classifies network events as either typical network events or DOS attacks, probes, U2R, and R2L. Three conditions are essential for machine learning: The information should be readily available. The information should be formatted. No fundamental numerical model exists for the data. On the basis of the presence or lack of labeled data and what we should predict based on the gathered information, AI innovation is frequently split into guided and unguided categories. The progression of IDS during the past two and a half years. In the subsequent part, we will provide a brief overview of the main machine learning techniques. Fuzzy logic and genetic algorithm are an added dimension to machine learning approach [13,14].

### 12.3.1 SUPERVISED MACHINE LEARNING TECHNIQUES

It is the process of using labeled data sets to train algorithms that accurately categorize or predict data. Adjust their weights until the model is appropriately calibrated, which is accomplished by cross-validation. Companies can use supervised learning to solve a variety of real-world challenges, such as separating spam emails into distinct categories. The training set is utilized by supervised learning to train the model to attain the desired results (Figure 12.1).

#### 12.3.1.1  Decision Trees

A tree that classifies instances by ordering them according to their include values. Each node in the tree corresponds to a section in the body. If we simply evaluate

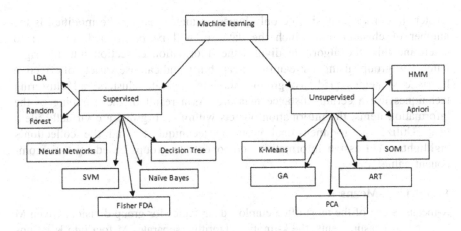

**FIGURE 12.1** Machine learning techniques.

"gain," an attribute with multiple values will be selected automatically. An alternative to ordering is to employ gain ratio, with each branch addressing a value that the hub can anticipate. Cases are organized by their main hub and their trademark values.

### 12.3.1.2 Neural Networks

Neural network is an approach to programming that is inspired by the human brain. A brain organization is composed of numerous neurons, each of which performs information, output, and initiation functions. The neural organization's contribution is applied to the information layer, and several estimations are conducted on the information and loads in the actuation region.

### 12.3.1.3 Support Vector Machines

It is the final strategy to be evaluated that transforms the data into more precise measurements and identifies the hyperplane that best separates the data. Using the concept of fields, backing vector machines seek to determine the largest distance between records. A support vector machine (SVM) revolves around the concept of "field" on both sides of the hyperplane that separates the two types of data. Increase the margins to create the greatest distance possible between the separating hyperplane and examples on one or both sides; each margin has been shown to reduce the maximum distances of the typical speculation error.

### 12.3.2 UNSUPERVISED MACHINE LEARNING

Unsupervised AI strategies utilize informative indexes that are not labeled and assign items to specified classifications. Regarding the optimality model, there is often no assurance that the optimal global configuration has been attained. This is a heuristic strategy since generally, all features of the data must be addressed, regardless of the sample size. The goal is to unearth concealed data groups. The recognized group is meaningless; it is up to the analyst to interpret the observed cluster. In cluster analysis, the only hyperparameter that can be modified is the number of clusters into which the data set will be partitioned. In order to determine this, the algorithm divides the information collection into the right number of groups using a streamlining capability and can use variety of effective heuristic strategies [15]. To group data into separate clusters, all clustering techniques use a certain distance measure. As a result of the grouping of the information items, the information objects within each group are virtually identical. Utilize the n-dimensional grouping technique to find the collection's highlights, then assign information components to groups based on their component value.

### 12.3.2.1   K-Means

K-means is one of the most often employed strategies for group division. Given M foci and N measurements, the k-implies algorithm separates M foci into K groups so as to restrict the number of squares within the bunches.

### 12.3.2.2   Self-Organizing Maps

Kohonen (1995) introduced self-organizing map (SOM) as a fundamental method for data organization. The fundamental concept is to set the facts on the framework and then alter the perceptions repeatedly (and the middle). Gatherings around this lattice lower the quantity of focus point growth and the number of focus points considered to be close to the network node. SOM is a fictional neural structure disguising itself as leaves. Through a single learning phase, its cells are extraordinarily tuned to diverse data instances or example classes. Only a single cell or a group of nearby cells respond definitively to the present information in the basic version.

### 12.3.2.3   Bayesian Clustering

Bayesian clustering is best suited for tasks involving unlabeled data preparation procedures, you should dismiss any strategies the system may use to classify labeled data.

### 12.3.3   Types of Classifiers

There are a variety of AI solutions that can be deployed in any combination to address the problem. AI problem-solving solutions can be categorized as straightforward, sentence-by-sentence, or mixed. Ways vary according to the quantity of problems and methods to be solved.

### 12.3.3.1   Single

These are less complicated solutions for addressing the current issue using AI technology. This AI strategy can be any collection, classification, or affiliation strategy. Singular working procedures are straightforward, quick, and simple to use, but they do not produce good critical thinking outcomes, hence they are rarely used nowadays. Ensemble, an additional technique to addressing concerns with AI tactics, is to integrate the findings of multiple weak classifiers; integrating multiple

training methods has a higher predictive performance than utilizing a single composition learning algorithm to generate the results. Combining the opinions of
several pupils will get the findings. We frequently employ simple classifiers, but
nevertheless get outstanding results. In spite of their parallel nature, the incorporated methodology for preparing and testing might save time when approaching
different processors. It can be implemented in two ways: preparing many classifiers
for a single informational collection, or preparing a single classifier for multiple
informational sets. It assigns the classes that most classifiers refer to during testing
after training the data set.

### 12.3.3.2 Hybrid
Hybrid approaches integrate two AI strategies to solve a problem; in this situation,
AI calculations collaborate rather than compete, as is the case with multiple strategies. Merging two methods in a cascade, grouping and then categorizing them, or
combining two distinct approaches might produce hybrid methods. Its performance
is superior to the other two.

## 12.4 FUNCTION SELECTION METHOD

Detecting intrusions is a clustering challenge that requires the development of
models that account for normal and abnormal behavior. It would be computationally
impossible to identify all of the functions present in the data set that can be used for
intruder detection. Researchers have developed and implemented a vast array of
feature selection techniques over many years. Exhibit a particular ant colony.
Currently, optimization algorithms, sepia algorithms, and evolutionary algorithms
are widely used, and algorithms for selecting features can be classified as filtering
techniques, envelope methods, or hybrid approaches [16].

The filtering approach chooses characteristics from the data collection regardless
of the classification algorithm used to represent the data. The filtering process
captures information with numerous characteristics and selects the relevant element
from the information collection based on a single characteristic. Use the inherent
qualities of the data collection to select a subset of attributes to classify individuals,
typically without considering the data mining technique. The filtering approach
analyzes unique characteristics without considering the classifier and determines
which characteristics should be maintained [17].

*Wrapper*: The packing approach employs a conventional data mining procedure
for evaluating a subset of the function of the created data set. These techniques are
typically the most effective since they identify characteristics that are more suited to
regular mining algorithms. The wrapper-based strategy generates superior functions, but is slower and more computationally costly [18]. Extraction of features is
an alternative to selection of features. In this technique, an n-dimensional data
collection is converted into a data set whose attributes do not correlate to the
genuine attributes of the original data set. The method [19–21] transforms an n-
dimensional informational index into a dimensional distance vector, which is
subsequently employed for testing and preparation. The changed segment is an
uncomplicated remix of the opening credits.

## 12.5  AVAILABLE DATA SET AND TOOLS

The following two subsections momentarily portray the apparatuses utilized for interruption identification and the various variants of the informational index. The convention attacks that exist in the informational index are additionally given as a table, which shows each trait of the informational index and the kind of significant worth utilized. This is additionally referenced.

### 12.5.1  DATA SET

Numerous data sets have been utilized to evaluate the practical efficacy of the technique. The majority of intrusion detection systems use passive ways to process intrusion detection, and IDS periodically receives data from the network on which it is placed. Some utilize mining techniques to discover intrusions. The public has access to numerous data sets for testing purposes. The following is a brief overview of the data set.

#### 12.5.1.1  KDDCup99 Data Set

The most broadly utilized and freely accessible interruption recognition informational collection is the KDDCup99 informational collection. The informational index is separated into two subsets; the preparation set contains 5 million informational collections, and the test set contains 3 million informational indexes. The attributes of information records can be isolated into four classifications: internal qualities, association span, convention type (TCP, UDP, and so on), and network administration (http, telnet, and so on).

#### 12.5.1.2  Corrected KDDCup99 Data Set

The KDDCup99 informational collection comprises of profoundly repetitive informational collections, which implies that learning calculations are outfitted toward regular informational collections, subsequently keeping them from learning uncommon informational indexes that are generally more ruinous to the organization, for example, U2R and R2L attacks [22]. This eliminates redundant records and reduces the possibility of system errors in the classifier.

#### 12.5.1.3  10% KDDCup99 Data Set

The total informational index is seldom utilized for preparing or testing purposes. This informational index doesn't utilize 10% of the full informational collection, yet lessens the quantity of attacks. Train the classifier on the worked on informational index to make it computationally plausible. The data sets contain the quantity of occasions in every variation of the informational collection and the quantity of explicit attacks in every variation. In each of the three forms of the informational index, attacks can be categorized as one of four classifications of attack.

### 12.5.2  ANALYZING THE ATTACK

One of the three protocols TCP, UDP, and ICMP can be used to mimic attacks in the KDDCup99 information record. Mohammad Hubeb [23] did a comprehensive

**TABLE 12.1**

**Array Matrix for Classification to Evaluate the Efficacy of IDS**

| Expected Level | Yes | No |
|---|---|---|
| No | TP | FN |
| Yes | FP | TN |

analysis of 10% of the KDDCup99 data set, which consists of 494,020 occurrences. 97277. Approximately 19.69% of the informational index consists of standard informational collections. The remaining attacks can be classified as DoS, U2R, R2L, or probe attack. There are 22 distinct training set attacks. Table 12.1 displays the frequency of each informational index attack.

### 12.5.3  TOOLS (INSTRUMENTS) AVAILABLE

#### 12.5.3.1  Weka

Weka is a collection of AI algorithms for data mining tasks. It is trivial to apply algorithms to informational collections or invoke them from Java code. Weka offers tools for data preparation, grouping, relapse, clustering, and affiliation controls, and is also suitable for developing new AI systems [24]. Customers favor Weka because it is a free tool with an intuitive graphical user interface. The client is not required to be an expert on the system computer in order to employ Weka.

#### 12.5.3.2  MATLAB

MATLAB has about one million customers in the scientific and industrial domains. It is a fourth-age programming language and multi-worldview mathematical figuring environment. The MATLAB application development language is MATLAB prearranging language. MATLAB has a completely different set of uses than Weka, but it's not as user-friendly and requires users to have a strong background in computer programming to be efficient [25].

### 12.6  PERFORMANCE PARAMETERS

Utilize a variety of performance metrics to evaluate the efficacy of IDS, and record the following results: Researchers utilize these indices to compare their results to those of established methodologies [26].

*True positive (TP)*: The positive instance is correctly assigned to the positive category.

*False positive (FP)*: The negative instance was mistakenly allocated to the positive class.

*True negative (TN)*: The negative instance is effectively doled out to the negative case.

*False negative (FN)*: The positive case was mistakenly delegated a negative case (Table 12.1).

List of most useful evaluation metrics parameter for classification algorithms are as follows:

1. *Accuracy (Acc)*: For the most part, exactness score estimates proportion of right expectation to add up to the number of all predictions.

$$Acc = \frac{TP + TN}{TP + FP + TN + FN} \tag{12.1}$$

2. *Error rate (Err)*: Degree of prediction error with respect to true model.

$$Err = \frac{FP + FN}{TP + FP + TN + FN} \tag{12.2}$$

3. *Specificity (Sp)*: Negative proportion or accuracy in certain fields, it is the extent of true negative rate that are effectively ordered.

$$Sp = \frac{TN}{TN + FP} \tag{12.3}$$

4. *Sensitivity (Sn)*: It is extent of correctly predicted positive rates from all the positive cases.

$$Sn = \frac{TP}{TP + FN} \tag{12.4}$$

5. *Precision (p)*: The positive mode that is accurately anticipated from all prediction in the positive class.

$$p = \frac{TP}{TP + FP} \tag{12.5}$$

6. *Recall (r)*: Ratio of positive rate from all actual positive rate.

$$r = \frac{TP}{TP + TN} \tag{12.6}$$

7. *F-Measure (FM)*: This number is the consonant average between the recovery value and the accuracy value.

$$FM = \frac{2TP}{2TP + FP + FN} \tag{12.7}$$

## 12.7   EMERGING PROBLEMS AND PROBABLE SOLUTIONS

Although there has been a lot of research on intrusion detection using machine learning technology, there are still many challenges that need to be further solved.

### 12.7.1   PROBLEMS

The existing systems have the following problems:

- An excessive number of false-positive results are generated by the vast majority of tested methods. This is because the paradigm suggests that every user activity is completely viewable and that legal behavior is distinct from intrusive behavior and user use [10,27,28].
- The detection speed of U2R and R2L attacks is slower with the current technology, posing an additional challenge which may be due to the fact that U2R and R2L attacks mimic normal data so closely that they are often misclassified as regular data or other categories. The low frequency of these attack categories may also contribute to the low detection rate [20,29,30], hence decreasing the detection rate.
- IDS is an asset that is vulnerable to attack. An attacker can attack IDS. If a hacking effort against IDS is successful, the network remains susceptible to attack, and IDS may consequently fail. The list of potential IDS attacks is large [7,31].
- Typically, IDS learns from reference data sets, and when deployed in a real-world environment, everything remains coherent under atypical circumstances. The performance of an IDS that is trained and tested in two unique situations will decrease.
- Multiple trials using the same classifier have had widely contrasting outcomes. However, the maximum accuracy or detection rate of the algorithm when used for this task is not disclosed.
- Since there are many different machine learning algorithms, and because research has not advanced to the point where classifiers are compared and one method is declared better to all others, no studies have been conducted on the best classifier for a certain environment.
- In the case of attacks, some attacks occur frequently but others occur seldom, limiting the ability of the classifier to recognize threats.
- The IDS generates an excessive number of alarms that cannot be managed by the administrator. Individual network administrator notifications for each attack will result in an unmanageable quantity of alarms for the administrator.
- There is no methodology that can be deployed in a real-world context because all learning methods need an inadvisable amount of time for training and testing.
- Even though more complex and advanced detection systems have been created, few researchers focused on the features of common linkages and attacks.
- Despite extensive research on anomaly detection, all current IDSs rely solely on abuse detection, as their models are built on labeled data that are absent from the actual network.

## 12.7.2 Possible Solutions

Several possible solutions to the problems discussed in the previous section are as follows:

- To reduce false positives, IDS must be capable of online learning, handling conceptual aberrations, and contextual adaptation.
- To increase the detection rate of R2L and U2R attacks, it is essential to combine feature extraction, feature selection, data transformation, clustering, classification algorithms, and the selection of extremely specific data properties.
- You may investigate the practicality of installing IDS as a distributed system in order to increase reliability, scalability, and remove single points of failure.
- To reduce classifier errors, IDS must be able to handle asymmetric class assignments.
- To reduce the amount of alerts administrators must handle by merging alarms and reporting risks per attack as opposed to each packet.
- To reduce time on training and testing, do not use the actual data attributes, rather convert and represent the data as a single point in space, and use the modified one-dimensional data set for training and testing (Figure 12.2).

After the study, some analyses were done on the KDDCup99 data sets and the following outputs were identified. The Python tool was used with 10% corrected KDDCup99 data sets (Figures 12.3 and 12.4).

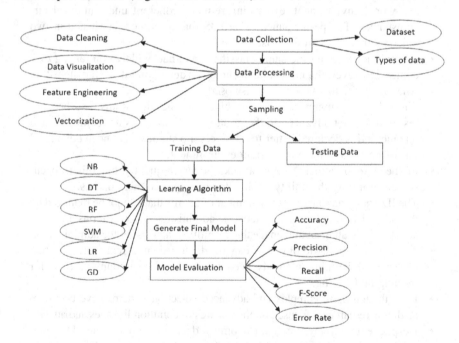

**FIGURE 12.2**   Methods involved in machine learning process for identifying network attacks.

```
Apply various machine learning classification algorithms such as Support Vector Machines, Random Forest,
Naive Bayes, Decision Tree, Logistic Regression to create different models.

Implementation of Guassian Naive Bayes

Training time Gaussian Naive Bayes:  0.014961719512939453
Testing time Gaussian Naive Bayes:  0.013972282409667969
Train score is: 0.49206097173705937
Test score is: 0.498041706361808
Training time Decision Tree:  0.0651249885559082
Testing time Decision Tree:  0.0013229846954345703
Train score is: 0.9598285169895204
Test score is: 0.9583994919021912
Training time Random Forest:  0.12805843353271484
Testing time Random Forest:  0.16969060897827148
Train score is: 1.0
Test score is: 0.9955541441727532
Training time Support Vector Classifier:  0.25743865966796875
Testing time Support Vector Classifier:  0.4568343162536621
Train score is: 0.9868212130835186
Test score is: 0.9870329205038637
Training time Logistic Regression:  0.5138204097747803
Testing time Logistic Regression:  0.0009999275207519531
Train score is: 0.9690377897745316
Test score is: 0.9666560812956494
Training time Gradient Descent:  5.228958606719971
Testing time Gradient Descent:  0.03690385818481445
Train score is: 1.0
Test score is: 0.9940192653752514
```

**FIGURE 12.3**  Output of various machine learning algorithm applied on 10% corrected KDDCup99 data set.

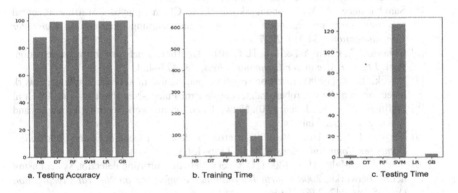

a. Testing Accuracy          b. Training Time          c. Testing Time

**FIGURE 12.4**  Based on the data set and machine learning approach showing comparison in term of accuracy, training, and testing time.

## 12.8  CONCLUSION AND FUTURE WORK

This chapter investigates intrusion detection systems by utilizing machine learning techniques. It examines a large number of related articles and categorizes them into one of three categories: independent, collaborative, or mixed. A data set is utilized for each piece of work, and the implementation of each system is selected. The chapter gives information about the environment, and the best performance metrics or the requirements used in making a good IDS-based attack identification in cloud or individual host environment. In addition to this, a comprehensive list of the attacks featured in the KDDCup99 record are discussed to show how these attacks can be trained and tested using a machine learning approach. Following an exhaustive analysis of the research, it has been determined that the hybrid machine learning method that employs the optimal algorithm for parameter selection can be implemented along with reducing the complexity by selection of best parameter and performance analysis. This chapter also makes an effort to draw attention to problems that are associated with already-established systems and to offer some direction for further research. This research can be further extended to identify attack at the top layer of cloud, i.e., at the cloud layer where authentication and API logs are the only ways to identify attacks while reducing the computing complexity.

## REFERENCES

[1] Tsai, C. F., Hsu, Y. F., Lin, C. Y., & Lin, W. Y. (2009, December 1). Intrusion detection by machine learning: A review. *Expert Systems with Applications*, 36(10), 11994–12000.

[2] Graham, R. (2000). FAQ: Network intrusion detection systems. http://www. robertgraham.com/pubs/network-intrusion-detection.html

[3] Heady, R., Luger, G., Maccabe, A., & Servilla, M. (1990). The architecture of a network level intrusion detection system (No. LA-SUB-93-219). Los Alamos National Lab., NM (United States); New Mexico Univ., Albuquerque, NM (United States). *Dept. of Computer Science*.

[4] Venter, H. S., & Eloff, J. H. (2003). A taxonomy for information security technologies. *Computers & Security*, 22(4), 299–307.

[5] Sangkatsanee, P., Wattanapongsakorn, N., & Charnsripinyo, C. (2011). Practical real-time intrusion detection using machine learning approaches. *Computer Communications*, 34(18), 2227–2235.

[6] ChiaMei, C., Chen, Y., & Lin, H. (2010). An efficient network intrusion detection. 4, sl. *Elsevier, Computer Communications*, 33, 477–484.

[7] Ptacek, T. H. (1998). Insertion, evasion, and denial of service: Eluding network detection. http://www.robertgraham.com/mirror/Ptacek-Newsham-Evasion-98.Html

[8] Stallings, W. (1995, January 10). Network and Internetwork Security: Principles and Practice. Prentice-Hall, Inc.

[9] Verwoerd, T., & Hunt, R. (2002). Intrusion detection techniques and approaches. *Computer Communications*, 25(15), 1356–1365.

[10] Shun, J., & Malki, H. A. (2008, October). Network intrusion detection system using neural networks. *2008 Fourth International Conference on Natural Computation* (Vol. 5, pp. 242–246). IEEE.

[11] Rajan, D. A., & Naganathan, E. R. (2022, April 2). Trust based anonymous intrusion detection for cloud assisted WSN-IOT. *Global Transitions Proceedings*.

[12] Rajwar, S. K., Manjhi, P. K., & Mukherjee, I. (2022). Comparative evaluation of machine learning methods for network intrusion detection system. Intelligent Systems and Sustainable Computing (pp. 531–541). Singapore: Springer.

[13] Koza, J. R., & Koza, J. R. (1992). Genetic Programming: On the Programming of Computers by Means of Natural Selection (Vol. 1). MIT press.

[14] Hamid, Y., Sugumaran, M., & Balasaraswathi, V. R. (2016, January 1). IDS using machine learning-current state of art and future directions. *British Journal of Applied Science & Technology*, 15(3),1–22

[15] Hartigan, J. A., & Wong, M. A. (1979, January 1). Algorithm AS 136: A K-means clustering algorithm. *Journal of the Royal Statistical Society. Series C (applied statistics)*, 28(1), 100–108.

[16] Kohavi, R., & John, G. H. (1997). Wrappers for feature subset selection. *Artificial Intelligence*, 97(1–2), 273–324.

[17] Li, Y., Xia, J., Zhang, S., Yan, J., Ai, X., & Dai, K. (2012). An efficient intrusion detection system based on support vector machines and gradually feature removal method. *Expert Systems with Applications*, 39(1), 424–430.

[18] Hall, M. A., & Smith, L. A. (1999, May). Feature selection for machine learning: Comparing a correlation-based filter approach to the wrapper. FLAIRS Conference (Vol. 1999, pp. 235–239).

[19] Luo, B., & Xia, J. (2014). A novel intrusion detection system based on feature generation with visualization strategy. *Expert Systems with Applications*, 41(9), 4139–4147.

[20] Lin, W. C., Ke, S. W., & Tsai, C. F. (2015). CANN: An intrusion detection system based on combining cluster centers and nearest neighbors. *Knowledge-Based Systems*, 78, 13–21.

[21] Tsai, C. F., & Lin, C. Y. (2010). A triangle area based nearest neighbors approach to intrusion detection. *Pattern Recognition*, 43(1), 222–229.

[22] Jeya, P. G., Ravichandran, M., & Ravichandran, C. S. (2012). Efficient classifier for R2L and U2R attacks. *International Journal of Computer Applications*, 45(21), 28–32.

[23] Siddiqui, M. K., & Naahid, S. (2013). Analysis of KDD CUP 99 data set using clustering based data mining. *International Journal of Database Theory and Application*, 6(5), 23–34.

[24] Holmes, G., Donkin, A., & Witten, I. H. (1994, November 29). Weka: A machine learning workbench. *Proceedings of ANZIIS'94-Australian New Zealand Intelligent Information Systems Conference* (pp. 357–361). IEEE.

[25] Higham, D. J., & Higham, N. J. (2016, December 28). *MATLAB guide*. Society for Industrial and Applied Mathematics.

[26] Liao, Y., Vemuri, V. R., & Pasos, A. (2007). Adaptive anomaly detection with evolving connectionist systems. *Journal of Network and Computer Applications*, 30(1), 60–80.

[27] Clifton, C., & Gengo, G. (2000, October). Developing custom intrusion detection filters using data mining. *MILCOM 2000 Proceedings. 21st Century Military Communications. Architectures and Technologies for Information Superiority (Cat. No. 00CH37155)* (Vol. 1, pp. 440–443). IEEE.

[28] Kumari, S. R., & Kumari, P. (2014). Adaptive anomaly intrusion detection system using optimized Hoeffding tree. *Journal of Engineering and Applied Sciences*, 95(17), 22–26.

[29] Horng, S. J., Su, M. Y., Chen, Y. H., Kao, T. W., Chen, R. J., Lai, J. L., & Perkasa, C. D. (2011). A novel intrusion detection system based on hierarchical clustering and support vector machines. *Expert Systems with Applications*, 38(1), 306–313.

[30] Wang, S. S., Yan, K. Q., Wang, S. C., & Liu, C. W. (2011). An integrated intrusion detection system for cluster-based wireless sensor networks. *Expert Systems with Applications*, 38(12), 15234–15243.

[31] Cheng, T. H., Lin, Y. D., Lai, Y. C., & Lin, P. C. (2011). Evasion techniques: Sneaking through your intrusion detection/prevention systems. *IEEE Communications Surveys & Tutorials*, 14(4), 1011–1020.

# Section C

---

*Security and Challenges Associated with Cloud Integration*

# 13 Decentralized Lightweight Blockchain
*IoT-Based Authentication System for Cloud-Based Supply Chain Management*

Inderpal Singh, Balraj Singh, and Prateek Agrawal

## 13.1 INTRODUCTION

Blockchains are permanent records of transactions. They are based on a secure network of secured nodes. Nodes are able to produce and read exchanges to compose transactions within a block according to a consensus protocol [1,2].

Technology developments, especially those involved with Industry 4.0, are provoking significant disruptions and leading to the development of new business models for supply chain management (SCM) companies. In this regard, blockchains stand out as a promising technology of the future. The idea of a blockchain was first introduced with the bitcoin technology (Nakamoto, 2008). It has been developed through the use of a distributed data structure that works in a peer-to-peer environment. Cryptographic hashes link the blocks and every node has a copy of all the blocks. Due to these characteristics, the transactions records are considered practically unalterable. In spite of the fact that the blockchain emerged with Bitcoins, its current applications are disruptive for a lot of different industries. Smart contracts operate according to the decentralization principle, in which intermediaries are eliminated. They assist in the automated transfer of assets when conditions are satisfied, based on the decentralization principle. Hence, smart contracts are redefining a number of business models, by enabling producers and consumers to conduct business without the need for an intermediary. The decentralizing and disinter mediating effects of blockchains can cause disruption in logistics and SCM, and support innovation and reconfiguration in the digital age. While the literature about blockchain technology in the SCM field is in its infancy, it is extremely promising with regard to its potential to promote changes in various types of supply chains through the introduction of new operation models. There is a lack of literature examining the growth of blockchains in SCM, and the impact of these disruptions in the SCM space.

## 13.2　STUDIES REGARDING THE APPLICATIONS OF IOT, CLOUD COMPUTING, AND BLOCKCHAIN WITH SCM

Today, SCM creates additional challenges in business domains for cost reduction, product quality, and accurate real-time visibility, therefore a cloud is offered for SCM development. Many firms use cloud computing to outsource software for good service. Cloud-based SCM improves IT support [3,4]. Integrating interactive processes reduces information inconsistency by ignoring undesired issues. It also builds and administers a database of user data by periodically treating hundreds of thousands of providers.

The Smart Contract model uses blockchain to give Circular supply chain model consumers trust and security [5]. SC and blockchain enable a more flexible value chain and data transparency and accounting in SC networks. The CSCM protects data and manages third and fourth logistical parties. It has a lower exchange cost and a trusted contractor to monitor without third parties. Blockchain accurately evaluates product quality during delivery and secures all data in the central database in CSCM. When an electronic moneylender combines transactions into a block, the blockchain terminates a transaction record through job authentication [6,7]. A well-organized SC provides better consumer service, product address, etc. Finally, it provides a decentralized intelligent transport system architecture.

## 13.3　IMPACT OF COVID-19 ON LOGISTICS

COVID-19, also known as coronavirus, is an infectious disease caused by the SARS-CoV-2 virus. COVID-19 symptoms are not very specific and can be very mild or sour. There are many ways the disease can spread, but it can also cause nasty pneumonia, and in the worst case, the disease can kill people. Most of the time, coronaviruses spread through airborne droplets (coughing, sneezing) and direct contact. Less often, the virus can spread through dirty surfaces. People over the age of 60 who have a weak immune system or long-term illnesses are at the highest risk of getting coronavirus or influenza. Any other illness makes it more likely that you will get sick. Children who are infected with coronavirus usually don't show any signs of it (World Health Organization – WHO). On December 31, 2019, the WHO reported an unknown microbial cause of death in Wuhan City, China. The WHO later said they also found a new kind of virus in samples taken from these patients. Since then, the outbreak has grown into a huge problem and spread quickly worldwide, which is very scary. People worldwide were concerned about a public health emergency that the WHO first declared on January 30, 2020. On March 11, 2020, the WHO officially declared a pandemic.

Clinical studies are done to discover more about the virus, its source, how it affects the body, and how it can be treated. For vaccines to be used in the real world, they usually have to go through research and testing first. In 2020, scientists set out on a race to make coronavirus vaccines safe and effective quickly. One hundred five vaccines were tested on humans at the end of October 2021. Forty-one vaccines reached the end of their tests. More than 75 vaccines that weren't tested on humans were tested on animals later. Zimmer C. and other people wrote about this in 2020.

## 13.4 CONVENTIONAL SUPPLY CHAINS FACE THE FOLLOWING CHALLENGES

1. A lack of transparency between upstream and downstream can result in a number of issues, including fraud and violations of codes of conduct.
2. Due to the effect of globalization, there are frequent changes in demand and indirect increases in operating cost due to lack of flexibility to these changes.
3. There is a lack of trust between stakeholders when it comes to security: Since there is a lack of trust, information cannot flow properly between parties.
4. Having an ineffective supply chain, risk management system will result in an inability for the system to predict risk. It is also unable to adapt to changing conditions (Figures 13.1 and 13.2).

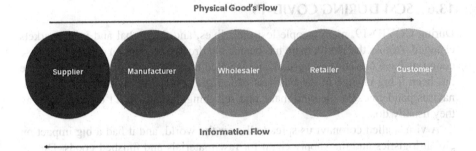

**FIGURE 13.1** Traditional supply chain management.

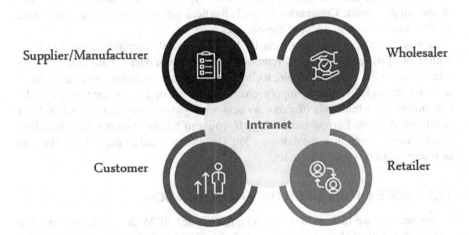

**FIGURE 13.2** Digital supply chain management.

## 13.5  IN REGARDS TO THE SUPPLY CHAIN, BLOCKCHAIN AND IoT PROVIDE THE FOLLOWING BENEFITS

1. Besides ensuring continuity and traceability of information, the immutability and irrevocability of blockchain facilitates the exchange of information among stakeholders, allowing products and information to be tracked without the need for inherent risk.
2. The transparency of the blockchain enables access to a great deal of information generated along the supply chain. A link between the flow of information and the flow of materials. The Internet of Things (IoT) provides a mechanism to link information flow and material flow at different stages of SC networks to increase their effectiveness.
3. Reduced code of conduct violations and fraud: Blockchain's transparent and auditable characteristics support the detection of fraud across the supply chain and the reduction of code violations.

## 13.6  SCM DURING COVID-19

During COVID-19, many people lost their lives, and the global and local markets changed. Across the world, there has been a big drop in production capacity because countries have closed their borders and isolated themselves from each other. There has been a big change in the business of logistics companies because of the coronavirus pandemic. People who make and sell things usually don't connect the way they usually do.

A virus called coronavirus spread all over the world, and it had a big impact on global logistics and the supply chain for raw materials and finished goods. During the crisis, the coronavirus affected supplies right away because it made them run out. There were losses and changes in one way or another for all businesses. The size of the losses and changes depended on the type of business and the complexity of the supply chain. Companies that sell medical supplies, food, and other basic needs were the first to adapt to the changes.

In recent years, the logistics industry has had a lot of complicated supply chains with a lot of different groups of remote suppliers. The model is based on complete interconnectivity between people, technology, and transportation, making it easier to move around the world. Supply chains work because of economies of scale. Containers from hundreds of cargo owners were put on one ship and taken from Southeast Asia to Europe reasonably. If you can't move goods other than life-support items, cargo flow went down a lot. The transport didn't get full, and the cost of transportation went up by a lot.

## 13.7  ROLE OF BLOCKCHAIN AND IoT IN SCM

In this section, we look at how blockchain, IoT, and SCM can work together. We assume that if blockchain can improve IoT security, it will also enhance the security of SC systems. Blockchain-based solutions use an IoT system to verify the identities of individuals and assets, according to Kshetri [8–11].

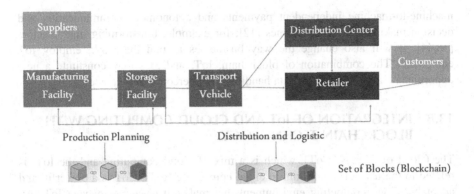

**FIGURE 13.3** Blockchain-enabled supply chain management.

Using the blockchain in an SC, it is possible to track the activities of each member of the SC. In addition, some key outcomes and performances may be accurately measured thanks to these features of SCM activities. The role of IoT and its impact on SCM was also examined by Ben-Daya et al. [12] applications and procedures. As a result, IoT for SCM will impact, as per Ben-Daya et al. SCM, including all the activities listed above, plus inventory control, quality assurance, and regular maintenance.

As a result of IoT technologies, SCM can have unparalleled access to all elements of the SC. However, the IoT for SCM is still in its infancy. Risks associated with IoT implementation in SCM exist in this case [13–15]. These risks are categorized into three clusters: The environmental, network related and organizational considerations. These dangers have an effect on Industry 4.0 (Figure 13.3).

The IoT [12,16,17] requires proper security to minimize environmental, network, and organizational threats. Ezmaeilian et al. [18–20] define IoT by "connecting and monitoring industrial items. The internet and physical gadgets." Key IoT security issues can be addressed with blockchain-based access management solutions.

M. Mahmud Hossain et al. [21–32] analyzed IoT security challenges and problems. During the study, security issues, requirements, attack surfaces, and challenges were also surveyed. Components of IoT along with security constraints in terms of hardware, software, and network were also explored. Security requirements regarding information, access level, and function were also presented in the study.

Such as those, connected with IP address spoofing [33–37] IoT devices must have an identifiable identity, according to. In this context, the term "blockchain" is the device's origin that can be tracked using decentralized identifiers (DIDs), especially crucial in high-risk settings. Because of this, blockchain has the potential to allocate and administer the device IDs, which is an essential component of this, and is a potential future use case for the blockchain. The sharing of services and resources is facilitated by using a blockchain and IoT combo. Innovating at the cutting edge of technology, opening the door for increased automation and innovation in a safe environment [38–42].

The blockchain-IoT combo is a formidable one, and it's only going to get stronger. IoT devices can perform autonomous transactions through smart contracts, providing machine-to-machine independent payments and autonomous communication and decision making between machines [12]; for example, transforming many sectors [38,44]. It will also change the way businesses around the world employ IoT equipment. The combination of blockchain, IoT, and SCs may constitute a new opportunity. Improvements in data handling for interconnected devices.

## 13.8   INTEGRATION OF IoT AND CLOUD COMPUTING WITH BLOCKCHAIN TECHNOLOGY

The Cloud of Things (CoT), which is a mix of cloud computing and the IoT, is related to the uses of blockchain in cloud computing (IoT). CoT is a powerful and adaptable cloud computing environment that makes it easier to manage IoT services. This means that CoT makes an IoT system work better. IoT is a system made up of many sensors, home appliances, vehicles, etc. that are all connected to each other. In an IoT system, the devices can connect to each other and share data over the Internet without any help from a person.

IoT systems are used by many industries to collect data from the environment, store it, and analyze it to get useful information that helps them take the right steps. But IoT devices don't have a lot of storage space, so they store large amounts of sensor data in the cloud. This is what makes CoT. There are many kinds of cloud services like public clouds, private clouds, and hybrid clouds.

In blockchain-based cloud computing, the blockchain network can be hosted as a Blockchain as a Service (BaaS) in the cloud. This makes it possible to use the blockchain for secure network management. IoT applications can use BaaS because it offers blockchain-enabled services like smart contract services, user transaction verification services, and cloud blockchain storage.

### 13.8.1   How Does Blockchain Facilitate the Management of Supply Chains?

The major downside of cloud computing is that it does not guarantee data protection. The data in the cloud are controlled on a server that may be hacked and attacked. Therefore, we know that anything accessible via the Internet is vulnerable to assault (Lee et al., 2015). By utilizing blockchain, it can be disposed of to some extent. To use an essential similarity, we fathom that it is simpler to take data kept secretively than taking that specific data from the public record. This is where blockchain has an effect (Kraft, 2016).

They simply propose that blockchain be linked to distribute computing so that its disseminated property of shared organization appears and information can be secured. It is possible to modify data on the framework by hacking a few cloud workers. However, nothing like this will happen if recorded on a public ledger such as a blockchain. When we try to answer that precise question, several hubs or "miners" in the framework will keep track of it, and the person attempting to hack will have hundreds of framework hubs, which is nearly inconceivable. Blockchain has a significant advantage (Kshetri, 2017).

We assessed the deployment of new technology in SC during COVID-19 and their influence on SC resilience and performance by conducting a comprehensive literature study. According to the conclusion of the studies, the adoption of blockchain technology in public distribution systems considerably minimizes pilferage and ghost demands. RFID (Radio Frequency Identification) technology can also help reduce grain shrinkage and misplacement (Kumar, 2020).

Using 5G-IoT integrated drones, Ray et al. (2020) found that medical deliveries may be possible and straightforward using blockchain in medical delivery drones. 5G-IoT is used to visit disaster-stricken areas, look after patients away from hospitals, aid hospital operations and facilitate the transportation of medicines, vaccinations, surgical instruments, and human organs.

### 13.8.2 WHAT ARE THE BENEFITS OF BLOCKCHAIN-BASED IoT DEVICES IN SCM?

Firms that can accurately predict future demand and consumption through big data analytics increase their supply chain agility, improving marketing sales, according to Hopkins (2020). Similar to the IoT, the sensors in containers, vehicles, and products can improve supply forecasting. On the other hand, blockchain technology is a powerful tool for enhancing supply chain collaboration and enhancing transparency, security, and accuracy of transactions. Additionally, during COVID-19, additive manufacturing was a critical component in response to the epidemic, as was using these new technologies. A long-term defense against this pandemic is an offer by integrating existing technology into existing manufacturing and delivery operations (Figure 13.4).

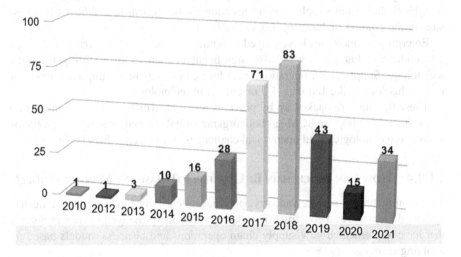

**FIGURE 13.4**   The number of blockchain projects created in each year.

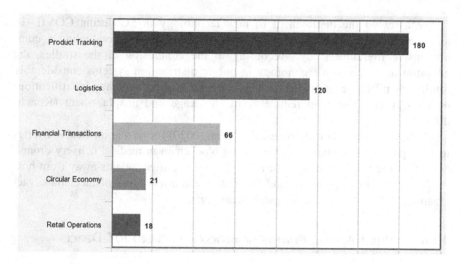

**FIGURE 13.5**  Role of blockchain in SCM.

### 13.8.3  What Are the Impacts of Emerging Technologies on Supply Chain Resilience at COVID-19?

The COVID-19 epidemic has strained global supply systems, causing disruptions and restrictions. Supply networks for various goods and services have been the most severely harmed by the COVID-19 epidemic. Retailers confront 12 significant operational obstacles in supplying adequate medical equipment supplies, and Kumar et al. (2020) argue that the deployment of Industry 4.0 as a countermeasure will help them overcome these challenges. He noted several significant hurdles in delivering medical equipment during the pandemic, including a lack of adaptability. IoT, blockchain, and supply-side information exchange can help address these issues in the context of Industry 4.0, as well.

Emerging technologies have played a significant role. Nineteen writers identified 19 pandemics, but there were also significant challenges in adopting this new technology. Supply chain operations may face challenges in the implementation of new technologies like Industry 4.0 or emerging technologies.

These findings are backed up by previous research, which shows that integrating blockchain technology in SCM has both organizational and end-user-related problems as well as technological and operational challenges (Wang et al., 2019) (Figure 13.5).

### 13.8.4  How Can Blockchain Be Used for IoT-Based SCM in the Future?

The manufacturing, service industry, pharmaceutical industry, electronic industry, agri-food industry, and construction industry are some of the well-known industries that have implemented new supply chain operations and business models based on evolving technologies.

In the process of SCM, new technologies are being used. The spread of the COVID-19 pandemic caused major disruptions in supply chains worldwide. Disruptions are a result of events that interfere with the normal flow of raw materials, finished commodities, and services within a system. Disruptions to the free movement of products and services at this extreme level have a severe and negative impact on business growth and the efficiency of the supply chain (Papadopoulos et al., 2017). As a result, new digital technologies are being deployed exponentially throughout global supply chains to deal with these types of disturbances and interferences.

## 13.9 CONCLUSION

COVID-19's impact on global manufacturing and supply chains was also examined in this study. Manufacturers and their supply chains around the world have been adversely affected by the n-CoV virus. We're seeing the effects of COVID-19 on a daily basis in our supply networks and industrial facilities. The COVID-19 pandemic has already disrupted the supply chain and prompted thousands of businesses in the United States and Europe to temporarily reduce or shut down their assembly lines. In both computing and healthcare, blockchain technology is still in its infancy. The qualities and properties of this technology have enormous potential in healthcare subsectors to solve important concerns. It is possible that technological advancements will have a profound impact on the entire environment. More research is needed in the early stages of its development, but it must also be conducted out in the health insurance and pharmaceutical supply chains. It's important to note that the application of blockchain technology has run into several problems, which will be addressed in future studies. Some of the concerns raised above about the study's validity could lead to better future research.

## REFERENCES

[1] Zhang, Y., and Wen, J. (2015). An IoT Electric Business Model Based on the Protocol of Bitcoin. 18th International Conference on Intelligence in Next Generation Networks (ICIN), 2015, pp. 184–191.

[2] Chen, L., Thombre, S., Järvinen, K., Lohan, E. S., Alén-Savikko, A., Leppäkoski, H., Bhuiyan, M. Z. H., Bu-Pasha, S., Ferrara, G. N., Honkala, S., Lindqvist, J., Ruotsalainen, L., Korpisaari, P., and Kuusniemi, H. (2018). Robustness, Security and Privacy in Location-Based Services for Future IoT: A Survey. *IEEE Access*, 5, 8956–8977.

[3] Murthy, C. V. B., Shri, M. L., Kadry, S. , & Lim, S. (2020). Blockchain Based Cloud Computing: Architecture and Research Challenges. *IEEE Access*, 8.205190-205205.

[4] Park, J. (2017). Blockchain Security in Cloud Computing: Use Cases. *Challenges, and Solutions Symmetry*, 9, 164.

[5] Cearnău, D.C. (2019). Block-Cloud: The New Paradigm of Cloud Computing. *Academy of Economic Studies. Economy Informatics*, 19(1), 14–22.

[6] Zhuo, Y. (2021). Blockchain-Enabled Access Management System for Edge Computing. *Electronics*, 10, 1000.

[7] Gupta, A. (2019). Cloud Computing Security Using Blockchain. *Journal of Emerging Technologies and Innovative Research*, 6(6).

[8] Rafique, H., Shah, M. A., Islam, S. U., Maqsood, T., Khan, S., and Maple, C. (2019). A Novel Bio-Inspired Hybrid Algorithm (NBIHA) for Efficient Resource Management in Fog Computing. *IEEE Access*, 7, 115760–115773.

[9] Salaht, F. A., Desprez, F., and Lebre, A. (2020). An Overview of Service Placement Problem in Fog and Edge Computing. *ACM Computing Surveys*, 53, 1–35.

[10] Bendechache, M., Svorobej, S., Takako Endo, P., and Lynn, T. (2020). Simulating Resource Management across the Cloud-to-Thing Continuum: A Survey and Future Directions. *Future Internet*, 12, 95.

[11] Nguyen, D. C., Pathirana, P. N., Ding, M., & Seneviratne, A. (2020). *Integration of Blockchain and Cloud of Things: Architecture, Applications and Challenges. IEEE Communications Surveys & Tutorials*, 22(4), 2521–2549.

[12] Meng, W., Tischhauser, E. W., Wang, Q., Wang, Y., and Han, J. (2018). When Intrusion Detection Meets Blockchain Technology: A Review. *IEEE Access*, 6, 10179–10188.

[13] Rathore, S., and Park, J. H. (November 2018). Semi-Supervised Learning Based Distributed Attack Detection Framework for IoT. *Applied Soft Computing*, 72, 79–89.

[14] Wang, T., Zhou, J., Liu, A., Bhuiyan, M. Z. A., Wang, G., and Jia, W. (2019). Fog-Based Computing and Storage Offloading for Data Synchronization in IoT. *IEEE Internet Things Journal*, 6, 4272–4282.

[15] Bittencourt, L., Immich, R., Sakellariou, R., Fonseca, N., Madeira, E., Curado, M., Villas, L., DaSilva, L., Lee, C., and Rana, O. (2018). The Internet of Things, Fog and Cloud Continuum: Integration and Challenges. *Internet Things*, 3-4, 134–155.

[16] Pham, C., Nguyen, L. A. T., Tran, N. H., Huh, E.-N., and Hong, C. S. (September 2018). Phishing-Aware: Aneuro-Fuzzy Approach for Anti-phishing on Fog Networks. *IEEE Transactions on Network and Service Management*, 15(3), 1076–1089.

[17] Aivazidou, E., Antoniou, A., Arvanitopoulos, K., and Toka, A. Using Cloud Computing in Supply Chain Management: Third-Party Logistics on the Cloud. *Second International Conference on Supply Chains, Aristotle University of Thessaloniki, Greece, 2012.*

[18] Sarmah, S. S. (2019). Application of Block Chain in Cloud Computing. *International Journal of Innovative Technology and Exploring Engineering*, 8(12), 4698–4704.

[19] Teseng, L., Wong, L., Otoum, S., Aloqaily, M., & Othman, J. B. (2020). Blockchain for Managing Heterogeneous Internet of Things: A Perspective Architecture. *IEEE Network*, 34(1), 16–23.

[20] Underwood, S. (2016). Blockchain Beyond Bitcoin. *Communications of the ACM*, 59(11), 15–17.

[21] Walsh, C., O'Reilly, P., Gleasure, R., Feller, J., Li, S., & Cristoforo, J. (2016). New kid on the block: a strategic archetypes approach to understanding the Blockchain.

[22] Leukel, J., Kirn, S., and Schlegel, T. (March 2011). Supply Chain as a Service: A Cloud Perspective on Supply Chain Systems. *IEEE Systems Journal*, 5(1), 16–27.

[23] Armbrust, M., Fox, A., Griffith, R., Joseph, A. D., Katz, R., Konwinski, A., Lee, G., Patterson, D., Rabkin, A., Stoica, I., and Zaharia, M. (February 2009). *Above the Clouds: A Berkeley View of Cloud Computing, Technical Report, EECS Department.* Berkeley: University of California, 1–23.

[24] Lucky, R. W. (May 2009). Cloud Computing. *IEEE Journal of Spectrum*, 46(5), 27–45.

[25] Dikaiakos, M. D., Pallis, G., Katsa, D., Mehra, P., and Vakali, A. (September/October 2009). Cloud Computing: Distributed Internet Computing for IT and Scientific Research. *IEEE Journal of Internet Computing*, 13(5), 10–13.

[26] Buyya, R. K., Yeo, C. S., and Venugopal, S. (2008). Market-Oriented Cloud Computing: Vision, Hype, and Reality for Delivering IT Services as Computing Utilities. *10th IEEE International Conference on High Performance Computing and Communications, HPCC.* Los Alamitos, CA: IEEE CS Press.

[27] Liu, S., and Wo, B. (May 7–9, 2010). Study on the Supply Chain Management of

Global Companies. *International Conference of E-Business and E-Government, Guangzhou, People's Republic of China*, 3297–3301.

[28] Supriya, A., and Djearamane, I. (May 2013). RFID Based Cloud Supply Chain Management. *International Journal of Scientific & Engineering Research*, 4(5), 2157–2159.

[29] Jun, C., and Wei, M. Y. (2011). The Research of Supply Chain Information Collaboration Based on Cloud Computing. *Procedia Environmental Sciences*, 10, 875–880.

[30] Bowersox, D. J., and Closs, D. J. (1996). *Logical Management: The Integrated Supply Chain Process*. New York, USA: McGraw-Hill Companies.

[31] Schramm, T., Wright, J., Seng, D., and Jones, D. Six Questions Every Supply Chain Executive Should Ask about Cloud Computing. *ACC10-2460/11-241*. Available: http://www.accenture.com/... ... /10-2460-Supply_Chain_Cloud_PoV_vfinal.pdf

[32] Buyya, R. K., Yeo, C. S., and Venugopal, S. (September 25–27, 2008). Market-Oriented Cloud Computing: Vision, Hype, and Reality for Delivering IT Services as Computing Utilities. *10th IEEE International Conference on High Performance Computing and Communications (HPCC 2008, IEEE CS Press, Los Alamitos, CA, USA)*, Dalian, China.

[33] Tuna, G., Kogias, D. G., Gungor, V. C., Gezer, C., Taşkın, E., and Ayday, E. (2017). A Survey on Information Security Threats and Solutions for Machine to Machine (M2M) Communications. *Journal of Parallel and Distributed Computing*, 109, 142–154.

[34] Avital, M., Beck, R., King, J. L., Rossi, M., & Teigland, R. (2016). Jumping on the Blockchain Bandwagon: Lessons of the Past and Outlook to the Future. In Proceedings/International Conference on Information Systems (ICIS).

[35] Makhdoom, I., Abolhasan, M., Abbas, H., and Ni, W. (2019). Blockchain's Adoption in IoT: The Challenges, and a Way Forward. *Journal of Network and Computer Applications*, 125(2019), 251–279.

[36] Morkunas, V. J., Paschen, J., and Boon, E. (2019). How Blockchain Technologies Impact Your Business Model. *Business Horizons*, 62(3), 295–306.

[37] Johansen, S. K. (2018). A Comprehensive Literature Review on the Blockchain Technology as an Technological Enabler for Innovation. *Department of Information Systems, Mannheim University*. Retrieved from https://www.researchgate.net/publication/312592741

[38] Schneider, S., and Sunyaev, A. (2014). Determinant Factors of Cloud-Sourcing Decisions: Reflecting on the IT Outsourcing Literature in the Era of Cloud Computing. *Journal of Information Technology*, 31(1), 1–31.

[39] Yli-Huumo, J., Ko, D., Choi, S., Park, S., and Smolander, K. (2016). Where Is Current Research on Blockchain Technology? A Systematic Review. *PloS One*, 11(10), 1–27.

[40] Shim, J. P., Avital, M., Dennis, A. R., Sheng, O., Rossi, M., Sørensen, C., & French, A. M. (2017). Internet of Things: Opportunities and Challenges to Business, Society, and IS Research. In ICIS.

[41] Gubbi, J., Buyya, R., Marusic, S., and Palaniswami, M. (2013). Internet of Things (IoT): Avision, Architectural Elements, and Future Directions. *Future Generation Computer Systems*, 29(7), 1645–1660.

[42] Atzori, L., Iera, A., and Morabito, G. (2017). Understanding the Internet of Things: Definition, Potentials, and Societal Role of a Fast Evolving Paradigm. *Ad Hoc Networks*, 56, 122–140.

# 14 IoT Cloud Platforms

## A Case Study in ThingSpeak IoT Platform

Varsha Pimprale, Sandhya Arora, and
Nutan Deshmukh

### 14.1 INTRODUCTION

There was an era where people used to get rid of things around them by throwing them in the thrash or in an unwanted place. Finding them again used to be a big task. But as soon as technology evolves, these things become important to us in all ways. The Internet of Things (IoT) is not only about things and RFID placed on it is just to find them, but much more than what we know about it [1,2].

Kevin Ashton is the inventor of the term *IoT*. There are multiple different definitions that describe IoT in their own words. Many definitions on the web talk about proposed systems for IoT but the reality is now the systems are REAL systems that are in use by many. The simplest definition is "Multiple intelligent devices (sensors, actuators etc.) having unique identifiers for each device are linked together using wireless networks for sharing information without human to human interface or human to machine interface in between the devices and using the shared data for further processing" [1–3].

In 1966, the first embedded system was designed using a microprocessor for the first time to control an electronic fuel injection system by Volkswagen. This embedded system was developed for vehicles and had a big remarkable contribution toward the evolution of embedded systems. Then, slow and steady, the concept of evolving embedded systems into intelligence began. There are many similar concepts but the IoT has become the most accepted term to describe and support this concept. The term came into existence in 1999, to assist the RFID concept. The popularity of IoT did not ramp up until 2010/2011 and reached shotgun advertising in early 2014. Machine to machine or industrial Internet is the concept that supports IoT, i.e., we can call them sub-segments of IoT.

But there are certain important parameters playing a major role in the system like intelligent things, network or Internet, devices, resources, and protocols. Every parameter plays a vital role in the system [1,2,4].

DOI: 10.1201/9781003341437-17

- *Things*: Things in IoT can be any intelligent device that has the ability to boot itself and read the information from the outside world and transfer it to the devices for further processing. Things can be a sensor, transducer, or any other component that can fulfill the given task.
- *Network/Internet*: An Internet is a global system of interconnected devices that forms a system into performing specific tasks. It connects devices all over the world. Through the Internet, people can communicate and share information easily.
- *Devices*: IoT gadgets include Wi-Fi sensors, software programs, actuators, and computer devices. They may be connected to a selected object that operates through the net, allowing the transfer of data amongst items or humans mechanically without human intervention. A couple of matters are related to the gadgets that help in imparting large amounts of information, and these facts are used for evaluation or further processing to get the desired paintings executed.
- *Resources*: Resources in IoT are the software that support every device or things to perform. It is as good as a device driver that supports the hardware to run.
- *Protocols*: Protocols are a medium of communication in between the devices connected in a system. There are various protocols used at various layers [1,2,5].

## 14.1.1 Cloud Computing Introduction

Cloud computing is a buzzword, where people store their data on the cloud and access it from anywhere by applying different methods. Online data storage has made life easy to go. In older days, people used to store data on desktop machines and then they used to copy it onto some pen drive or floppy disk and then carry the data wherever they wanted. But now, carrying data everywhere is easy because of cloud computing. There are multiple different types of services provided by the cloud. Computing resources can be easily shared and used over the Internet [11].

## 14.1.2 Cloud Computing

It is a method that relies on sharing computing resources rather than using traditional methods like local servers, personal machines/devices, and other appliances. Cloud here refers to the Internet. In short, we can say that cloud computing is nothing but processing your data on the Internet and applying it at various places as needed. There are several different applications that connect you to the cloud in various domains. Huge data is stored in the cloud on various servers, storage spaces with the help of applications connected to it. Nowadays online business is making a boom only because of cloud computing. This era is an online era, where people talk to each other online, see each other online, share their happy moments, sad moments together, meetings are done together, deals are cracked far away, etc. This all is possible only because of different services provided by cloud computing [3,6,8].

### 14.1.3 CONNECTING IoT TO CLOUD

Cloud computing is one element that helps the IoT to succeed. Users can use services offered via the Internet to execute computing chores thanks to cloud computing. The combination of cloud technology and the IoT has become somewhat of a catalyst. The IoT and cloud computing are now interconnected. These are real future technologies that will bring many benefits [3,6,8].

## 14.2 BENEFITS AND FUNCTIONS OF THE IoT CLOUD

The benefits of integrating these services are numerous.

1. IoT cloud computing offers numerous connecting choices, which suggests a huge network. One of the various tools people use to access cloud computing resources is a mobile, tablet, or laptop device. However, this brings up the problem of a lack of network access points.
2. IoT cloud computing is readily accessible to developers. In other words, it is a web application that doesn't require any assistance or additional authorization to utilize. Only having access to the Internet is necessary.
3. Adjusting the service to user needs and demands is possible. Fast and versatile allow you to change the user count, expand storage capacity, and alter software preferences. This characteristic enables the provision of deep computing and storage.
4. Cloud computing implies resource sharing. It enables users to cooperate more successfully and builds stronger relationships.
5. Security issues arise when the use of automation and IoT devices increases. Cloud solutions for businesses provide authentication and encryption techniques.
6. Last but not least, IoT cloud computing is practical since you get what you pay for. This indicates that fees change according to use because the provider tracks your usage patterns. An ever-expanding network of objects with IP addresses is necessary for the Internet and the data flow between its parts.
7. It is important to emphasize that dependability, security, economy, and performance optimization depend on cloud architecture; it must be well-designed. Structured services, CI/CD pipelines, and sandboxed environments enable agile development [3,6,8].

## 14.3 IoT CLOUD PLATFORMS

### 14.3.1 THINGWORX IoT PLATFORM

The ThingWorx platform is a complete platform, which is meant for the IoT. It provides various technologies and tools that upgrade the businesses to develop quickly and execute the important applications experiences.

ThingWorx is essential for the rapid creation and application of intelligent, networked devices. It supports the networking, production, analysis, and other elements of IoT development with a wide range of integrated IoT development tools. SQUEAL, which stands for Search, Query, and Analysis, is the search engine that ThingWorx employs. Users recommend SQUEAL for data analysis, data filtering, and record-specific searches. The ThingWorx IoT platform also includes a collection of elements that offer the convenience, effectiveness, and adaptability necessary for the development of IoT applications [9–14].

ThingWorx is the first objective that brings people, systems, connected operations, connected products, and applications together. The major benefit from ThingWorx is that it reduces the risk, time, and also cost, which occurs majorly while building any IoT- and cloud-based applications. It deploys the application very rapidly with model-based development. The ThingWorx IoT platform is also flexible and scalable to adapt that application in the future [15].

Key features of ThingWorx:
- It provides smart and complete platform furnishing.
- Rapid deployment of applications.
- Bringing people, systems, and machines together.
- Evolving and growing your application over time.
- Intelligence technique based on searching.
- Collaboration with others.
- Flexible options for connected products and applications.

### 14.3.2 Microsoft Azure IoT Suite

The Microsoft Azure IoT Suite is a collection of Microsoft-based cloud services that connect, manage, and govern a number of the IoT assets under Microsoft's management. IoT devices that connect to cloud-hosted back-end services make up an IoT solution. A cloud-hosted back end may virtually communicate with any device, thanks to Azure IoT Suite. The value of IoT requires many sets of services, as well as open-source client libraries that make it simple to communicate with the Azure IoT Suite. Microsoft Azure is also capable of changing the current business to a flexible intelligent system to achieve comfortability and scalability. Also, it allows Microsoft Azure Intelligent System Service and the services that build IoT systems and its applications to collect, store, and process the data [9].

#### 14.3.2.1 Cloud Connectivity with Azure

Microsoft Azure IoT service provides trustworthy, secure, and safe two-directional communications between millions of IoT devices and a cloud-based solution [14]. These services are provided without any human intervention, just-on-time provisioning of devices to the correct IoT hub without any manual involvement [14]. These facilities allow customers to provide robustness, security, and scalability to many devices. IoT Hub is a major component, and the user can use it to fulfill IoT implementation challenges such as:

- Rich set of device connections and its management.
- Increase in telemetry ingestion.

- Commanding and controlling of connected devices.
- Security for device implementations.

The fundamental concept of Microsoft IoT foundation is Microsoft Azure cloud platform. With the help of Microsoft Cloud Compute facility, processing, and analysis of the data, scalability of data collection can be covered easily and accurately for any business model. Cloud technology provides the solutions for data storage, its processing, its consumption, and its analysis on real time or latest data [9,14].

Like any other cloud platforms, Azure believes in virtualization. Most of the computer hardware can be emulated in software. The cloud is a set of physical servers in one or more data centers. The data centers execute virtualized hardware for customers.

### 14.3.3    GOOGLE CLOUD'S IOT PLATFORM

IoT on Google Cloud is a cloud-based IoT platform. It is intended to handle businesses' recording, analysis, and storage of business data from multiple devices. It offers real-time performance optimization and intelligent forecasting of equipment maintenance needs. The Google Cloud product line offers solutions for IoT problems that consumers and their partners can handle in the future.

With the help of Google Cloud technologies, their partners and consumers can adapt some IoT solutions to their unique needs [14]. With Google's highly scalable and dependable infrastructure, developers can build, test, and deploy their apps. Even Google uses it [16]. Additionally, it provides products that can support edge messaging, analytics, and insight analysis leveraging Google Cloud's superior AI/ML intelligence. For securely syncing and controlling IoT devices for small to big applications, Google Cloud IoT Core is a fully managed service [9].

#### 14.3.3.1    Components

Google Cloud IoT consists of two primary parts. The device manager and protocol bridges are two examples. These are what they are:

- *Device manager*: To register devices with the service for monitoring and configuration, a device manager is necessary.
- *Protocol bridges*: Google Cloud IoT uses two different protocol bridges. Devices must connect to Google Cloud Platform using the HyperText Transfer Protocol (HTTP) and Message Queuing Telemetry Transport (MQTT).

Telemetry information from the devices is also regarded as a component of the cloud area that can be used to trigger cloud functions. An open and partner-driven IoT strategy is being developed by Google Cloud, which can be compared to how they approach many of their other cloud services. Customers benefit from a wide range of options, less vendor lock-ins, and more fully featured contributions.

Advantages of Google Cloud for IoT applications:

- *Security is excellent*: The sector is well renowned for the security of Google Cloud. Every cloud and edge service that Google Cloud provides always puts security first.
- *Increase-in AI/ML products*: IoT creates an expanding data pipeline for machine learning (ML) and artificial intelligence (AI). Google's AI and ML tools make device data usable, enabling improved automation and effective solutions.
- *Cost-effective*: The strength of the IoT with cloud is a professional and microservices-based IoT platform that has been known to all of the major cloud providers. Therefore, none of the cloud is more reliable and less expensive than that of the Google Cloud.
- *Data occupancy is governed*: Google Cloud is popular as it has the most extensive fiber backbone in the world. It is implementing the edge locations and points of presence (PoPs) rapidly around the world.
- *Location service facility*: Location is an important parameter for many IoT applications. It is used where Google's suite of location-centric products is the most comprehensive and accurate from Google Maps and Google Earth. It is applicable not only for indoor but also for outdoor data visualizations. It is performed due to rich APIs for optimized routing and multi-source, non-GPS location.

### 14.3.4  SALESFORCE IoT CLOUD

Salesforce (Cloud CRM) IoT cloud [17] was launched in 2015 in its annual Dreamforce user conference. The idea behind this is to provide a platform to users to store and process data from connected devices, websites, sensors, applications, and customers. This is powered by a real-time processing engine, which is highly scalable. This platform initiates real-time response actions for the data generated in large volumes by websites, sensors, devices, applications, and customers. Real-life applications of this can be seen in wind turbines that change their behavior based on real-time weather data or dealing with connecting flights for airline passengers. Delay or cancellation of connecting flights can be rebooked before the planes they are on have landed. This platform can capture billions of events every day. You can create rules that specify which events to handle and which actions to take.

Everything in Salesforce IoT cloud is self-contained and connected, but autonomous at the same time. Reasons to implement Salesforce IoT cloud for your business are as follows:

- It creates a proactive engagement and personalized relationship between the customer and the organization by sending offers, information ahead of deadlines.
- It considers customer location, customer history, service history, and data from IoT devices to give you a complete picture of what your customers

want. This capability guides organizations to make customer-friendly decisions and meet their needs.

- It uses low code approach technology. IoT actions are used to send data from the IoT device to the service cloud or the marketing cloud, which automatically creates a lead for the customer.
- Data is analyzed effectively with Einstein Analytics. Cloud collects and processes data from various sources, such as sensors, portals, Salesforce CRM, and ERP, which is helpful for Salesforce IoT Cloud to produce visualization reports, predictions, trends, and patterns.
- It helps businesses to use visual dashboards, which is a 360° bird's-eye view for the organization to see how IoT products respond with changing customer experiences.

### 14.3.4.1  Integrate Salesforce CRM with Enterprise Cloud Protected Features

- Create a connected app in Salesforce, Dev Hub, Org, authorize, and complete the Salesforce client steps.
- To call the function, create a service account to control access to services and resources on the Google Cloud.
- To set up your scratch org and code deployment, enable the Dev Hub. You can do it from Setup in your Salesforce org by entering Dev Hub in the Quick Find box.
- Download the generated keystore on your local computer by downloading the salesforce.jks file.
- Save the Cloud Function's HTTP trigger endpoint at the remote site URL.

### 14.3.5  Kaa IoT Platform

The Kaa IoT Cloud environment allows users to add their devices to the cloud, facilities to manage their status and activity, telemetry tracking, user management, data analysis, custom dashboard creation, and many more. It is a developer-friendly cloud environment that addresses all these concerns using an easily configurable and secure IoT PaaS environment. It keeps users free from setup, hosting, and configuration troubles for their IoT projects. Start-ups and small companies can launch or migrate their products/projects quickly by using this platform. It is also helpful for personal IoT solutions, including smart metering, smart building, fleet management, air quality monitoring [18,19], and smart home.

Kaa IoT Cloud offers you the following:

- Real-time tracking of telemetry, location, and other device data
- Remote configuration of devices
- Condition and event based alerts setting
- Custom dashboards creation for IoT use case
- Managing users and their access rights
- Allowing to use pre-built IoT templates for popular solutions

Kaa IoT device management gives you a 360° view of your device inventory as this helps to find the exact device needed from thousands of others available in the application by keeping track of its operational status, executed commands history, etc. Using various dashboard widgets, Kaa IoT Cloud allows users to visualize their device's live data. These widgets are configurable to fulfill small and advanced needs of data visualization. Flexible, configurable widgets are available in Kaa IoT Cloud for remotely running commands on your devices, updating device software and for uploading and downloading data. Kaa IoT Cloud has the feature of providing alerts to notify users immediately if their live device data deviates from normal. Instant analytics of Kaa IoT Cloud helps to filter out noisy data by performing detailed analysis of device's telemetry and understanding trends.

### 14.3.5.1  Working with Kaa IoT Cloud

Working with Kaa IoT Cloud [18] requires first connecting a device simulator to the Kaa Cloud server and then sending and visualizing the device simulated data on the web dashboard (WD). Simulated devices can be connected to the Kaa platform using the default MQTT-based protocol.

You can create a digital twin of your device, connect it, send some metadata attributes, and view it in the Kaa web interface.

You can collect telemetry data from a simulated device to the Kaa platform and can transform collected data into well-structured time series and visualize them on the Kaa web interface. Then custom WD can be implemented and integrated with the Kaa platform. For IoT notifications, you can integrate your own microservice with the Kaa IoT Platform and can send email notifications for events from your device.

The Endpoint Register (EPR) service maintains a database of all endpoints registered within the solution as well as their associated key/value attributes (metadata). You can use the EPR REST API to perform these operations. The Kaa visualization feature is implemented by the Kaa WD microservice. WD implements a web interface for dashboard and data visualization, device management, endpoint configuration management, command invocation, etc. Managing the Kaa platform, as a front-end component, WD integrates with many microservices of the Kaa platform via a REST API.

### 14.3.6  ORACLE IoT PLATFORM

It is a cloud-based Platform as a Service (PaaS) provided by Oracle to connect and manage your devices and data over the cloud. Users may quickly make crucial business decisions and strategies by integrating data into corporate applications, web services, or other Oracle Cloud Services. This cloud has a business intelligence service that provides real-time analytical tools for incoming data stream correlation, synchronization, aggregation and filtering. Each device is given a distinct digital identity by the Oracle IoT Cloud service in order to create trusted bi-directional communication between the cloud and the device. Due to the cross-protocol capacity of this communication, users can connect devices without regard to firewall or network protocol limitations.

#### 14.3.6.1   Accessing Oracle IoT Cloud Service

Users can access and control Oracle IoT Cloud Service data and functionality from your corporate apps by using REST API calls. REST APIs can be used to safely link connected devices with business applications. It is assumed that users have already set up an instance of Oracle IoT Cloud Service before doing this operation. By logging onto http://cloud.oracle.com and choosing a classic cloud account from the list, you can access Oracle Cloud. Choose the data center where the service is located from the Data Center list. Click Go after entering the identification domain from your welcome email in the appropriate field in my services. Sign in by entering your username and password. Click the and select Cloud Services from the list under the IoT Enterprise menu item.

### 14.3.7   ThingSpeak IoT Platform

Users can talk to Internet-connected devices using ThingSpeak, an open source IoT analytics platform service. In the cloud, you can collect, display, and examine real-time data streams. Sending data to ThingSpeak allows you to send alerts and instantly visualize real-time data. To handle and analyze incoming data online, you can execute MATLAB code in ThingSpeak. The following are some of ThingSpeak's salient characteristics [20,21]:

- Common IoT protocols can be readily configured on devices to send data to ThingSpeak and display real-time sensor data.
- Data collected on demand from other sources.
- It makes use of MATLAB's capabilities to interpret your IoT data.
- IoT analytics can be done automatically based on schedules or occurrences.
- Building a prototype or IoT system without a server.
- Uses third-party services such as Twilio and Twitter to automatically process data and communicate [22,23].

#### 14.3.7.1   Working with ThingSpeak

ThingSpeak allows you to interact with devices, social media, and web services. Users can create and configure a channel to send, receive, and retrieve data from the channel. You can publish your channel to share data. To create, update, and delete channels as well as their feeds, you can utilize REST API functions like PUT, GET, POST, and DELETE. You may also update the channel feed and sign up to receive messages when the channel is changed using the MQTT (MQ Telemetry Transport) publish and subscribe methods.

This interface is used by a server to provide data in the format required in response to requests made by web browsers or other clients. To explore and display channel data, the MATLAB Analysis and Visualization App can be used.

The ThingSpeak MQTT brokers can be used to allow users to update and receive channel feeds. A client device can connect to an MQTT broker, publish on a channel, and subscribe to updates from that channel [20].

## 14.3.8   CASE STUDY OF THINGSPEAK IOT PLATFORM

This case study is related to temperature and humidity monitoring, visualization, and alerting system using the ThingSpeak IoT platform.

IoT provides a solution for monitoring atmospheric parameters like temperature and humidity remotely. The system uses a DHT11 sensor for measuring atmospheric temperature and humidity. With the help of an inbuilt Wi-Fi module present in Raspberry Pi, recent readings are sent to ThingSpeak, an IoT analytics service platform that allows us to aggregate and visualize data streams in the cloud. For notifying users about abnormal parameters, an email alert system is implemented. Also, for local monitoring, the system uses a buzzer to alert the observers about the sensed parameters.

Monitoring atmospheric parameters is a basic step in many high-scale applications like weather prediction, smart farming, etc. For weather forecasting, current and past readings of these parameters are required. So, keeping a record of every value accurately and continuously is a very important step. In a smart farming or gardening system, weather monitoring can help people to plan the irrigation and other agricultural activities based on the current weather, in order to use the resources efficiently. Also, the system is used in large food-storage areas, for maintaining suitable atmospheric conditions for preserving food.

### 14.3.8.1   System Design

Hardware requirements:
- 5 V/3.3 V power supply
- Raspberry Pi (with inbuilt Wi-Fi module)
- DHT11 temperature humidity sensor
- Buzzer
- Jumper wires
- Breadboard
- Desktop monitor

Software requirements:
- Raspbian OS
- Chromium browser
- Python3
- Adafruit_DHT: Python library
- Thonny: Python IDE
- ThingSpeak channel

### 14.3.8.2   Purpose and Requirements

i. *Purpose*: To build a temperature-humidity monitoring system using IoT for tracking atmospheric parameters remotely and to visualize them.

ii. *Requirements*
- Behavior: The system should sense atmospheric temperature and humidity constantly and give alerts about extreme atmospheric conditions. The system should also be able to visualize the temperature humidity data over time, in the form of charts.
- Requirement for system management: The system must provide features for remote monitoring, alerting, and visualization.
- Data analysis should be carried out locally by the system, as per the requirement.
- Program deployment requirements ask for local deployment of the application but distant data visualization.
- Security requirement: Since the program does not handle any confidential or sensitive information, neither authentication nor security is necessary.

iii. *Process specification*: In this stage, the IoT system's use cases are officially described, based on, and deduced from the requirement and purpose specifications. In Figure 14.1, the process specification is displayed.

iv. *Domain model specification*: The domain model provides an abstract representation of the key ideas, entities, and objects in the IoT system's domain along with their relationships. Figure 14.2 tells us more about the same.

v. *Information model*: The IoT system's entire database shown in figure 14.3 is organized according to the information model. By outlining their attributes and relations, it gives the virtual entities more specifics (Figure 14.3).

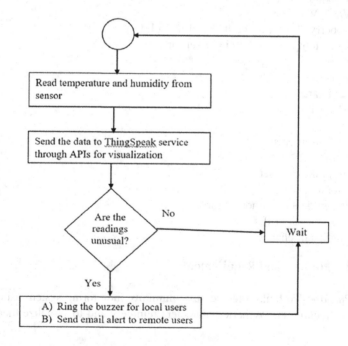

**FIGURE 14.1**  Process specification.

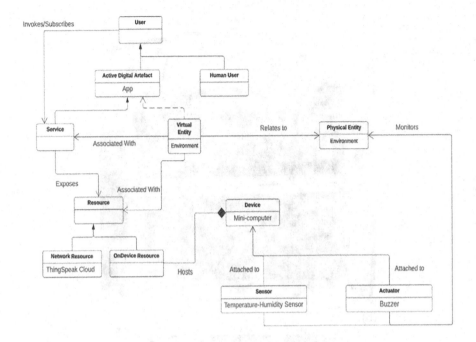

**FIGURE 14.2**  Domain model specification.

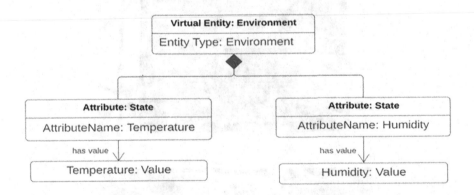

**FIGURE 14.3**  Information system.

  vi. *Device & component integration*: The real connection between IoT
      devices is specified in this phase as shown in Figure 14.4).
 vii. *Application development*: This step includes the development of an
      application as shown in figure 14.5, 14.6 and 14.7 for using the IoT
      system.

Layout of the application that can be developed further (Figures 14.5–14.7):

(a)

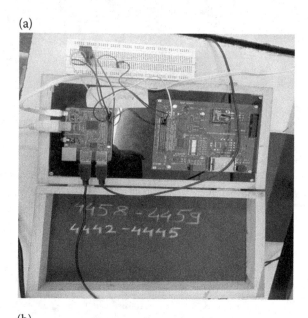

(b)

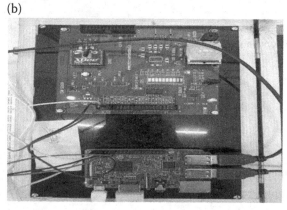

(c)

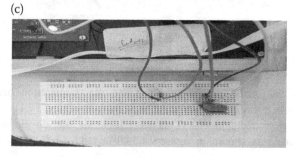

**FIGURE 14.4** (a) Actual implementation of temperature and humidity monitoring, visualization, and alerting system. (b) Actual implementation of temperature and humidity monitoring, visualization, and alerting system. (c) Actual implementation of temperature and humidity monitoring, visualization, and alerting system.

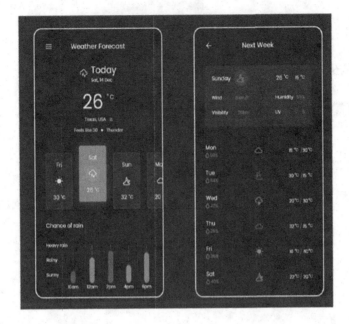

**FIGURE 14.5**  Application developed for case study.

**FIGURE 14.6**  ThingSpeak view.

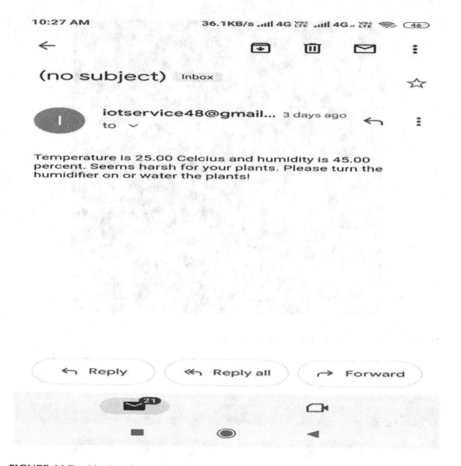

FIGURE 14.7   Alerting through mail.

## 14.4   CONCLUSION

The integration of IoT and cloud computing technologies, which is currently fixing a number of corporate difficulties and presenting new commercial and research prospects, is where the future of the Internet lies. New programs and services are being developed at each stage to deal with the issues at hand. Prior to reaching their full potential, IoT and the cloud still have a ways to go.

## REFERENCES

[1] Deshmukh, N. H. (2022), "Internet of Things – Essential IoT business guide with different case studies." *Computing Technologies and Applications: Paving Path towards Society 5.0.* Chapman and Hall: London, UK, 2021, pp. 71–93.

[2] Sapkal, S., Arora, S. (2022), "Research issues in IoT." *Computing Technologies and Applications: Paving Path towards Society 5.0.* Chapman and Hall: London, UK, 2021, pp. 93–103.

[3] Pflanzner, T., Kertész, A. (2016), "A survey of IoT cloud providers." *39th International Convention on Information and Communication Technology, Electronics and Microelectronics (MIPRO)*, pp. 730–735.

[4] Aazam, M., Khan, I., Alsaffar, A. A., Huh, E.-N. (2014), "Cloud of Things: Integrating Internet of Things and cloud computing and the issues involved." *Proceedings of 11th International Bhurban Conference on Applied Sciences & Technology* (IBCAST). Islamabad, Pakistan.

[5] Sahmim, S., Gharsallaoui, H. (2017), "Privacy and security in Internet-based computing: Cloud computing, Internet of Things, Cloud of Things: A review." *International Conference on Knowledge Based and Intelligent Information and Engineering Systems*. France.

[6] Yangui, S. (2020), "A panorama of cloud platforms for IoT applications across industries." *Sensors* 20 (9), 2701–2720.

[7] Darwish, A., Hassanien, A. E., Elhoseny, M., Sangaiah, A. K., Muhammad, K. (2019), "The impact of the hybrid platform of Internet of Things and cloud computing on healthcare systems: Opportunities, challenges, and open problems." *Journal of Ambient Intelligence and Humanized Computing* 10, 4151–4166.

[8] Shah, J. (2022), "Cloud technology and management." *Computing Technologies and Applications: Paving Path towards Society 5.0*. Chapman and Hall: London, UK, 2021, pp. 3–21.

[9] Hurel, L. M. (2018), "Architectures of security and power: IoT platforms as technologies of government." Thesis for MSc Media and Communications (Data and Society). doi: 10.13140/RG.2.2.28293.29920

[10] Ray, P. P. (2016), "A survey of IoT cloud platforms." *Future Computing and Informatics Journal* 1 (1-2), 35–46.

[11] Peng, J., Zhang, X., Lei, Z., Zhang, B., Zhang, W., Li, Q. (2009), "Comparison of several cloud computing platforms." *2009 Second International Symposium on Information Science and Engineering*, pp. 23–27.

[12] Bisong, E. (2019), "An overview of Google Cloud platform services." *Building Machine Learning and Deep Learning Models on Google Cloud Platform*, 7–10.

[13] Houidi, I., Mechtri, M., Louati, W., Zeghlache, D. (2011), "Cloud service delivery across multiple cloud platforms." *IEEE International Conference on Services Computing*, pp. 741–742.

[14] Nakhuva, B., Champaneria, T. (2015), "Study of various Internet of Things platforms." *International Journal of Computer Science & Engineering Survey* 6(6), 61–74. doi: 10.5121/ijcses.2015.6605

[15] Edson, B. (2020), "Creating the Internet of your things." Microsoft Corporation.

[16] Gupta, D., Bhatt, S., Gupta, M., Kayode, O., Tosun, A. (2020). Access control model for Google Cloud IoT. pp. 198–208. doi: 10.1109/BigDataSecurity-HPSC-IDS49724.2020.00044

[17] Choudhary, N., Arya, V. (2021), "Salesforce IoT cloud platform." *Integrated Intelligence Enable Networks & Computing*, pp. 301–309. doi: 10.1007/978-981-33-6307-6_31

[18] Rasyid, M., Mubarrok, M., Hasim, J. (2020), "Implementation of environmental monitoring based on KAA IoT platform." *Bulletin of Electrical Engineering and Informatics* 9(6), 2578–2587. doi: 10.11591/eei.v9i6.2578

[19] Sadawi, A. A., Hassan, M. S., Ndiaye, M. (2022), "On the integration of blockchain with IoT and the role of Oracle in the combined system: The full picture." *IEEE Access* 10, 92532–92558. doi: 10.1109/ACCESS.2022.3199007

[20] De Nardis, L., Caso, G., Di Benedetto, M.-G. (2019), "ThingsLocate: A ThingSpeak-based indoor positioning platform for academic research on location-aware Internet of Things." *Technologies* 7, 50. doi: 10.3390/technologies7030050

[21] Shewchuk, J., "Internet of Things." Microsoft Corporation.

[22] Ganguly, P. (2016), "Selecting the right IoT cloud platform." *International Conference on Internet of Things and Applications (IOTA)*, pp. 316–320.

[23] Sikarwar, R., Yadav, P., Dubey, A. (2020), "A survey on IOT enabled cloud platforms." *IEEE 9th International Conference on Communication Systems and Network Technologies (CSNT)*, pp. 120–124.

# 15 Cloud-Based E-Store Using Distributed Indexing Technique for Tribal Art Globalization
## A Boon for Tribes

Kishor Mane and Urmila Shrawankar

## 15.1 INTRODUCTION

In recent years, cloud technology captures the market with rapid speed due to its low-cost solutions without investing the large amount of the capital. This technology is based on the concept model of pay only for use. It offers various services such as any software can be accessible from a remote location without installation, any hardware configuration along with operating system will be accessed virtually, it can increase the processing power with an increase in the resources such as memory, processors, storage, etc. Currently, all the companies are switching from their old infrastructure to the cloud platform by either adapting the public, private, or combination of both as a hybrid model of the cloud environment. It will save the operating cost of the companies. There are many e-platforms available based on the cloud infrastructure for purchasing the products through online mode without intervention of dealers or brokers. The vendor can sell their products directly to the customers through this mode of platforms.

In India, the tribal art getting the much attention due to their attractive handmade design, eco-friendly material, smooth finishing, etc. features. Table 15.1 shows few samples of the tribal products purchased through the market and used images of it for spreading the awareness related to the tribal products and their quality. All the credit goes to the tribal artists who have made these products. But very few tribal art products are available on these platforms for selling and purchase because of illiteracy of the technical knowledge, unavailability of the hardware infrastructure, etc. Also, these platforms are lagging in the accuracy of retrieving the correct products without getting many irrelevant products.

So, there is a need of the indexing-based retrieval mechanism, which can accept keyword text input or the image as an input. Indexing is used for improving the search accuracy when the user want to search the products from the big data set of the variety of the products.

DOI: 10.1201/9781003341437-18

**TABLE 15.1**

**Sample Tribal Art Products (Credit Goes to Tribal Artists Who Have Made These)**

Sample Images of Tribal Products

| | | | |
|---|---|---|---|
|  | 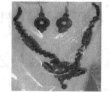 |  |  |
| It is the embroidery work of Gujarat state. | It is Terracotta jewellery. | It is a home décor tribe product. | It is a Joha rice from Assam state of India. |
| 1. Gujarat embroidery | 2. Terracotta ornament | 3. Home decor | 4. Food – Joha rice |
|  |  |  |  |
| It is the embroidery work of West Bengal. | It is a mushroom from Maharashtra state of India. | It is a bamboo product. | It is the embroidery work under woolen. |
| 5. Katha work – West Bengal | 6. Food –mushroom | 7. Bamboo products | 8. Woolen rumal |

Figure 15.1 shows the basic mechanism for the indexing and retrieval of the images with the help of the content of images. The image data set has been considered as an input for extracting the features after pre-processing. These features are used as an input for the indexing mechanism. Any indexing mechanism such as B+ tree, Hash tree, R tree, etc. [1] can be considered for indexing of the features.

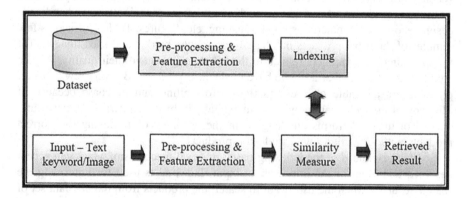

**FIGURE 15.1**    Schematic of indexing and retrieval mechanism based on content.

Once indexing is done, the structure is ready to search the data from it. In the retrieval mechanism, the input can be considered as any text keyword or image. It has undergone through the pre-processing and process of extraction of features from it which can be helpful for finding similar features in the indexing structures through the similarity measure. Once the features are matched, the same images are retrieved and displayed as a result.

In this chapter, the distributed indexing mechanism has been used for searching the tribal products through the big data. This approach of indexing having benefits such as faster search time, availability of the data even through one node fails, scalability, fetching the appropriate results within less time, time required to index the new item will be reduced.

## 15.2   CURRENT PLATFORMS FOR E-SHOPPING OF TRIBAL ART PRODUCTS

Recently in the period of lockdowns due to COVID-19 restrictions, the people of India are very much familiar with the different e-platforms, which are used to get the essential items required to survive. The people also benefited due to the "Digital India" and "Make in India" campaign run by the Indian government to get awareness for doing online payments using UPI payment interfaces and applications. Nowadays, people are buying different products through the different e-platforms easily. Following are a few of the e-platforms for selling and purchasing the tribal art products:

1. amazon.in – This platform provides one separate section for selling the tribal platform.
2. flipkart.com – It provides paintings and cloths related to the tribal products.
3. tribeindia.com – This platform is created by the ministry of tribal affairs for selling the tribal products. This platform started in the year 2020.
4. trulytribal.in – It started in 2015 and has been developed for filling the communication gap between artist and customer.
5. universaltribes.com – It provides different categories of products, including painting, organic foods, handcraft, etc.

Many other platforms are available for the tribal products.

## 15.3   LIMITATIONS OF CURRENTLY AVAILABLE E-PLATFORMS

Currently many e-platforms are available for tribal art products, including the above-mentioned platforms. But they are lagging in the relevance of the retrieved results. Following are the different limitations are the available platforms:

- *Only text keyword-based search*: The current platform supports only the text keyword-based platform, but it provides only 20–30% accuracy of the products and 70–80% results are irrelevant of the search keywords.

- *Missing content-based search*: The search facility based on the query image is not available on these platforms. If any customer want to search similar products as seen in the image, then it is very hard to search it through these platforms.
- *Unavailability of event-based search facility*: If the customer is interested in the tribal products related to the specific events, such as "marriage," then it is a tedious process to search each product separately.
- *Missing geo-location-based search facility*: The tribal products are not able to be searched by selecting the location of the region.
- *Non-availability of theme-based search facility*: The tribal products are not categorized based on the theme, such as Maharashtrian products based on "Kokan" theme.
- Not able to correctly identify the semantics of the product.
- Missing the opportunity to apply machine learning techniques to increase the system's accuracy.
- Lagging in the indexing mechanism used for the retrieval of the similar products.
- Does not provide the facility to retrieve the products based on the description.
- Fewer number of tribal products available on these platforms due to technical illiteracy of the tribal people.

So, to overcome the above limitations, there is a need for the cloud-based solution.

## 15.4 PROPOSED ARCHITECTURE OF THE E-STORE

### 15.4.1 System Model

The cloud-based tribal products' e-store has been designed and developed to overcome the limitations of the currently available e-platforms, as shown in Figure 15.2. The different concepts, algorithms, and technologies have been used in the design of the e-store. It consists of different stages of processing as follows:

1. *Data set creation*: The product data set has been created by taking the input from the user using the product image, product keyword, and description of the product along with the cost. This input data can be entered through the Android mobile application interface or the web interface. Currently, many tribal people are used to the Android app, but those who do not have any knowledge of it can enter their data with the help of the gram panchayat centers or Asha worker or inside the common service center through the use of a web-based interface.
2. *Client-end backup*: This is used to store the data on the device local storage when the network is not available in the tribal areas. When network is available, it will be automatically stored on the cloud.
3. *Mobile backend*: It is responsible to fetch the data from the mobile, which is saved in offline mode synchronization operation.

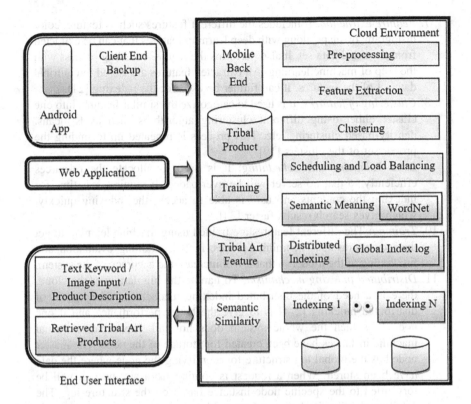

**FIGURE 15.2**  System architecture for the cloud-based e-store for tribal art.

4.  *Text preprocessing*: When the text keyword or the product description is passed as an input by the user, then they need to apply the preprocessing on the input. It includes the different operations such as converting the data in lowercase, applying tokenization, stopping word removal from the keywords, removal of numbers, special characters, and punctuations, transforming the keywords to the root form using lemmatization or stemming, weight calculation, etc.

5.  *Image preprocessing*: This step is essential when the input query image or the input data set images are not in the specific dimensions. It requires resizing the images to a specific size, grayscale conversion if required, enhancement in the contrast using histogram equalization, reduction of noise, normalizing the image into a fixed range of the pixel along with different augmentation operations such as flip, zoom, etc. to increase the size of data set.

6.  *Semantic meaning extraction with WordNet*: Sometimes, the text keywords give the wrong results due to not understanding the meaning of the keyword. This task is done by the semantic meaning extraction process with the use of WordNet. It is the lexical database that can find the meaning and relationship of the keyword along with its context [29,30].

7. *Feature extraction*: It includes the different features such as texture, color histogram, or shape along with deep learning features that can be extracted from the tribal data set. It also performs the feature encoding process with the help of machine learning. All extracted features are stored into a tribal data set of the features. It can further be used for the indexing [21].

8. *Clustering of features*: It is used to categorize the similar features into one cluster either using different clustering algorithms such as K-means, density-based clustering, etc. This process is repeated up to finding the proper set of the clusters [19].

9. *Load balancing and scheduling*: It is used to allocate the resources efficiently so that no server will be overloaded. It requires less time for indexing the contents and user is able to access the indexing quickly, which gives search results faster [34].

10. *Training*: The different features are trained using machine learning to get the accurate results. The training process includes training, evaluation, and fine-tuning of the model so that it will increase the accuracy of the system.

11. *Distributed indexing mechanism*: To handle the big data over the cloud, there is a need of the distributed indexing mechanism. The benefit of distributed indexing [2–4] is to give the better performance and if one node fails then the whole system does not fail The separate virtual machine instances have been created for storage of the node. The master node has the global log structure for identifying the node where the data have been stored. When a request is coming from any user, it will be forwarded to the specific node instance based on the structure log. The detail mechanism is shown in Figure 15.3. The master server instance is responsible for monitoring the capacity and load of each virtual node instance [28]. The instance connect is responsible for the communication between the main server instance and the node instances. Each node has the separate storage for storing the index [7,8,10].

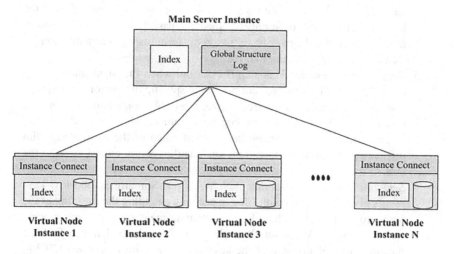

**FIGURE 15.3**  Schematic of distributed indexing mechanism.

12. *Semantic similarity*: This step has been used while matching the input query features with the indexing features to retrieve the similar products, including in the same cluster. It is very much important step for identifying the same products which are very much similar with input query image. The distance can be measured using a different similarity measure coefficient [13,16].

The different cloud environment can be used for implementation of the e-store, including Solr, ElasticSearch, CloudSearch, algolia, Elatic cloud, Google cloud, OpenStack, etc.

## 15.5 TRIBAL ART GLOBALIZATION

Tribal art is the pride of Indian people. It is one of the rare art forms that vanish rapidly due to less publicity. So, our system is one of the attempts to spread the tribal art products throughout the globe by developing the cloud-based platform. While developing this e-store, the tribal product information data set has been created with different categories.

### 15.5.1 TRIBAL ART CATEGORIES

The tribal e-store includes the different categories, including product categories, theme-based categories, event-based categories, etc. Figure 15.4 shows the different sample tribal products along with categories of the tribal products.

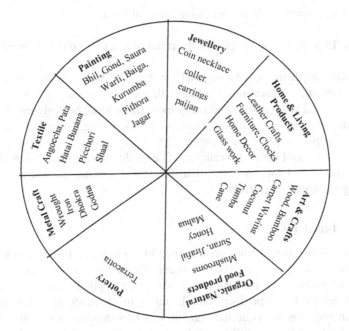

**FIGURE 15.4** Sample tribal products along with categories.

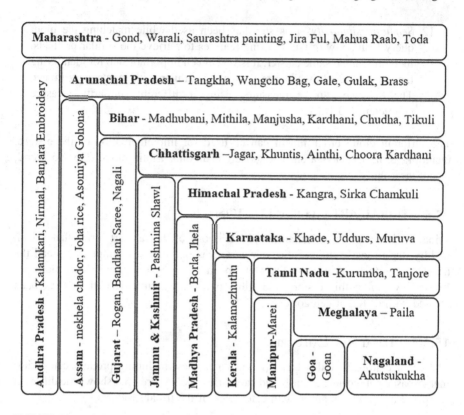

**FIGURE 15.5** Tribal products from various states of India.

Figure 15.5 shows the samples of the tribal products from the different states of India.

The different theme-based categories are designed based on the specific theme, such as Gujrati, Maharashtrian, Odisha theme, eco-friendly product, bamboo, glasswork, metal work theme, and many more themes can be designed. The event-based categories include different event occasions, where the products are placed under one umbrella, as shown in Figure 15.6. All the products are matched and the event names are sold under this category. The products are also categories based on the state name and location. So, such different categories are considered while designing the tribal product data set.

## 15.5.2 TRIBAL DATA SET

The tribal product data set has been created by considering the 26 states and four union territories. More than 10,000 product information has been collected. This information includes the product name, product description, product photo image, keywords related to the products, and the rating of the products. In the first stage, the Indian products are collected; later it will be extended to the different other countries' tribes, along with their product.

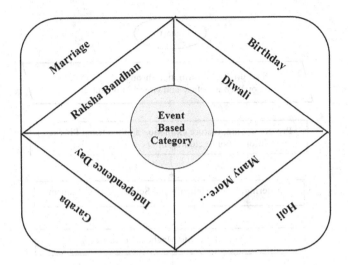

**FIGURE 15.6**   Event-based categories of tribal products.

## 15.6   RESULTS AND DISCUSSION

### 15.6.1   IMPLEMENTATION

The proposed system of tribal product e-store has been implemented and tested using the following experimental setup:

- The Android application has been developed using the Android studio IDE and Java language.
- The web application GUI has been developed using the HTML, Python, and PHP language.
- The Google cloud/AWS/OpenStack-free service can be used for testing purposes.
- The master node virtual instance and other node instances are created with the help of Google cloud platform/AWS/OpenStack.
- The Python language has been used for preprocessing and sematic checking along with retrieval of the tribal products.
- The tribal product big data has been created for testing the applications, as discussed in the above section.

The design and implementation of the e-store has been done using the following dataflow, as shown in Figure 15.7. It shows the distributed indexing mechanism for implementation of the e-store for the tribal products using the different services provided by the cloud. The tribal product information for the data set will be taken from the tribe people through the use of the Android app or using the web-based interface. It includes the product image, description, and keywords related to the product. They can use the help of the others for providing the tribal product information available with them.

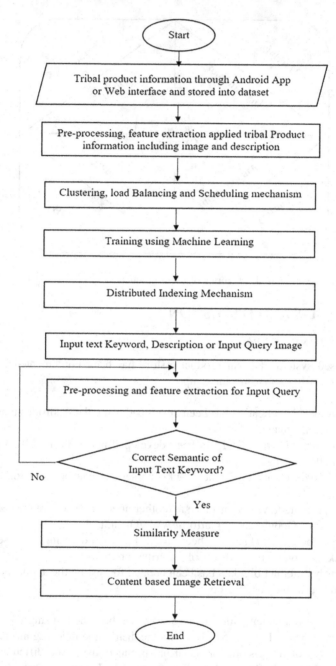

**FIGURE 15.7** Dataflow of the cloud-based e-store for tribal products using distributed indexing.

**TABLE 15.2**
**Comparative Result Analysis**

| | Amazon.in | Flipkart.com | Tribe india.com | Truly tribal.in | Universal tribes.com | Proposed E-Store |
|---|---|---|---|---|---|---|
| Input | Text | Text | Text | Text | Text | Text, image, and description |
| Tribal product data set | Few products support | Few products support | Few products support | Few products support | Few products support | More than 10,000 products support |
| Retrieved results relevant with input query | 20–30% | 10–20% | 50–60% | 20–30% | 30–40% | 70–85% |
| Accuracy % | 23.48 | 22.39 | 28.57 | 7.17 | 28.45 | 79.86 |

## 15.6.2 RESULTS ANALYSIS

The proposed system of the e-store has been tested with the tribal data set mentioned above. The different queries are fired on the available platform and on proposed e-store and given the results by comparing all the platforms. The accuracy of the result has been measured using the following formula as:

$$\text{Accuracy} = (\text{No. of Correct Retrieved Images})$$
$$/(\text{Total Number of Tribal products in data set}) \quad (15.1)$$

The comparison of the different platforms with the proposed e-store is shown in Table 15.2.

The comparison in Table 15.2 shows that the proposed e-store gives 81.63% accuracy, which is best as compared with the other platforms. The samples are randomly tested based on the random input queries. Figure 15.8 shows the graph for the accuracy comparison of the different platforms.

## 15.7 ADVANTAGES

The proposed cloud-based e-store has the various advantages over the currently available platforms:

1. It fetches the results by using text keyword as well as using the description of the tribal products.
2. This system also supports the content-based retrieval of the tribal products using the image query.

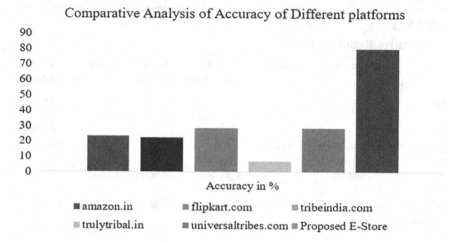

FIGURE 15.8  Comparative analysis of accuracy of different platforms.

3. The accuracy of the search results increases by using the semantic meaning extraction using the WordNet dictionary.
4. The machine learning has been used for training the data for increasing accuracy of the feature clustering.
5. Distributed indexing approach increases the performance of the system, capacity of processing of data, load balancing over the cloud.
6. The product information can be registered either using the android application interface or web interface.
7. It will increase the number of products due to easy registration process.
8. The theme-based, event-based, and state-wide tribal products will be available through the e-store.
9. The geo-location-based products can be searched by using the user's location, which is mapped with the state.

## 15.8  RESEARCH CHALLENGES

The proposed system faces some research challenges such as:

1. The different combinations of indexing mechanisms need to be tested for getting the best distributed indexing mechanism along with optimization for improving the search result accuracy.
2. The different machine learning algorithms, including deep learning, artificial intelligence, neural network, etc. need to be tested for performing the training of the data.
3. The number of different preprocessing steps needs to be added to decrease the percentage of the noisy data at a time of input query.
4. The load balancing, scheduling, and migration mechanisms need to be improved for efficient and optimized management of the distributed indexing mechanism.

5. The biggest challenge in this research is to automatically enroll the tribal product information without accessing any application or the web interface. The IoT sensor-based automatic capture of the product image along with the speech-to-text conversion of the product description needs to be implemented, which can solve the tribe illiteracy toward technology.

6. The various clustering algorithms need to be tested for checking the effectiveness of the clustering mechanism while being divided into the clusters.

## 15.9   SOCIAL BENEFITS

The proposed e-store of the tribal products is the first step for getting the direct marketplace for the tribe artist. This online store establishes the direct communication between the tribe artist and the customer, which destroys the model of the intermediator. It will be beneficial to the tribe artist and customer, i.e., the tribe artist will get a sufficient amount of the product cost and the customer can get the product at a reasonable cost. Since mobile phones have reached the tribe, they can easily register their products after a few training sessions. It will grow the tribe economy along with upliftment in the lifestyle along with their cultural values.

## 15.10   SUMMARY

In recent years, cloud computing replaced the distributed, grid, and cluster computing approaches. Many businesses are shifting to the cloud environment. In this chapter, the different available e-platforms are explained along with the limitations. The design and implementation of the e-store for the tribal art product has been presented in detail, along with the advantages and challenges. Multi-model inputs can be used, including text keyword, product description, and image query. This e-store includes the distributed indexing mechanism along with machine learning over the cloud for improving the performance and accuracy of the search results. The result shows that the accuracy increases up to 40–50% as compared with the currently available e-platforms. This e-store will be helpful for increasing the growth of the tribal economy along with the standard of living.

## ACKNOWLEDGMENT

The images of the tribal products shown in this chapter are the products purchased from the tribal people. The credits go to the tribal artists who have made these excellent products that inspired us to write this chapter. The intention is to use the tribal images to promote the tribal products over India and globe.

## REFERENCES

[1] S. Khawandi, F. Abdallah, A. Ismail. (2019). A Survey on Image Indexing and Retrieval Based on Content Based Image. *International Conference on Machine Learning, Big Data, Cloud and Parallel Computing (COMITCon)*, pp. 222–225.

[2] D. J. Ladani, N. P. Desai. (2020). Stopword Identification and Removal Techniques on TC and IR applications: A Survey. *6th International Conference on Advanced Computing and Communication Systems (ICACCS)*, pp. 466–472.

[3] P. Saktel, U. Shrawankar. (2012). An Improved Approach for Word Ambiguity Removal. *International Journal of Human Computer Interaction (IJHCI)* 3(3), 7182.

[4] M. M. Nashipudimath, S. K. Shinde, J. Jain. (2020). An Efficient Integration and Indexing Method Based on Feature Patterns and Semantic Analysis for Big Data. *Array* 7, 100033, ISSN 2590-0056.

[5] M. Á. Castillo-Martínez, F. J. Gallegos-Funes, B. E. Carvajal-Gamez. (2020). Color Index Based Thresholding Method for Background and Foreground Segmentation of Plant Images. *Computers and Electronics in Agriculture* 178, 105783, ISSN 0168-1699.

[6] K. Kimmatkar, U. Shrawankar. (2015). Multiple Applications Sharing for Effective Load Balancing in Secured Distributed Environment. *Procedia Computer Science* 78, 763–770.

[7] Z. Hou, C. Huang, J. Wu, L. Liu. (2020). Distributed Image Retrieval Based on LSH Indexing on Spark. In Tian, Y., Ma, T., Khan, M. (Eds.), *Big Data and Security. ICBDS 2019. Communications in Computer and Information Science*, vol. 1210, Singapore: Springer.

[8] C. Feng, C. D. Li, R. Li. (2018). Indexing Techniques of Distributed Ordered Tables: A Survey and Analysis. *Journal of Computer Science and Technology* 33, 169–189.

[9] S. Ghosh, A. Eldawy, S. Jais. (2019). AID: An Adaptive Image Data Index for Interactive Multilevel Visualization. *IEEE 35th International Conference on Data Engineering (ICDE)*, pp. 1594–1597.

[10] U. Shrawankar, C. Dhule. (2021). Virtualization Technologies for Cloud based Services. *Cloud Computing Technologies for Smart Agriculture and Healthcare*. Boca Raton: CRC Press/Taylor & Francis.

[11] P. K. Sadineni. (2020). Comparative Study on Query Processing and Indexing Techniques in Big Data. *3rd International Conference on Intelligent Sustainable Systems (ICISS)*, pp. 933–939.

[12] H. B. Abdalla, A. M. Ahmed, M. A. Al Sibahee. (2020). Optimization Driven MapReduce Framework for Indexing and Retrieval of Big Data. *KSII Transactions on Internet and Information Systems* 14(5).

[13] S. R. Dubey. (2022). A Decade Survey of Content Based Image Retrieval Using Deep Learning. *IEEE Transactions on Circuits and Systems for Video Technology* 32(5), 2687–2704.

[14] M. AlMousa, R. Benlamri, R. Khoury. (2022). A Novel Word Sense Disambiguation Approach Using Wordnet Knowledge Graph. *Computer Speech & Language* 74, 101337, ISSN 0885-2308.

[15] N. M. Varma, A. Mathur. (2020). Survey on Evaluation of Similarity Measures for Content-Based Image Retrieval Using Hybrid Features. *International Conference on Smart Electronics and Communication (ICOSEC)*, pp. 557–562.

# 16 Optimized Fake News Detection Model for Inspecting Data on the Cloud Using Machine Learning Techniques

*Deepali Goyal Dev and Vishal Bhatnagar*

## 16.1 INTRODUCTION

Because of the advancement of IT, the number of individuals utilizing the Internet has dramatically increased. As a consequence, both news presenters and news-readers are more comfortable and productive. It transforms people's traditional information and news-consuming habits into digital ones. The system produces a lot of fake news reports in addition to being practical. Fake news is one of the most important topics right now because it has the power to undermine governments and hurt contemporary society. For instance, it has been found that the impact of fraudsters during the election campaign significantly increased the prominence of the phrase "fake news." Online news is widely available on the Internet. Contrary to the past, the news is not currently printed on paper. Internet-based platforms are being used more and more by newspaper offices. Readers may easily access content through the Internet at any time and from any location. Today, it's simple for people to rapidly share news content on websites like the WWW, Google, YouTube, and Google+ as well as social networks like Facebook, Twitter, Instagram, and Line. The threat of false news to democracy has eroded public confidence in media, governments, and civil society everywhere [1]. Fake news that contains conspiracies, lies, and violent perspectives is becoming more prevalent. The identification and mitigation of the impacts of false positives are one of the current major concerns that is garnering a lot of attention.

This digitalization allows for globalization. Because of this advancement, people can now access the entire world's information with a single click. Despite its benefits, this shift has presented some challenges. Fake news is one of the issues confronting today's digital society. Fake news is pervasive propaganda that spreads false information and manipulates public opinion through social media platforms. Social media can be used to inform the public about current events or, on the other

DOI: 10.1201/9781003341437-19

hand, it can be used to disseminate false information. Furthermore, its ease of use and lack of oversight on the Internet facilitates the spread of "false news." The growth and advancement of mobile devices and high-speed Internet have significantly increased the number of individuals who use digital media. According to the [2] Digital Global Report 2020, 301 million individuals utilized social media in 2020, bringing the total number of digital media users to 4.75 billion. Fake news has been a major issue in the media for the previous three years. Only 54% of individuals are said to be capable of spotting deceit on their own, according to surveys. In order to discriminate between fake and authentic news, an accurate automated system is needed. Although there have been a number of studies, additional analysis and inquiry are needed. The suggested study intends to prevent the spread of rumors and misleading information while also supporting readers in identifying whether a news source is trustworthy by automatically categorizing the content [3,4].

They found that the normalization process was crucial in getting the data ready for classification by ML. With a 99.90% accuracy rate throughout data gathering, the support vector machine (SVM) model fared the best. Their tests produced the best accuracy results (72.93%). Actual application cases for Thai false news were not included in the report. It is challenging to build false news identification. Since there are no spaces between words in Thai, one of the most difficult languages, it is considerably more challenging to identify false information in the actual world. In this work, we suggest a strategy for creating an automated system for spotting bogus Thai news online [5].

Online fake news is produced using three steps: collection and preparation of the data along with analysis of data using different type of algorithms. The contributions made by this study are as follows: (1) Our main contribution is the paradigm we provide for identifying fake news online. (2) This study's natural language analysis produced a feature selection technique.

## 16.2 LITERATURE REVIEW

### 16.2.1 Fake News

People are connecting to the Internet and social networks increasingly often as part of their daily routines in the digital age. More people are using the Internet because it is so simple to distribute, access, and share news via social networks. This makes exchanging information on these sites without any restrictions possible. However, the data could contain both accurate and false information. Some dishonest users utilize the Internet and social media to spread untrue information about people, organizations, and political leaders. The diverse formats and domains of disinformation include fake news, clickbait, and false rumors, and earlier research has concentrated on domain-specific modeling. Even though these domains may have diverse formats and even serve distinct objectives, such as "This is a farce" vs "Clickbait," their common objective is to trick readers. Examples of these formats and purposes include long essays versus condensed headlines and tweets. Because of this, literature has developed that shares comparable language characteristics, such as the utilization of fascinating subjects to spark readers' attention or evoke powerful emotional responses. As a result, several academics suggested a technique for identifying bogus news and halting its dissemination. As social media grows, so does online news. False news can be produced by malicious users who diverge from the original. It is challenging to spot fraud when phony news is automatically extracted from the Internet. The development of automated disinformation or false news identification involves several ideas and methodologies [6–8].

1. *Cloud computing*: The growth of data sources has occurred concurrently with an increase in data volume, giving rise to the term "big data." Big data has demonstrated the importance of this idea in many fields, including economics, and it is likely to continue to expand in the future. As a result, of more people exchanging data on social networks, data lakes have formed, allowing for their storage and accessibility anywhere, anytime. This has made cloud computing possible. A rise in social network data sharing, a rise in user numbers, the development of data lakes, and as a result, their storage and presentation across locations and times (Figure 16.1).

    a. *IaaS*: It exemplifies the infrastructure requirements that serve as the cornerstone for the provision and management of physical storage facilities, servers, and cloud computing through the Internet. IaaS is frequently used in data storage, backup, and recovery situations, large data analysis, high performance computing, online applications, testing, and development activities to avoid unexpected data losses [9].

    b. *PaaS*: This platform's offerings include software, database management systems, business development tools, business intelligence tools, and AI and ML technologies. More business intelligence and analysis processes are presented in this section [10,11].

    c. *SaaS*: This service is typically used by individuals that utilize and exchange different databases and office tools online to identify bogus news.

    d. *Public cloud*: The public cloud offers quick access to resources for information technology (IT). Users of these services don't have to buy infrastructure because service providers own and take care of these

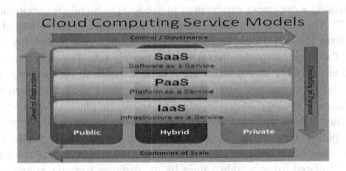

**FIGURE 16.1**   Cloud computing.service models and the dimensions [23].

necessities. Users of public cloud services do not need to buy hardware, software, or supporting infrastructure because providers already own and control these crucial components. This kind of service offers cutting-edge SaaS business applications for a range of uses, including data analysis for the detection of fake news and source and process management. It is appropriate for cloud-based application development and distribution environments and is frequently used for short-term storage services [12].

e. *Private cloud*: The private cloud is goal-oriented and better suited for personal or more private use in a business setting. The most productive utilization of resources is made possible in this manner. In order to execute more effective data analysis and get the right outcome, the small user base is crucial. The adaptability and capacity to plan and evaluate for the aims are the most fundamental aspects of this service. The user can take the initiative to accomplish the goal and security is optimized because they are aware of the necessity [13].

f. *Hybrid cloud*: The private cloud serves as the foundation of the hybrid cloud, but this service also incorporates and makes use of public cloud services. In general, resources in the hybrid cloud type are not treated separately from those in the public cloud. The management of workloads on both the private and public clouds has led to the adoption of the hybrid cloud as cloud computing usage grows in the business world. The studied data and important applications can essentially be housed in a private cloud or a regular data center environment, thanks to the hybrid cloud. For instance, the public cloud environment is used to store previously studied and non-critical data, whereas a private cloud should be used to store critical and secret data.

2. *Information retrieval*: Databases classify data from a variety of publications. It could be difficult to locate important information, such as search phrases or example papers, during a document search. Users can organize and preserve documents using a piece of software called an IRS. A query may employ full-text or other content indexing. Data overload is reduced via an automated IR system. A group of words known as index terms that represent a document can be used to use texts to highlight important ideas in IR. The content of a document can be described using a variety of index phrases [14–17]. Boolean models, vector models, and probability models are the three categories into which IR models fall. The search terms and the terminology of the index are a perfect match in the Boolean model. Boolean information retrieval is used to forecast each document's relevance. A strategy uses language or words in place of characteristics (terms). The terms that were searched for have been weighed or measured for phrase frequency. Document queries are replaced by weight values. The association between the queries conducted against the database record is calculated using weight values by the distance formula, sometimes referred to as a similarity measure.

3. *Natural language processing*: A subfield of linguistics, computer science, data engineering, and artificial intelligence is known as natural language processing (NLP). NLP is concerned with how people and machines communicate. Large-scale natural language data processing and analysis is done using NLP [18–21]. Text extraction is a fundamental step in natural language processing.

4. *Machine learning*: Various types of ML techniques are as follows:

1. *K-nearest neighbors* (KNN) is an easy, parameter-free classification technique. To utilize KNN, we must first select an acceptable K value, and the result of the classification is based on this value. The KNN operates as is seen below. (1) Read a data record to identify categories. (2) Calculate the separation between each training data record and the record used for classification. (3) Choose the K-narrowest distance. (4) Categorize the data according to the labels of the K nearest data records, which received the most votes [10,11].

2. *Rule-based classifiers* (RBC) consist of a group of laws with the syntax IF X, then Y. We can train a rule-based system to become an RBC using a classification training data set. RBC requires a rule-based algorithm to create a classification scheme that may be expressed as a series of IF-THEN rules. The occurrences in the data set may then be categorized by applying the stated rule to each one. CN2 is one of the most used rule induction techniques. Not all training samples will be appropriately classified using the given criteria. It functions superbly even with the fresh, unexpected facts. To reduce noise, the CN2 will only accept limits that are very rigorous. A rule list that is sorted or unordered may also be created using CN2 [22,23].

3. *Decision tree classifier* (DTC) is a recursive partition of the data space that represents a tree-like model. A rooted tree is produced by the highest discriminant node in a decision tree. A root node at the very top of a tree has no connections to any extending branches, links, or edges [12,13]. There is just one incoming edge for each other node. Test nodes or intermediate nodes are nodes having outgoing edges. Nodes are called leaves, and they act as decision nodes at the most fundamental level. Three well-known decision tree induction techniques are ID3, C4.5, and C5.

4. *Random forest* (RF) a top algorithm for classification challenges. The core idea of RF is that a group of weak learners may produce a strong learner. Large data sets may be classified precisely and correctly using RF. Each tree in RF functions as a classifier by using a random vector value. RF builds a number of random selections of attribute values to forecast the outcome of the modality. The forecast is created by averaging all decision trees and the results of the majority vote.

5. *Naïve Bayesian* (NB) is a straightforward probabilistic method based on the explicit assumption that attributes are conditionally independent of one another and the Bayes rule. Applications for categorization can utilize the estimation. NB seems to be a good solution in many real-world deployments [24,25].

6. *Multilayer perceptron* (MLP) is a type of artificial neural network (ANN) created using computer programs that replicate how the human brain functions. A few of the specific taught problems that an ANN may utilize to apply what it has learnt from training data are classification, regression, and clustering. Because of how it works, MLP is sometimes called a "black box." A feed forward network, often known as an MLP, employs a number of different calculation methods [25–27].

7. *SVM* is built upon understanding statistical theory. Different academics have applied SVM in numerous applications for data classification and pattern identification. These are the theoretical components of SVM. The idea of structural risk minimization defines the likelihood of making mistakes when learning as well as the size of the risk. The SVM learning process determines how judgments should be made in order to lower error rates. An essential idea in vector machine support strategies is the optimal margin hyper plane [28,29].

8. *Long short-term memory* (LSTM) may capture the reliance of sequence data, such as time series and natural languages, by using hidden state feedback as input. RNN can process sequential data in addition to a single data point. Anomaly detection in network data, sentiment analysis from documents, handwriting recognition, audio recognition, and other processes may all be performed with LSTM [30–34].

## 16.3 PROPOSED FAKE NEWS DETECTION FRAMEWORK

It is challenging to create ML as a false news detection system since misinformation or fake news contents are so diverse and dynamic. However, a trustworthy news classifier may be created. Because news providers share and put their content online, people may quickly and easily get news from anywhere on the Internet. Both accurate and fraudulent news are stored on cloud servers by the Internet and social media. On the news website, comments are posted by users, who then share them on social media. We provide an IR, NLP, and ML based strategy for identifying bogus news. Based on the user-supplied news query, the IR module obtains news-related information from the Internet. The search query retrieves pertinent news stories from several online news sources. The gathered documents are subsequently segmented, cleaned, and characteristics are extracted using the NLP module. The ML module also classifies news as either real, suspicious, or fake. The suggested process for identifying bogus news is shown in Figure 16.2. News training and collecting and ML prediction are the two processes in putting false news detection into practice. The IR, NLP, and ML modules are used by each. In order to train ML as a false news detection model, web crawlers simultaneously collect data from social media and the Internet in the first phase. The user query provides access to the training data. A user search will be available for each news search. This indicates that the web crawler will search the Internet for news lists pertinent to the news request. The feature data is used to produce a training set and a test set. During the training phase, the ML model is trained, and cross-validated, and its performance is assessed using the test set. When NLP receives news content, it parses it, cleans it up, and extracts features before analyzing it. The featured data are obtained

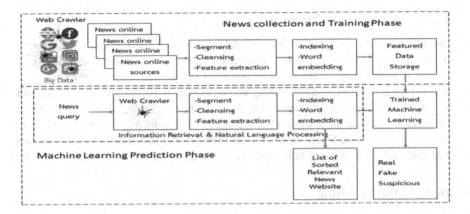

**FIGURE 16.2** Fake news detection framework [2,15]. India fake news data set proposed framework [11,17,18].

by the trained ML model, which divides them into three categories: real, fake, or suspicious. Learning is developed. Using our research, we labeled the highlighted data as fake, real, or questionable (Figure 16.1) [23].

Since there isn't a data set for Indian news particularly, we proposed one to bridge the study gap. To obtain news about India, we just choose the India news column, and we have also set up a filter to omit other news. We manually requested cross-verification of the data set we collect from a number of topic annotators. We obtained data from several different factors, such as the title, publication date and time, source, link, picture link, and label (true/false). LDA (Linear Discriminant Analysis) topic modeling is also used to incorporate the news category. Five categories were developed using LDA topic modeling: election, politics, COVID-19, violence, and other (Figure 16.3) [35].

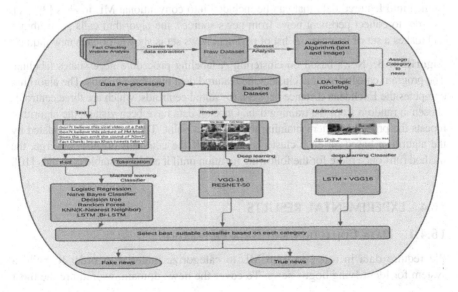

**FIGURE 16.3** Shows the proposed workflow that was used to create the IFND data set [35].

### 16.3.1 INFORMATION RETRIEVAL

Our difficult challenge is to develop a model for detecting bogus news. Then, we may employ it to identify bogus news online and caution users against disseminating or sharing it with others. Retrieval of information is essential to the framework. It is required for access to social networking and news content on the Internet. The Internet not only contains legitimate news, but also fake news. According to web crawlers, information retrieval is a more effective method of gathering news content from Internet news sources. Online news sources provide information on big data. The web data collected by web crawlers is delivered to the data preparation procedure [36–38].

### 16.3.2 ML MODELING

Using an ML engine, news is divided into three categories: dubious, true, or fraudulent. The NLP module sends feature data to the ML module, which then turns the text input into document vectors. In this work, ML models include both traditional classifiers and advanced deep learning models.

### 16.3.3 DATE PRE-PROCESSING AND ALGORITHMIC MODEL

We provide three algorithms:

**Algorithm 1:** An information retrieval method that uses crawlers gets a user's news query. The system dispatches crawlers to websites, where they retrieve the pertinent news and metadata. This algorithm determines how closely user news queries and the information that is returned are related and then returns the news metadata with similarity ratings [16].

**Algorithm 2:** Using NLP-based feature extraction, the news documents are transformed into featured data that can be included into conventional ML models [39–41]. In order to collect pertinent news from news sources, the algorithm calls Algorithm 1 and makes a set of inquiries. A list of pertinent news set is shown for each new inquiry.

**Algorithm 3:** News based on clustering A labeling procedure necessitates labeling. The program categorizes and clusters the featured data into three groups. The algorithm computes the Euclidean distance between the initial centroids, which are three centroids chosen at random from the training data. Once all data have been visited, the algorithm repeats the procedure after obtaining the next data point. The centroids are updated by the algorithm based on each cluster's member. If the centroids do not converge, the method runs once more for the following iteration until it achieves stable centroids [10].

## 16.4 EXPERIMENTAL RESULTS

### 16.4.1 DATA COLLECTION AND DATA PREPARATION

We require data in order to train ML to categorize material in order to build a system for identifying bogus news. To cover the news domain, we require the most

**TABLE 16.1**
**Sample Data Collected**

| Labels | No. Samples |
|---|---|
| Fake | 15,000 |
| Real | 15,000 |
| Suspicious | 15,000 |
| Total | 45,000 |

data possible. We achieved this by collecting data via web robot crawlers. Details of the information retrieval process that Algorithm 1 explains utilizing web crawlers. Thai does not have spaces between words, therefore understanding it might be difficult. We provided our Thai word segmentation tool. We divided Thai keywords using a custom lexicon and the maximum matching technique with a vocabulary size of 75,936 words utilized in this investigation (Table 16.1).

### 16.4.2 EXTRACTED FEATURE DATA

NLP analyzes the information collected through web crawling. Word segmentation is the process of dividing text into tokens of individual words. Segmented tokens are cleaned even further throughout the purification process by getting rid of superfluous words and letters. During the feature extraction procedure, import traits are taken out of news articles.

The targeted categories include suspect, legitimate, and false. It should be noticed that the objectives are connected to the extracted characteristics. Both the fake and actual classes have a good association with the sim matched. With regard to class fake, score, and domain fake characteristics show respective predictive influences of 0.76 and 0.77. The correlation between the class real and the score real and domain real characteristics is 0.16 and 0.11, respectively.

It suggests that the data can accurately represent both genuine and fictitious classes. Class suspicion, however, is negatively correlated with characteristics. It would be challenging to distinguish the shady bunch (Tables 16.2 and 16.3).

### 16.4.3 ML MODELING COMPARISONS

We created a false news detection system after collecting data, identifying features from it, and doing analysis on it. F1-measure, recall, accuracy, and precision are a few of the performance metrics employed. Tables 16.3, 16.4, 16.5, and 16.6 show examples of test performance results based on RBC, SVM, RF, and LSTM. It has been discovered that sampling models can categorize phony and questionable classes accurately and effectively, but not the real class. Table 16.7 compiles the results of all ML models. Figure 16.6 shows a box plot for a tenfold cross-validation based on test accuracy. It reveals that the LSTM model was the most effective at achieving a score of 100% accuracy.

**TABLE 16.2**

**Feature Data Correlation**

|  | Domain Real | Fake | Real | Suspicious | Score Fake | Score Real | Sim Matched | Domain Fake |
|---|---|---|---|---|---|---|---|---|
| Domain real | 1 | .11 | .11 | − .25 | .15 | .86 | .22 | .2 |
| Fake | .11 | 1 | − .62 | − .49 | .7 | .04 | .27 | .76 |
| Real | .11 | − 0.62 | 1 | − .38 | − .43 | .16 | .3 | − .47 |
| Suspicious | − .25 | − 0.49 | − .38 | 1 | − .35 | − .22 | − .65 | − .38 |
| Score fake | .15 | .7 | − .43 | − .35 | 1 | .07 | .35 | .91 |
| Score real | .86 | .04 | .16 | − .22 | .07 | 1 | .16 | .1 |
| Sim matched | .22 | .27 | .3 | − .65 | .35 | .16 | 1 | .37 |
| Domain fake | .2 | .76 | − .47 | − .38 | .91 | .1 | .37 | 1 |

**TABLE 16.3**

**Test Performance of RBC**

|  | Precision | Recall | F-Measure |
|---|---|---|---|
| Fake | .98 | .95 | .96 |
| Real | .87 | .97 | .86 |
| Suspicious | .97 | .92 | .89 |
| Weighted avg | .92 | .90 | .91 |
| Accuracy |  | .90 |  |

**TABLE 16.4**

**Test Performance of SVM**

|  | Precision | Recall | F-Measure |
|---|---|---|---|
| Fake | .99 | .99 | .99 |
| Real | .89 | .99 | .94 |
| Suspicious | .99 | .90 | .94 |
| Weighted avg | .96 | .96 | .96 |
| Accuracy |  | .96 |  |

Data used in fake news is quite dynamic. The development of a false news detection algorithm that generalizes to any unknown data is difficult. The feature extraction approach uses five features – fake news score, true news score, similarity matching, false news domain length, and true news domain length – to extract news data. It validates the efficacy of the proposed NLP-based feature selection method for categorizing misleading news. Additionally, the most effective test was

**TABLE 16.5**
**Test Performance of RF**

|  | Precision | Recall | F-Measure |
|---|---|---|---|
| Fake | .99 | .99 | 1.00 |
| Real | .90 | .99 | .94 |
| Suspicious | 1.00 | .99 | .94 |
| Weighted avg | .97 | .96 | .96 |
| Accuracy |  | .96 |  |

**TABLE 16.6**
**Test Performance of LSTM**

|  | Precision | Recall | F-Measure |
|---|---|---|---|
| Fake | 1.00 | 1.00 | 1.00 |
| Real | 1.00 | 1.00 | 1.00 |
| Suspicious | 1.00 | 1.00 | 1.00 |
| Weighted avg | 1.00 | 1.00 | 1.00 |
| Accuracy |  | 1.00 |  |

**TABLE 16.7**
**Comparison of ML Models**

| Metrics vs Models | DT | RF | KNN | RBC | NB | LR | MLP | SVM | LSTM |
|---|---|---|---|---|---|---|---|---|---|
| Accuracy | .94 | .95 | .95 | .90 | .81 | .93 | .97 | .96 | 1.00 |
| Precision | .94 | .97 | .95 | .91 | .85 | .93 | .97 | .96 | 1.00 |
| Recall | .94 | .95 | .95 | .92 | .80 | .93 | .97 | .96 | 1.00 |
| F-measure | .94 | .95 | .95 | .91 | .81 | .93 | .97 | .96 | 1.00 |

achieved using LSTM employing concatenated text from pertinent news stories that were quite similar to the news query.

Users' questions to assess if news is phony or true are among the system's primary features. The entire process could take 3 to 10 seconds, depending on structure of new enquiry. It should be noted that we chose LSTM rather than BERT since we categorize the type of news using ML. In order to have the optimal user experience, a user needs a speedy answer when they submit a news query into the system. BERT or GPT may be unable to categorize news rapidly if there are too many factors. Just to carry out a classification task, and we opted for LSTM. The website offers well-known actual and false news stories that are now becoming more and more famous in social media groups.

## 16.5 CONCLUSION

It might be difficult to recognize bogus news because news articles are often updated. This study offers a novel, trustworthy strategy for combating unreliable information. To create automatic online bogus news identification, we use three main techniques. We initially apply information retrieval as a technique to extract data from a social networking platform and an online news website. After the collected news was subjected to a natural language processing study, separate feature data was generated. ML separates the news items into three groups after getting the feature data: real, fake, and suspicious. We used a web crawler to crawl the data and pre-classified it into categories for genuine, fake, and questionable classifications for 41,448 samples. For reaching 100% accuracy, precision, recall, and f-measure on test data, we found that LSTM was the optimal model.

We'll concentrate more on deep learning models in the future. How to get deep learning to comprehend news as well as people does is a research question that has to be answered. The machine can anticipate the news's nature and explain why it reacts in a certain manner. Additionally, the machine must accurately analyze and react whether the news information consists of text, sound, and video. We also plan to learn the language so that we can comprehend it better. It will be necessary to use a more complicated architecture, such as BERT and GPT. Future research is still possible in this situation.

## REFERENCES

1. Akhter MP, Zheng J, Afzal F, Lin H, Riaz S, Mehmood A. Supervised ensemble learning methods towards automatically filtering Urdu fake news within social media. PeerJ Comput Sci. 2021;7:1–24. 10.7717/peerj-cs.425
2. Aphiwongsophon S, Chongstitvatana P. Detecting fake news with machine learning method. In: 2018 15th Inter Con Electrical Engineering/Electronics, Computer, Telecommunications and Information Technology (ECTI-CON). 2018. pp. 528–531. 10.1109/ECTICon.2018.8620051
3. Salton G, Wong A, Yang CS. A vector space model for automatic indexing. Commun ACM. 1975;18(11):613–620. 10.1145/361219.361220
4. Robertson S, Zaragoza H. The probabilistic relevance framework: BM25 and beyond. Foundations TrendsR Inf Retrieval. 2009;3(4):333–389. 10.1561/1500000019.
5. Jing K, Xu J. A survey on neural network language models. ArXiv190603591 Cs. 2019. arXiv:1906.03591. Accessed March 20, 2020.
6. Zhang F, Fleyeh H, Wang X, Lu M. Construction site accident analysis using text mining and natural language processing techniques. Autom Constr. 2019;99:238–248. 10.1016/j
7. Chirawichitchai N, Sanguansat P, Meesad P. Developing an effective Thai document categorization framework base on term relevance frequency weighting. In: Eighth Int Con ICT and Know Eng. 10.1109/ICTKE.2010.5692907
8. Lample G, Ballesteros M, Subramanian S, Kawakami K, Dyer C. Neural architectures for named entity recognition. ArXiv160301360 Cs. 2016. arXiv:1603.01360. Accessed April 21, 2021.
9. Quinlan JR. Improved use of continuous attributes in C4.5. J Artif Intell Res. 1996;4:77–90. 10.1613/jair.279

10. Yang H, Xu A, Chen H, Yuan C. A review: the effects of imperfect data on incremental decision tree. In: Ninth Inter Con P2P, Parallel, Grid, Cloud and Internet Computing. 2014. pp. 34–41. 10.1109/3PGCIC.2014.34
11. Ahmad I, Yousaf M, Yousaf S, Ahmad MO. Fake news detection using machine learning ensemble methods. Complexity. 2020;2020:e8885861. 10.1155/2020/8885861
12. Svetnik V, Liaw A, Tong C, Culberson JC, Sheridan RP, Feuston BP. Random forest: a classification and regression tool for com- pound classification and QSAR modeling. J Chem Inf Comput Sci. 2003;43(6):1947–1958. 10.1021/ci034160g
13. Sharma Y, Agrawal G, Jain P, Kumar T. Vector representation of words for sentiment analysis using GloVe. In: Int Con Int Com and Comp Tech (ICCT). 10.1109/INTEL CCT.2017.8324059
14. Chormai P, Prasertsom P, Rutherford A. AttaCut: a fast and accurate neural Thai word segmenter. ArXiv191107056 Cs. 2019, arXiv:1911.07056. Accessed April 21, 2021.
15. Phatthiyaphaibun W, et al. PyThaiNLP v2.3.1 release!. Zenodo. 2021. 10.5281/zenodo.4662045. Accessed April 29, 2021.
16. Kleinbaum DG, Klein M. Logistic regression: a self-learning text. 3rd ed. Springer; 2010.
17. LaValley MP. Logistic Regression. Circulation. 2008;117(18):2395–2399. 10.1161/CIRCULATIO
18. Guo G, Wang H, Bell D, Bi Y, Greer K. KNN model-based approach in classification. In: On the Move to Meaningful Internet Systems 2003: CoopIS, DOA, and ODBASE, 2888, R Meersman, Z Tari, DC Schmidt, Eds. Berlin, Heidelberg: Springer Berlin Heidelberg; 2003. pp. 986–996.
19. Wright RE. Logistic regression. In: Reading and Understanding Multivariate Statistics. Washington: American Psychological Association; 1995. pp. 217–244.
20. Clark P, Boswell R. Rule induction with CN2: some recent improvements. In: Machine Learning – EWSL-91. Berlin: Heidelberg; 1991, pp. 151–163. 10.1007/BFb0017011.
21. Misra S, Li H. Chapter 9—noninvasive fracture characterization based on the classification of sonic wave travel times. In: Misra S, Li H, He J. (Eds). Machine Learning for Subsurface Characterization. Gulf Professional Publishing. 2020. pp. 243–287.
22. Shrivastava D, Sanyal S, Maji AK, Kandar D. Chapter 17 – Bone cancer detection using machine learning techniques. In: Paul S, Bhatia D. (Eds). Smart Healthcare for Disease Diagnosis and Prevention. Academic Press. 2020. pp. 175–183.
23. Kim HC, Ghahramani Z. Bayesian classifier combination. In: Artif Intell and Stat. pp. 619–627. 2012. http://proceedings.mlr.press/v22/kim12.html. Accessed April 24, 2021.
24. Yager RR. An extension of the naive Bayesian classifier. Inf Sci. 2006;176(5):577–588. 10.1016/j.ins.2004.12.006
25. Zhang H. The optimality of naive Bayes. In: Proc FLAIRS. 2004. p.6.
26. Hagan MT, Demuth HB, Beale MH, Jesús OD. Neural network design. 2nd ed. Wrocław: Martin Hagan; 2014.
27. Morshedizadeh M, Kordestani M, Carriveau R, Ting DSK, Saif M. Power production prediction of wind turbines using a fusion of MLP and ANFIS networks. IET Renew Power Gener. 2018;12(9):1025–1033. 10.1049/iet-rpg.2017.0736
28. Zhang L, Tian F. Performance study of multilayer perceptrons in a low-cost electronic Nose. IEEE Trans Instrum Meas. 2014;63(7):1670–1679. 10.1109/TIM.2014.2298691
29. Rodríguez ÁI, Iglesias LL. Fake news detection using deep learning. ArXiv. 2019. arXiv:1910.03496.
30. Allcott H, Gentzkow M. Social media and fake news in the 2016 election. J Econ Perspect. 2017;31(2):211–236. 10. 1257/jep.31.2.211

31. Jiang T, Li JP, Haq AU, Saboor A, Ali A. A novel stacking approach for accurate detection of fake news. IEEE Access. 2021;9:22626–22639. 10.1109/ACCESS.2021. 30560

32. Rahman MS, Halder S, Uddin MA, Acharjee UK. An efficient hybrid system for anomaly detection in social networks. Cyber- security. 2021. 10.1186/s42400-021-00074-w

33. Lakshmanan LVS, Simpson M, Thirumuruganathan S. Combating fake news: a data management and mining perspective. Proc VLDB Endow. 2019;12(12):1990–1993. 10.14778/ 3352063.3352117

34. Sharma DK, Garg, S (2021). IFND: a benchmark data set for fake news detection. Complex & Intelligent Systems, 1–21.

35. Yanagi Y, Orihara R, Sei Y, Tahara Y, Ohsuga A. Fake news detection with generated comments for news articles. In: IEEE 24th Inter Con Intelligent Engineering Systems (INES). 2020. pp. 85–90. 10.1109/INES49302.2020.9147195

36. Umer M, Imtiaz Z, Ullah S, Mehmood A, Choi GS, On BW. Fake news stance detection using deep learning architecture (CNN-LSTM). IEEE Access. 2020;8:156695–156706. 10.1109/ACCESS.2020.3019735.

37. Shu K, Wang S, Liu H. Beyond news contents: the role of social context for fake news detection. In: Proc ACM Inter Conon Web Search and Data Mining. 2019. pp. 312–320. 10.1145/

38. Clark P, Niblett T. The CN2 induction algorithm. Mach Learn. 1989;3(4):261–283. 10.1023/A:1022641700528.

39. Hamsa H, Indiradevi S, Kizhakkethottam JJ. Student academic performance prediction model using decision tree and fuzzy genetic algorithm. Procedia Technol. 2016;25:326–332. 10.1016/j.protcy.2016.08.114

40. Myles AJ, Feudale RN, Liu Y, Woody NA, Brown SD. An introduction to decision tree modeling. J Chemom. 2004;18(6):275–285. 10.1002/cem.873

# 17 Cloud Computing and Its Applications to E-Learning

*Laxman Singh, Sovers Singh Bisht, Pavan Shukla, Yaduvir Singh, Vinod M. Kapse, and Priyanka Chandani*

## 17.1 INTRODUCTION

Education is a basic part of life as it prepares us for everything we need to create. One of the best examples in education is e-learning, which involves the deliberate use of information and communication technology (ICT) in education and learning. Education and learning will be including online learning, virtual learning, and distributed learning networks in combination with web-based learning. E-learning has seen an increase in interest over the past ten years from a variety of sources. Programs for distance learning consider it as a natural progression from activities for distance learning. On-campus educational institutions also see e-learning as a way to increase access to and acquire programs. The use of e-learning is proposed as a re-emerging tool to deliver online, hybrid, and interactive learning, regardless of physical location, time of day, or type of digital reception or delivery device [1].

The expansion of ICT access and cost savings are related to the rise of e-learning. The fact that ICT can enable multimedia resource-based education and learning is another sign of the rising popularity of e-learning. More educators are utilizing technology in their classrooms. Making programs available across various dispersed systems, whether on campus, at home, or anyplace else that incorporates other community learning or resource centers, can be advantageous for organizations. My desire to learn at anytime and anywhere has become a reality, thanks to ICT. Even so, I have a lot of constraints and am interested in e-learning.

The main obstacle to the development of e-learning is the lack of access to the required technological infrastructure. Without e-learning, there would be no education. If there are not enough adequate or adequate technical resources available, it can hurt teachers, students, and the learning process. We always require communication model along with the storage medium so that we can understand the use and the structure of a portal being utilized over cloud for e-learning [2].

The cost is the number of hardware and software is reduced, and in many cases, no further costs are considered in the use of e-learning ventures. The most crucial of them are infrastructure support and upkeep, as well as appropriate personnel

DOI: 10.1201/9781003341437-20

training to make the most of technology. The literature defined within the cloud does not have a clear definition which is an important task in the areas of research, and it would help to explore new domains for the use of the cloud architecture [3]. Portraying cerebrum cancer districts involving surface examination in magnetic resonance imaging is to extricate surface highlights from attractive reverberation imaging (X-ray) outputs of patients with mind cancers and use them to prepare a characterization model for supporting an early finding over the cloud is easier [4,5].

Cloud computing is a new way of using interconnected computers that can be quickly and easily provisioned, and which provides a shared pool of resources for users. The cloud architecture has also given the medical component of segmenting masses in mammograms which now can deliver AI-based high-end diagnosis of ailments [6]. A network server, software, platforms, infrastructure, or service segments can all be considered resources [7]. States many cloud-based architectures understanding your business needs while deployment is not an easy task and security is always issue with a cloud-based architecture. With the right network access, data resources, and environment, cloud computing service delivery may be autonomous and demand-based, offering enough flexibility. By consolidating the storage, memory, and processing capability of personal computers and servers, this technology aids in the improvement of computing efficiency and cost-effectiveness. Many techniques nowadays are available over the cloud with APIs as well as the portals in the medical diagnosis system, where machine learning and artificial intelligence have contributed in the growth of early diagnosis of cancer [8]. With the benefits of cloud computing, we expect this technology to revolutionize online education. Cloud applications provide a lot of flexibility for everyone in the education sector, including universities, schools, and educational institutions. Organizations may leverage on-campus cloud platforms to offer a more effective deployment approach and infrastructure for their changing demands. The advantages of cloud computing may aid educational institutions in resolving issues like cost savings, quick and efficient communication, security, confidentiality, flexibility, and accessibility. Cloud computing has now become a cornerstone for medical prognosis as many breasts cancer in mammograms are detected over the cloud [9].

In this context, we explore how cloud computing can benefit online education. Detection and understanding over the edge computing in cloud has additionally given the clinical part of fragmenting masses in mammograms, which presently can convey man-made intelligence-based very good quality determination of breast cancer [10]. Our research shows that cloud computing may enhance the efficiency and usability of online education, making it more readily available and reasonably priced for students. We go over the benefits and drawbacks of utilizing the cloud in education and give case studies of well-known cloud services that are employed in this setting. We also talk about potential difficulties, such as the dangers and difficulties of cloud schooling. We can say that cloud architectures apart from the e learning portals have become a massive hit with the medical image processing data and has now been accepted widely for education as well as AI-based applications are being used as content, which is being taught over the cloud portals [8].

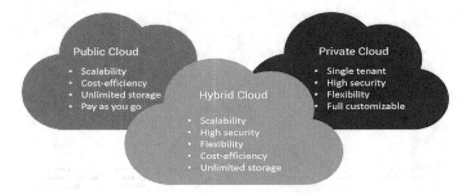

**FIGURE 17.1**   Cloud architecture.

There are four basic types of cloud computing. The list of cloud computing is as follows:

1. Private cloud
2. Public cloud
3. Hybrid cloud
4. Multi-cloud

There are also three essential types of cloud services:

Infrastructure as a Service (IaaS), Platforms as a Service (PaaS), and Software as a Service (SaaS) (Figure 17.1).

1. The term "public cloud" refers to clouds that are neither owned nor managed by the end user. The most well-known public cloud providers include Amazon Web Services (AWS), Google Cloud, IBM Cloud, Alibaba Cloud, and Microsoft Azure. Public cloud providers are increasingly beginning to offer cloud services on client data centers. Traditionally, public clouds have always been housed offshore.

2. Private clouds are a particular kind of cloud environment that are exclusive to one person or organization. This environment normally operates behind the firewall set up by the user or group. When the underlying computer infrastructure is devoted to a single client with isolated access, a private cloud is established.

3. Hybrid clouds: A virtual private network (VPN), wide area network (WAN), local area network (LAN), and/or application programming interfaces (API) are some of the connections that make up hybrid clouds, which are different computing environments made of various settings.

4. Multi-cloud: Multiple cloud services and cloud providers, both public and private, make up the cloud approach. All hybrid clouds are multicolored clouds, however, not all composite clouds are hybrid clouds. When many clouds are joined in some way, they can develop into hybrid clouds. Figure 17.1 Makes us understand the different cloud types and how we can make efficient use of their characteristics.

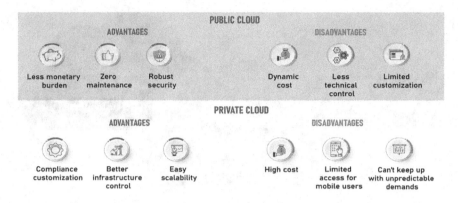

**FIGURE 17.2**   Cloud advantages and disadvantages.

Benefits of cloud computing:

The following are some of the many benefits of cloud computing:

1. Flexible infrastructure
2. Scalable infrastructure
3. Increase in the availability of the resources
4. Cost savings
5. High speed
6. Deployment in a quick manner
7. Unlimited storage capacity

Disadvantages of cloud computing is depicted in (Figure 17.2):

1. Internet connectivity
2. Security risk in cloud
3. Downtime
4. Variation in the performance of the system

## 17.2   BASIC CLOUD PROPERTIES

1. Applications interact with the infrastructure using APIs; therefore, there is no need to understand the infrastructure's inner workings.
2. These systems' "flexibility and elasticity" enables them to scale up and down at whim while leveraging a variety of resources, including databases, servers, load balancing, storage, and CPU power.
3. Utility computing and network-based computing that are "always on! anyplace and anywhere" and "pay as much as utilized and needed," respectively.
4. Users and apps can be produced with branded products, closed-source software or hardware, or plain old Computers; the cloud is transparent and is all about **declaring clear service thresholds**.

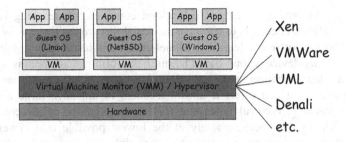

**FIGURE 17.3** Virtualization stack over cloud.

5. They are often constructed using groups of PC servers, commercially available parts, open-source software, together with proprietary applications and/or system software.

## 17.3   VIRTUALIZATION IN GENERAL

- *Virtual workspaces*: The act of creating a virtual (rather than a physical) version of something, such as a server, desktop, storage device, operating system, or network resources, is known as virtualization. Virtualization is a technology that allows many people and enterprises to share a single physical instance of a resource or application. When necessary, it accomplishes this by giving a logical name to a physical storage and providing a reference to that physical resource. An execution environment abstraction that may be dynamically made available to authorized clients via well-defined protocols, resource quotas (such as CPU and memory share), and program settings (such as operating system and offered services).
- *Implement on virtual machines (VMs)*: Any VM may be used to abstract an actual host computer. The hypervisor manages VMs, VMWare, Xen, etc. by intercepting and emulating instructions from VMs.
- *Provide infrastructure API*: Cloud management of APIs has an advantage over other systems due to plug-ins to hardware and support structures (Figure 17.3).

## 17.4   CLOUD COMPUTING AND E-LEARNING

Today, education associations around the world are transitioning to blended or fully remote learning due to the COVID-19 outbreak. The principal advantage of utilizing distributed computing in the business world is that clients don't have to spend enormous beginning speculation to construct a data innovation framework devices, and clients just have to lease the stage given by the cloud specialist organization [11]. This makes it more difficult to provide secure access and sufficient repositories to support real learning outcomes. Educational institutions also need to host their teaching equipment in a fully scalable and secure environment to enable cost-effective learning. Using cloud computing in teaching is a great choice as it allows educators to leverage the scalability, reliability, and security of the cloud to support early learning. Model-accessible learning is anytime, anywhere, from any device. Cloud-based learning platform management is one of the great ideas that an educational institution or a commercial learning and development department can offer. It allows teachers to upload a large amount of learning content in colorful types and formats to organize online courses and interact with their learners remotely at the lowest possible cost. Twenty-first-century education must be accessible and digestible, relevant, and scalable. The difficulties happened on account of the unfortunate web speed and the low level of the IT foundation in India, at the point when you plan the framework, you can keep these things in mind with the mindfulness level about distributed computing is still exceptionally low in India, online instruction is required in this day and age [12].

Most traditional learning formats are not suitable for current scenarios, as technology changes from day to day. Therefore, both learners and trainers need to consider alternative ways to benefit from it. Cloud computing and e-learning have changed the way users develop and access applications. These learning techniques improve the efficiency of the system and can be accessed regardless of person or location. With regard to the needs (foundational, stage, or administrational), as well as the cost and risk, the executives have an influence on how the arrangements for distributed computing-based e-learning are produced; there are particular tasks that deal with locating providers. This is due to the fact that e-learning programming projects are affected by the usage of distributed computing in e-learning setups [13].

In light of cloud computing, a web-based learning system, the cloud system or cloud learning framework is divided into three categories, namely:

1. Unified cloud learning framework or brought together as a single cloud system which act as a one unit.
2. A conveyed cloud system in which numerous servers are connected directly but not having a single server.
3. An intermediate system is used in which all the servers and all the clients are connected by sharing the information.

Cloud computing benefits students and lecturers by providing them with access to services and resources that are available whenever and wherever they need them, such as a variety of free and simple-to-use tools, applications, and programs. The execution of plan advancement of ADDIE informative model utilizing task learning move toward in the material information subject was finished progressively. The underlying phase of exploration and advancement is to dissect the necessities of instructors and understudies in the growing experience, and it shows outcome that 68.75% of the understudies expressed need the plan advancement of the ADDIE informative model utilizing a task learning approach,on material information subject to permit understudies to get illustrations well [14].

There are various advantages of adopting cloud computing for online learning, including the following:

- In this paradigm, learning providers serve as educational service centers, managing educational resources while guaranteeing that education becomes more effective and efficient.
- On a cloud-based online learning system, lecturers' duties include filling in the system's material depending on student requests, assessing the learning experience, and producing learner performance reports.
- The incorporation of the flipped plan into a language study hall will possibly improve the adequacy of language learning; also, flipped learning strategy offers more than adequate open doors for students to rehearse the language more informatively and cooperatively [15].
- Cloud computing will make it easier for parents to track their child's academic progress. Parents will get more active in assisting the learning process as a result of this easiness.
- Using Internet-based technologies, such as cloud computing, the public will be able to easily control the progress of education at the educational institution.
- All that is needed is to set up a cloud computing architecture at the center since cloud computing technology enables users to virtually share infrastructure. Teachers, students, parents, and the general public can only access the full functionality of the program at the web level.
- Resource effectiveness research: Cloud computing is used for most learning processes. In addition to all learning resource resources, cloud computing includes learning evaluation processes, student learning progress reports, and information sharing with other instructors, so educational institutions need to be in classrooms and practice rooms. You can manage learning materials, learn resources, and manage study time accordingly. Maximize the benefits of lack of temporal and spatial flexibility to suit your needs and conditions.
- Collaboration and sharing of e-learning: Because all work is meticulously documented, this technology makes it easier for stakeholders in education to engage in and share e-learning, collaborate across institutions, and conduct evaluations.
- Because the basis of using cloud computing technology is simplicity, the efficient use of cloud computing in a learning system needs an interface with a clear and easy-to-understand modular structure so that the application is simple to use and learn, rather than cumbersome.

The idea and execution of cloud computing demonstrate that the technology may be used to improve the quality of learning and information, as well as make all operations at universities and companies more reliable and controllable. Focusing on e-learning as a curriculum and adopting infrastructure principles incorporating instructional delivery mode, time, and flexibility are the key components of education sector e-learning [16] (Figure 17.4).

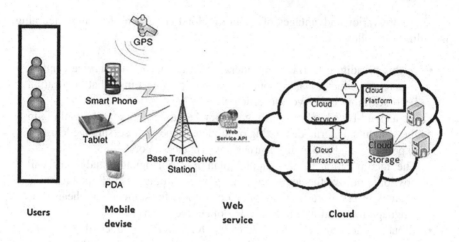

**FIGURE 17.4**   Mobile cloud computing architecture.

There are still challenges in implementing cloud computing. In particular, there are technical limitations associated with the computing technology infrastructure, including restricted Internet connection for both broadband and dial-up. Data that isn't really evident is spread so much since individuals will generally spread data disregarding its exactness and, as indicated by Pennycook and partners, this is particularly valid for individuals who need decisive reasoning abilities and are less instructed [17]. This technology is not widely used due to the partial lack of Internet connectivity. Even when not in use, it is limited to web-based applications (Software as a Service – SaaS) and is still widespread in PaaS (Platform as a Service – PaaS) and (Infrastructure as a Service – IaaS) models. . Additionally, the adoption of cloud computing in the educational sector is constrained by techno- logical challenges, particularly those related to virtualization and worries about the security assurance offered by this technology. Education assists with seeing life's different peculiarities and shaping an assessment on them. Collected information in this manner prompts the improvement of decisive reasoning, which implies that things are not underestimated, and the choices are settled on as per the choice creator's information [18,19]. The elastic cloud compute has a facility to expand when needed , this is related to mainly pay as you go service and is more technically related. This allows the elastic cloud compute to provision more resources as de- manded by the user [7].

Project-based Internet learning frameworks give numerous chances to get to show materials by learning residents. Numerous stages and online media can be gotten to by means of the web by instructors and understudies [20]. The problem of university data loss or corruption can be resolved if the data is stored in a relatively secure location rather than directly on a potentially corrupt server. Universities can use computer infrastructure and computer networks. Or, of course, because you can use cloud computing technology supported by Internet networks, university ex- ecutives don't have to provide expensive infrastructure and rent multiple facilities needed to develop applications from vendors. Use a variety of cloud computing that provides services such as Amazon, Salesforce, and GSuite. Cloud services has the following characteristics:

- Users may automatically identify their computing capabilities via on-demand self-services, eliminating the need to interact with service providers. AWS can give adaptable, reasonable innovation arrangements that helps their center mission and follow through on their most vital institutional needs (AWS Cloud Services).
- *Broad network access*: As long as a device is linked to the Internet network, services can be accessed from a range of devices at any time and from any location.
- *Resource polling*: To utilize the system to deliver services to various clients in a multi-tenant model, solution suppliers must be able to distribute and consolidate cloud computing services efficiently.
- *Rapid elasticity*: To adapt to changing client demand, a computer service must be able to scale up or down quickly.
- *Measured service*: Depending on the type of service utilized, cloud computing improves measurement capabilities at various levels to optimize and control the use of computer resources. Cloud computing advantages for learning systems technology related to cloud computing is crucial for education, particularly for intellectual pursuits. One advantage of employing cloud computing in education is accessibility. As much you have access to the Internet, you can access your data whenever and wherever you choose. The term "scalability" describes the power of cloud computing to store more data without the need to install new hardware, such as hard drives. Your cloud computing service provider ensures the security of your current data.

One Drive, Google Docs, Dropbox, and different cloud computing offerings are substantially applied in any education program due to the fact they're easy to use, economical, and dependable. Because those offerings are extensively utilized by students, they may be less complicated to evolve if they're used withinside the coaching and gaining knowledge of process. High availability, low reaction time, and scalability are only some of the blessings that make cloud computing so attractive to use. Google Programs for Education and Microsoft Office 365 both include online apps that aid individual productivity, such as word processing, spreadsheets, and displays that may be used in class. As a result, cloud computing is critical, with inside the monetary sector. As a result, cloud computing is extraordinarily crucial, on the subject of storing touchy facts that calls for intense protection. Because of the practicality of blended learning during the coronavirus pandemic, the flipped classroom is the most appropriate approach in SMK Negeri 14 Medan City. This adequacy is obtained in light of the fact that the flipped study hall is upheld by four mainstays of imaginative learning: adaptable climate, learning society, purposeful substance, and expert teacher, in view of a constructivist learning approach and its plan enacts and creates thinking abilities [21]. Kubernetes, one of the breakthroughs now being employed in the IT sector, may be used to carry out with the execution of e-learning in a cloud climate; instructive organizations no longer need to pay for the arrangement of the framework since the institution has been given by the cloud specialist organization of e-learning and offices that wish to utilize it just compensation as per the utilization by the institution [22]. Ordinary garage media has downsides, particularly if the device is destroyed or lost, while Internet-primarily-based totally garage media, additionally called cloud computing, may be accessed from everywhere and at any time without the threat of dropping the garage device. Cell phone enslavement adversely affects understudy learning and by and large scholastic execution, the more prominent the utilization of a telephone while examining, the more prominent the adverse consequence on learning, and the abilities and mental capacities of understudies required for scholastic achievement are adversely impacted by unnecessary telephone use [23]. Implementation of e-learning education in institutions and universities no longer has access to provisions of infrastructure because most of it has been provided by the cloud service provider of e-learning portal and agencies, and you can use it to pay according to the usage as per usage mode [22].

## 17.5 CONCLUSION

Cloud computing is critical for educational institutions. Because the use of cloud computing–based technologies in education may boost efficiency and effectiveness, instructors and students should learn more about it. Cloud computing benefits include high availability, massive storage capacity, exceptional accessibility, guaranteed data protection, reliable and trustworthy systems, and low-cost operations, particularly for educational institutions. Technology based on cloud computing may support educational institutions and assist in resolving a number of issues. Efficiency and effectiveness in the management of the learning process are essential for enhancing and sustaining the quality of learning results. The use of technology in the provision of education must be encouraged in an effective way to achieve maximum performance. The results when there is no DoS server attack, it runs well with great throughput in a e-portal server . When a DoS attack is carried out, the throughput value decreases and the more the greater the number of attacks, the lower the throughput value of cloud servers. This shows that the cloud server that has been built still vulnerable to DoS attacks [24]. Various cloud-based implementations have arisen in the past few years where e-commerce and e-learning portals have come into existence and are growing rapidly today in our life. Since many of the portals provide free services to the students hence learning has become more advanced and it's transforming our life with new AI driven technologies and structures where recorded content is available. Many portals such as Coursera, YouTube, Udemy, and many more are creating content using the cloud architecture and its services, every application is now an API, where you can just access any content of your choice with a click of a button. Cloud computing is mastering and is becoming a dynamic scaleable and attractive technology for the future using the resources effectively. In today's environment the significant development of technology in the educational perspective with quick and economical access to various applications using web pages on demand has lowered the cost on education and burden to the masses. Now there are various ways where we can collect economic data through online services and use the principles of cloud computing in universities and government institutions, which will help us to understand correct status and utilize cloud technology, which includes outsourcing and eye-catching email services. With the low-cost software licenses and hardware cost, great flexibility is invested upon the universities and corporate management. With this message, we can say that cloud computing is the next big event that is going to be valued on demand as a technology service and product being utilized with the data center facilities. This chapter generally presents the impact of how e-learning solutions development depends upon cloud-based services and platforms.

## REFERENCES

[1] Wagner, E. (2008). Delivering on the Promise of E-Learning. White Paper. http://www.adobe.com/education/pdf/elearning/Promise_of_eLearning_wp_final.pdf

[2] Armbrust, M., Fox, A., Griffith, R., Joseph, A., Katz, R., Konwinski, A., Lee, G., Patterson, D., Rabkin, A., Stoica, I., and Zaharia, M. (2009). Above the Clouds: A Berkeley View of Cloud Computing. UCBerkeley Reliable Adaptive Distributed Systems Laboratory.

[3] Vaquero, L., Rodero-Merino, L., Caceres, J., and Lindner, M. (January 2009). A Break in the Clouds: Towards a Cloud Definition. *ACM SIGCOMM Computer Communication Review*, 39 (1), 50–55.

[4] Singh, L., Jaffery, Z. A., and Zaheeruddin (2009). Segmentation and Characterization of Brain Tumor from Medical Imaging. IEEE International Conference on Advances in Recent Technologies in Communication and Computing, Kottayam, India, October 27–28.

[5] Singh, L., Arora, P., Singh, Y., Kapse, V., and Bisht, S. (2021). Computer Assisted Health Care Framework for Breast Cancer Detection in Digital Mammograms. Healthcare and Knowledge Management for Society 5.0. 10.1201/9781003168638-8

[6] Singh, L., and Jaffery, Z. A. (2017). Hybrid Technique for the Segmentation of Masses in Mammograms. *International Journal of Biomedical Engineering and Technology*, 24 (2), 184–195.

[7] Toby, V., Anthony, V., and Robert, E. (2009). Cloud Computing: A Practical Approach. ISBN13: 978-0-07-162694-1, 353 Pages.

[8] Singh, L., Bisht, S., and Pandey, V. (2021). Comparative Study of Machine Learning Techniques for Breast Cancer Diagnosis. Healthcare and Knowledge Management for Society 5.0. 10.1201/9781003168638-11

[9] Singh, L., Jaffery, Z. A., and Zaheeruddin (2010). Segmentation and Characterization of Breast Tumor in Mammograms. IEEE International Conference on Advances in Recent Technologies in Communication and Computing, Kottayam, India, October 16–17, 2010.

[10] Singh, L., and Jaffery, Z. A. (2018). Computerized Diagnosis of Breast Cancer in Digital Mammograms. *International Journal of Biomedical Engineering and Technology*, 27 .3, 233-246.

[11] Rumetna, M. S. (2018). Pemanfaatan Cloud Computing Pada Dunia Bisnis: Studi Literatur. *Jurnal Teknologi Informasi dan Ilmu Komputer (JTIIK)*, 5 (3), 305–314.

[12] Yuhua, L., Lilong, C., Kaihua, X., and Xi, Z. (2010). Application Modes, Architecture and Challenges for Cloud Educational System. The 2nd International Conference on Computer Research and Development-2010. 331–334.

[13]  Pocatilu, P. et al. (January 2010). Measuring the Efficiency of the Cloud Computing for the E-Learning Systems. *WSEAS Transaction on Computers*, 9,1,(89-159).

[14]  Ampera, D. (2017). Addie Model through the Task Learning Approach in Textile Knowledge Course in Dress-Making Education Study Program of State University of Medan. *International Journal*, 12 (30), 109–114.

[15]  Makruf, I., Choiriyah, S., and Nugroho, A. (2021). Flipped Learning and Communicative Competence: An Experimental Study of English Learners. International Journal of Education in Mathematics. *Science and Technology*, 9 (4), 571–584.

[16]  Naidu, S. (2006). E-Learning a Guidebook of Principles, Procedures and Practices. CEMCA.

[17]  Ginting, H. (2020). Perubahan Perilaku sebagai Respon terhadap Wabah COVID-19. Tulisan Edukasi HIMPSI di Masa Pandemi COVID-19 Seri 14 (Online), Tersedia. Retrieved June 22, 2021, from https://Covid19.go.id/edukasi/masyarakatumum/perubahan-perilaku-sebagai-respon-terhadap-wabahCovid19

[18]  John, P.2009 Cloud Computing – What Is It and What Does It Mean for Education? http://erevolution.jiscinvolve.org/wp/files/2009/07/clouds-johnpowell.pdf

[19]  Amazon Web Services. AWS in Education. http://aws.amazon.com/education/

[20]  Arizona, K., Abidin, Z., and Rumansyah, R. (2020). Pembelajaran online berbasis proyek salah satu solusi kegiatan belajar mengajar di tengah pandemi covid-19. *Jurnal Ilmiah Profesi Pendidikan*, 5 (1), 64–70.

[21]  Nurhayati, N., Ampera, D., Chalid, S., Farihah, F., and Baharuddin, B. (2021). Development of Blended Learning Type and Flipped Classroom-Based Cultural Arts Subjects. *International Journal of Education in Mathematics, Science and Technology*, 9 (4), 655–667.

[22]  Selviandro, N., Hasibuan, Z. (2013). Cloud-Based E-Learning: A Proposed Model and Benefits by Using E-Learning Based on Cloud Computing for Educational Institution. Information and Communication Technology. 7804 192 201 10.1007/978-3-642-36818-9_20

[23]  Chan, N. N., Walker, C., and Gleaves, A. (2015). An Exploration of Students' Lived Experiences of Using Smartphones in Diverse Learning Contexts Using a Hermeneutic Phenomenological Approach. *Computers & Education*, 82, 96–106.

[24]  Sharif, J. (2015). Membangun Private Cloud Computing dan Analisa Terhadap Serangan DoS, Study Kasus SMKN 6 Jakarta. *IncomTech, Jurnal Telekomunikasi dan Komputer*, 6 (3), 270–291.

# 18 Smart Rural Structures Using IoT and Cloud Computing

*Vikrant Shokeen, Sandeep Kumar, Amit Sharma, Sonali Mathur, and Mohit Mittal*

## 18.1 INTRODUCTION TO CLOUD COMPUTING AND IOT

Cloud computing is a computing model that allows users to access and use shared computing resources, such as servers, storage, applications, and services, over the Internet. In this model, the computing resources are owned and maintained by a third-party provider, who offers them to users on a pay-per-use basis. Cloud computing is based on the idea of virtualization, which allows multiple users to share a single physical server, storage device, or network. The cloud provider manages the hardware, software, and infrastructure, and users access the services and resources over the Internet using a web browser, a mobile app, or other client software. Cloud computing offers several benefits, including increased flexibility, scalability, and cost-effectiveness. It allows users to access computing resources quickly and easily, without the need for significant upfront investment in hardware, software, or infrastructure. Cloud computing can also improve the reliability, security, and performance of computing systems by leveraging the expertise and resources of cloud providers.

There are three main types of cloud computing services: Infrastructure-as-a-Service (IaaS), Platform-as-a-Service (PaaS), and Software-as-a-Service (SaaS) [1]. IaaS provides users with access to virtualized infrastructure resources, such as servers, storage, and networking. PaaS provides a platform for developing, testing, and deploying applications, without the need for managing the underlying infrastructure. SaaS provides users with access to software applications over the Internet, without the need for local installation or maintenance.

Cloud computing has revolutionized the way businesses and individuals use and manage IT resources. With its ability to provide on-demand access to a vast pool of shared resources, cloud computing has become a go-to solution for organizations looking to streamline their IT operations, reduce costs, and increase scalability. In this chapter, we will provide an overview of cloud computing, its various deployment models, and the services it offers. Cloud computing has transformed the way organizations think about IT infrastructure. Its on-demand scalability, reduced costs, and increased agility make it a compelling choice for businesses of all sizes.

DOI: 10.1201/9781003341437-21

As this chapter has shown, there are many different types of cloud services and deployment models available, and it is important for organizations to choose the right mix for their needs. By understanding the basics of cloud computing, businesses can take full advantage of the benefits it offers, while also ensuring that their infrastructure remains secure and compliant with relevant regulations.

Cloud computing has become a key technology for businesses and individuals alike. This technology enables users to access computing resources and services over the Internet, without the need for on-premises infrastructure. This essay will explore the history of cloud computing, its benefits and drawbacks, and its potential impact on future technology.

The origins of cloud computing can be traced back to the 1960s, with the development of time-sharing technology. This allowed multiple users to access a single computer at the same time, providing a cost-effective way of sharing resources. In the 1990s, the Internet provided a platform for remote computing services, leading to the development of application service providers (ASPs) that offered software applications and other services over the Internet. However, it wasn't until the mid-2000s that cloud computing began to gain popularity, with the launch of Amazon Web Services (AWS) and other similar services [2].

Cloud computing offers a wide range of benefits, including scalability, cost savings, and flexibility. With cloud computing, users can quickly scale up or down their computing resources to meet changing business needs, without the need for significant investment in hardware or infrastructure. Cloud computing also provides a cost-effective way of accessing IT services, as users only pay for the resources they use, with no need for upfront capital expenditure. This technology also offers flexibility, as users can access resources and services from any location, if they have an Internet connection.

However, cloud computing also has its drawbacks, including security concerns, limited control, and potential downtime. With cloud computing, users are entrusting their data and applications to third-party providers, which can raise concerns about data privacy and security. Additionally, users have limited control over the infrastructure and services they are using, which can lead to issues with customization and integration. Finally, cloud services are reliant on Internet connectivity, which can lead to potential downtime in the event of connectivity issues.

The impact of cloud computing on future technology is likely to be significant. As the technology becomes more widely adopted, we can expect to see increased innovation in areas such as artificial intelligence (AI), machine learning (ML), and the Internet of Things (IoT). These technologies require significant computing power and resources, which can be provided through cloud computing. Additionally, as more businesses and individuals adopt cloud computing, we can expect to see increased collaboration and data sharing, leading to more efficient and effective use of resources.

In conclusion, cloud computing has become a key technology for businesses and individuals, providing a cost-effective and flexible way of accessing computing resources and services. While there are potential drawbacks, the benefits of cloud computing are significant, and the impact of this technology on future innovation is likely to be significant. As such, it is important for businesses and individuals to understand the basics of cloud computing, in order to take full advantage of its benefits, while also ensuring that their data and applications remain secure and compliant with relevant regulations. Overall, cloud computing has transformed the way organizations use and access computing resources, offering a flexible, scalable, and cost-effective way to meet their computing needs.

The IoT refers to a network of interconnected physical devices, machines, and objects that are embedded with sensors, software, and connectivity, enabling them to collect and exchange data over the Internet [3]. These devices can include anything from smart home appliances, wearables, and vehicles to industrial machines, healthcare devices, and smart city infrastructure. The IoT allows for the creation of an intelligent and interconnected world, where data can be collected, analyzed, and acted upon in real-time. This data can be used to improve efficiency, optimize operations, and enhance user experiences. For example, in the healthcare industry, IoT devices can be used to monitor patient health remotely, improving patient outcomes and reducing the need for hospital visits [4].

The IoT ecosystem comprises three key components: the physical devices or "things," the network that connects them, and the software and services that enable data collection, processing, and analysis. The devices are embedded with sensors and communication technologies, such as Wi-Fi, Bluetooth, or cellular connectivity, that allow them to communicate with each other and with the cloud-based services that manage and analyze the data. The adoption of IoT has been driven by advancements in technology, such as the development of low-cost sensors, cloud computing, and machine learning. The IoT has the potential to transform multiple industries, from manufacturing and logistics to healthcare and transportation, offering benefits such as increased efficiency, cost savings, and improved user experiences.

However, the IoT also presents challenges, such as data privacy and security concerns, interoperability issues, and the need for standardized protocols. Despite these challenges, the potential benefits of the IoT have led to significant investment and growth in the industry, making it an exciting and rapidly evolving field.

## 18.2 TRANSFORMATIONAL ASPECTS OF THE USE OF SMART TECHNOLOGY

Cloud computing and IoT are two technologies that have transformed the way businesses operate, and their convergence has led to new opportunities for businesses to innovate, optimize, and expand their operations. In this chapter, we will explore how cloud computing using IoT is changing the way businesses operate.

As discussed in previous section, IoT refers to the interconnectedness of devices and machines that collect and share data, while cloud computing refers to the delivery of computing services over the Internet. IoT devices generate large amounts of data, which can be processed, stored, and analyzed in the cloud, making cloud computing a natural fit for IoT. The integration of these two technologies creates a powerful combination that enables businesses to operate more efficiently, provide better services to customers, and gain valuable insights into their operations.

The gateway then sends the data to the cloud servers, which store and process the data using cloud computing technologies. The processed data can then be accessed by applications or services that use the data to provide insights, control IoT devices, or make decisions. This is a basic representation of the architecture of cloud computing and IoT. The actual architecture of a smart city may be much more complex and involve many more components [5].

One application of cloud computing using IoT is in the area of smart cities. With IoT devices such as sensors, cameras, and smart traffic systems, cities can collect and analyze data on traffic flow, air quality, and energy usage, and use this data to optimize their operations. The cloud can be used to store and process this data, making it accessible to city planners and other stakeholders, who can use the insights gained to improve city infrastructure, reduce congestion, and promote sustainability.

Cloud computing and the IoT are both important technologies for building smart cities. Cloud computing provides a way to store, process, and analyze large amounts of data generated by IoT devices, while IoT devices are the sensors and actuators that collect and transmit data to the cloud. Together, these technologies can enable smart city applications that improve urban living, such as traffic management, waste management, energy management, and public safety.

Smart cities rely on IoT devices to collect data from a variety of sources, such as sensors that monitor air quality, traffic flow, and energy usage. The data collected from these devices can be processed and analyzed in the cloud, allowing city officials to gain insights into the operation of the city and make informed decisions about how to improve it.

For example, in a smart traffic management system, sensors embedded in the roads can detect traffic congestion and send that data to the cloud for analysis. The cloud-based system can then use that data to adjust traffic signals and reroute traffic in real-time, reducing congestion and improving traffic flow.

Similarly, in a smart waste management system, sensors can detect when waste bins are full and send that information to the cloud. The cloud-based system can then use that information to optimize waste collection routes, reducing fuel consumption and costs while ensuring that waste is collected efficiently.

Cloud computing and IoT are essential components of smart cities, enabling a wide range of applications that improve urban living. By leveraging these technologies, cities can become more efficient, sustainable, and livable for their residents.

Another area where cloud computing using IoT is making a significant impact is in healthcare. IoT devices such as wearables and sensors can collect data on patients' health status and transmit it to the cloud, where it can be analyzed and used to provide personalized care. Cloud-based healthcare systems can also provide real-time access to medical professionals, regardless of their location, enabling remote consultations and telemedicine services. This not only improves patient outcomes but also reduces healthcare costs and increases access to healthcare for patients in remote and underserved areas.

Cloud computing and the IoT have significant potential to transform healthcare by providing advanced monitoring, analytics, and data sharing capabilities [6]. Here are a few examples of how cloud computing and IoT are being used in healthcare:

1. *Remote patient monitoring*: IoT devices such as wearables, sensors, and mobile apps can collect patient data and transmit it to cloud servers in real-time. This data can be analyzed to track patient health status, identify potential health risks, and trigger alerts for healthcare providers [7].

2. *Telemedicine*: Cloud-based video conferencing platforms can enable remote consultations between healthcare providers and patients, allowing for greater access to care, particularly in remote or rural areas [8].

3. *Smart hospitals*: IoT sensors and devices can be used to monitor and control hospital environments such as temperature, humidity, and lighting, reducing energy costs and creating a more comfortable environment for patients [9].

4. *Electronic health records (EHRs)*: Cloud-based EHR systems can securely store and share patient data among healthcare providers, reducing errors and improving patient outcomes [10].

5. *Personalized medicine*: Cloud-based analytics tools can analyze large volumes of patient data to identify patterns and insights that can inform personalized treatment plans and improve patient outcomes [11,12].

In all these cases, cloud computing and IoT work together to improve the efficiency and effectiveness of healthcare delivery, ultimately improving patient outcomes and reducing costs. However, it is essential to ensure that the data collected and analyzed is protected, and patient privacy is maintained. Therefore, implementing strong security and privacy measures is crucial to ensure the safety and trust of patients and healthcare providers.

In the manufacturing industry, cloud computing using IoT is being used to optimize production processes and reduce downtime. IoT sensors can be used to monitor machines and equipment, collect data on performance, and detect issues before they lead to failures or downtime. The cloud can be used to store and process this data, allowing manufacturers to analyze and optimize their operations in real time. This can lead to increased efficiency, reduced costs, and improved product quality.

Cloud computing and the IoT are rapidly transforming the manufacturing industry by providing new capabilities for collecting, analyzing, and sharing data. Here are a few examples of how cloud computing and IoT are being used in the manufacturing industry:

1. *Predictive maintenance*: IoT sensors can be used to monitor the health of manufacturing equipment in real-time, collecting data on variables such as temperature, vibration, and energy consumption. Cloud-based analytics tools can then process this data to detect potential equipment failures before they occur, allowing manufacturers to perform maintenance proactively and avoid costly downtime [13].

2. *Supply chain optimization*: IoT sensors and cloud-based analytics can be used to track goods as they move through the supply chain, providing real-time visibility and transparency to manufacturers. This data can be used to optimize inventory management, reduce waste, and improve overall supply chain efficiency.

3. *Quality control*: IoT sensors can be used to collect data on product quality, such as temperature, humidity, and pressure. Cloud-based analytics tools can then process this data to identify quality issues and provide insights to manufacturers on how to improve product quality [14].

4. *Real-time performance monitoring*: IoT sensors can be used to collect data on manufacturing processes in real time, such as production rates, energy consumption, and machine utilization. This data can be analyzed in the cloud to provide manufacturers with real-time insights into their operations, allowing them to make more informed decisions and improve overall efficiency.

5. *Remote monitoring and control*: Cloud-based IoT platforms can enable remote monitoring and control of manufacturing processes, allowing manufacturers to adjust settings and parameters in real time from anywhere in the world.

In all these use cases, cloud computing and IoT are providing manufacturers with new capabilities for collecting, analyzing, and sharing data, ultimately improving efficiency, reducing costs, and enhancing overall performance. However, it is essential to ensure that the data collected and analyzed is protected, and privacy and security measures are in place to prevent data breaches and unauthorized access. Therefore, implementing strong security and privacy measures is crucial to ensure the safety and trust of manufacturers and customers.

In the retail industry, cloud computing using IoT is being used to provide a personalized shopping experience for customers. IoT devices such as beacons and smart shelves can be used to collect data on customer behavior, such as browsing habits and purchase history, and transmit this data to the cloud. Retailers can use this data to provide personalized recommendations and offers to customers, improving customer engagement and loyalty.

In conclusion, cloud computing using IoT is a powerful combination that is transforming the way businesses operate. By leveraging IoT devices and the cloud, businesses can collect and analyze large amounts of data, gain valuable insights into their operations, and provide better services to customers. As these technologies continue to evolve and become more widely adopted, we can expect to see even more innovative applications and use cases in a variety of industries.

## 18.3 SMART RURAL STRUCTURES USING IOT AND CLOUD COMPUTING

Smart rural structures using IoT and cloud computing is a concept that involves the integration of various technologies to create efficient and sustainable living environments in rural areas. The idea is to leverage the power of IoT devices and cloud computing to provide essential services to rural communities, including smart energy management, agricultural monitoring, and remote healthcare.

There are several reasons why we need smart rural structures enabled with IoT and cloud computing:

1. *Improving agricultural efficiency*: With the help of IoT and cloud computing, farmers can monitor crop health, soil moisture, and weather conditions in real time. This information helps farmers to make more informed decisions about irrigation, fertilization, and other factors that affect crop

growth. By improving agricultural efficiency, farmers can increase yields and reduce waste, which can ultimately lead to increased profits and food security.

2. *Enhancing livestock management*: Smart rural structures enabled with IoT and cloud computing can also be used to monitor the health and behavior of livestock. Sensors and cameras can be used to track the movement of animals, monitor their vital signs, and detect any signs of distress. This information can help farmers to provide better care for their animals, detect diseases early, and prevent the spread of diseases [15].

3. *Improving resource management*: With the help of IoT and cloud computing, farmers can monitor their energy and water usage, as well as their waste output. This information can be used to optimize resource usage, reduce waste, and improve sustainability.

4. *Increasing connectivity*: Smart rural structures can help to connect rural communities to the wider world, providing access to e-commerce, tele-medicine, and other services that might not be available locally. This can help to reduce isolation and improve quality of life in rural areas.

Overall, smart rural structures enabled with IoT and cloud computing can help to improve efficiency, sustainability, and quality of life in rural areas. They can also help to bridge the digital divide between urban and rural areas, and provide new opportunities for economic growth and development.

One example of a smart rural structure using IoT and cloud computing is a smart irrigation system for agriculture. This system would consist of a network of IoT devices, such as soil moisture sensors, weather stations, and drones, that collect data on weather patterns, soil moisture levels, and crop growth. This data would then be sent to the cloud, where it would be analyzed by ML algorithms to generate insights on optimal irrigation schedules and crop management strategies. Farmers would then receive alerts and recommendations on when and how much to irrigate, helping them save water and maximize crop yields.

Another example of a smart rural structure using IoT and cloud computing is a remote healthcare system. In many rural areas, access to healthcare is limited, which can lead to serious health issues going untreated. By leveraging IoT devices, such as wearable health monitors and remote medical consultation platforms, healthcare providers can monitor patients remotely and provide care as needed. This data can be transmitted to the cloud, where it can be analyzed to identify potential health risks and provide personalized treatment recommendations.

Also, smart energy management systems can also be used in rural areas to optimize energy usage and reduce costs. IoT devices, such as smart meters and energy monitoring systems, can be used to collect data on energy consumption patterns, which can then be sent to the cloud for analysis. This data can be used to identify areas where energy consumption can be reduced, and smart controls can be implemented to optimize energy usage. This can result in significant cost savings and reduced environmental impact.

In conclusion, smart rural structures using IoT and cloud computing can help to create sustainable and efficient living environments in rural areas. By leveraging the power of IoT devices and cloud computing, it is possible to provide essential services such as smart energy management, agricultural monitoring, and remote healthcare. As technology continues to advance, there is significant potential for these systems to become more sophisticated and effective, providing even greater benefits to rural communities.

### 18.3.1 SMART IRRIGATION SYSTEM USING IoT AND CLOUD COMPUTING

A smart irrigation system using IoT and cloud computing is an innovative solution that can help optimize the water consumption of crops, gardens, and lawns. The system leverages IoT sensors and cloud computing to monitor environmental factors, such as soil moisture, temperature, and humidity, and control the water flow to the plants accordingly [16].

Here are the main components of a smart irrigation system using IoT and cloud computing:

1. *IoT sensors*: These sensors are placed in the soil to measure various parameters, such as soil moisture, temperature, and humidity. The sensors can be wireless and battery-powered to provide real-time data to the cloud.
2. *Microcontrollers*: These devices are used to collect and process data from the IoT sensors and control the irrigation system. They can be connected to the cloud to receive commands and updates.
3. *Cloud computing*: The cloud is used to store and process the data collected by the IoT sensors. It also provides a platform for managing and controlling the irrigation system. Cloud-based software can analyze the data and generate recommendations for optimal watering schedules.
4. *Watering systems*: The irrigation system can be controlled by microcontrollers connected to solenoid valves or pumps. These components can be programmed to activate the watering system based on the data collected by the IoT sensors.

Benefits of a smart irrigation system using IoT and cloud computing include the following:

1. *Reduced water consumption*: The system can optimize the watering schedule based on real-time data, reducing water waste and conserving resources.
2. *Improved crop yields*: By providing the right amount of water at the right time, the system can help improve the quality and yield of crops.
3. *Remote monitoring and control*: The system can be accessed and controlled from anywhere with an Internet connection, allowing farmers and gardeners to manage their irrigation systems remotely.
4. *Predictive maintenance*: The system can detect issues before they become critical, allowing for proactive maintenance and reducing downtime.

## 18.3.2   RURAL REMOTE HEALTHCARE SYSTEM USING IOT AND CLOUD COMPUTING

A rural remote healthcare system using IoT, and cloud computing can be an effective solution to overcome the challenges of providing healthcare services in remote and underserved areas [17]. The system leverages IoT sensors and cloud computing to monitor and track the health status of patients, and provide real-time access to healthcare professionals, regardless of their location.

Here are the main components of a rural remote healthcare system using IoT and cloud computing:

1. *IoT sensors*: These sensors can be used to monitor vital signs, such as heart rate, blood pressure, temperature, and oxygen saturation. They can also be used to track medication adherence, physical activity, and other health-related parameters.
2. *Wearable devices*: These devices can be used to collect data from the IoT sensors and transmit it to the cloud. Examples of wearable devices include smartwatches, fitness trackers, and other wireless medical devices.
3. *Cloud computing*: The cloud can be used to store and process the data collected by the IoT sensors. It can also provide a platform for remote consultation and telemedicine services. Cloud-based software can analyze the data and generate alerts or notifications when necessary.
4. *Mobile applications*: Patients can use mobile applications to access their health data, communicate with healthcare professionals, and receive personalized recommendations for their health and wellness.
5. *Telemedicine platforms*: Healthcare professionals can use telemedicine platforms to provide remote consultations, monitor patients' health status, and prescribe medication or other interventions as needed.

Benefits of a rural remote healthcare system using IoT and cloud computing include the following:

1. *Improved access to healthcare*: Patients in remote and underserved areas can access healthcare services from anywhere with an Internet connection, reducing the need for travel and increasing convenience.
2. *Real-time monitoring*: The system can provide real-time monitoring and tracking of patients' health status, allowing for early detection and intervention in case of health issues.
3. *Personalized care*: The system can provide personalized recommendations based on the patient's health data, promoting preventive care and proactive management of chronic conditions.
4. *Reduced healthcare costs*: The system can help reduce healthcare costs by minimizing hospitalizations and emergency room visits, and promoting early intervention and prevention.

Overall, a rural remote healthcare system using IoT and cloud computing can improve the quality of healthcare services, increase access to care, and promote preventive and personalized care in underserved communities.

### 18.3.3 SMART ENERGY MANAGEMENT SYSTEM USING IoT AND CLOUD COMPUTING

A smart energy management system using IoT and cloud computing is an innovative solution that can help optimize energy consumption and reduce costs in commercial, industrial, and residential buildings [18]. The system leverages IoT sensors and cloud computing to monitor and control the energy usage of various devices and appliances and make adjustments based on real-time data.

Here are the main components of a smart energy management system using IoT and cloud computing:

1. *IoT sensors*: These sensors can be installed in various locations in a building, such as lighting fixtures, HVAC systems, and appliances, to measure energy consumption and other parameters, such as temperature and humidity.
2. *Energy monitoring devices*: These devices can be used to collect and transmit data from the IoT sensors to the cloud. They can also be used to control the energy usage of various devices and appliances.
3. *Cloud computing*: The cloud can be used to store and process the data collected by the IoT sensors. It can also provide a platform for analyzing the data and generating recommendations for energy-saving measures.
4. *Control systems*: The energy management system can be controlled by microcontrollers connected to devices such as light switches, thermostats, and energy meters. These components can be programmed to activate and deactivate devices based on the data collected by the IoT sensors.
5. *Mobile applications*: Building managers and residents can use mobile applications to monitor energy usage, receive notifications about energy-saving opportunities, and control devices remotely.

Benefits of a smart energy management system using IoT and cloud computing include the following:

1. *Reduced energy consumption*: The system can optimize the usage of devices and appliances based on real-time data, reducing energy waste and lowering energy bills.
2. *Improved energy efficiency*: The system can identify inefficiencies in energy usage and recommend improvements, such as upgrading to energy-efficient devices or adjusting settings.
3. *Predictive maintenance*: The system can detect issues before they become critical, allowing for proactive maintenance and reducing downtime.
4. *Remote monitoring and control*: The system can be accessed and controlled from anywhere with an Internet connection, allowing building managers and residents to manage their energy usage remotely.

Overall, a smart energy management system using IoT and cloud computing can help reduce energy consumption, lower energy costs, and promote sustainable energy use in commercial, industrial, and residential buildings.

## 18.4  LIMITATIONS OF IOT AND CLOUD COMPUTING

While IoT and cloud computing have transformed many industries, there are some drawbacks associated with using these technologies, including:

1. *Security risks*: IoT devices are often designed with minimal security features, which makes them vulnerable to cyber-attacks. Moreover, the use of cloud computing involves the transfer of data over the Internet, which makes it susceptible to security breaches and hacking.
2. *Reliance on Internet connectivity*: Both IoT devices and cloud computing rely heavily on Internet connectivity. In the absence of a reliable and stable Internet connection, the devices and services may fail to function properly.
3. *Complexity and interoperability*: IoT devices often operate on different protocols, which makes it difficult to ensure interoperability between them. Moreover, the integration of multiple IoT devices with cloud computing requires a high level of technical expertise and can be complex.
4. *Privacy concerns*: The data collected by IoT devices is often sensitive and personal. The storage of this data on the cloud raises privacy concerns, and there is a risk that the data could be accessed or misused by unauthorized parties.
5. *Cost*: The deployment of IoT devices and the use of cloud computing can be expensive. The cost of the devices, sensors, and infrastructure required for their operation can be significant, and ongoing maintenance and updates may also be costly.

Overall, while IoT and cloud computing offer many benefits, organizations should carefully consider the potential drawbacks before implementing these technologies. Proper security measures, reliable connectivity, and skilled technical expertise are essential to ensure a successful deployment.

## 18.5  CONCLUSION

Smart rural structures using IoT and cloud computing is a promising approach to enhancing the quality of life in rural areas. The use of IoT devices and cloud computing technologies can provide farmers and rural residents with access to real-time data, advanced analytics, and intelligent decision-making tools.

The implementation of smart rural structures can improve agricultural productivity, reduce water and energy consumption, increase food safety, and enhance overall sustainability. Additionally, smart rural structures can provide better access to healthcare, education, and other essential services, bridging the rural-urban divide.

However, the adoption of smart rural structures is not without challenges. The high cost of implementing IoT devices, lack of technical expertise, limited connectivity, and privacy and security concerns are some of the obstacles that need to be overcome.

Overall, smart rural structures using IoT and cloud computing have the potential to transform rural communities and create new opportunities for economic growth and social development. The key to success is developing sustainable and scalable solutions that address the specific needs and challenges of rural areas while balancing technological innovation with social, economic, and environmental considerations.

## REFERENCES

[1] Singh, Dilawar, Shweta Sinha, and Vikas Thada. 2022. "A Novel Attribute Based Access Control Model with Application in IaaS Cloud." *Journal of Integrated Science and Technology* 10 (2): 79–86. https://www.iaras.org/iaras/home/cijc/a-novel-attribute-based-access-control-model-with-application-in-iaas-cloud.

[2] Mishra, Shilpi, Manish Kumar, Niharika Singh, and Stuti Dwivedi. 2022. "A Survey on AWS Cloud Computing Security Challenges & Solutions." In *Proceedings – 2022 6th International Conference on Intelligent Computing and Control Systems, ICICCS 2022*, 614–617. 10.1109/ICICCS53718.2022.9788254.

[3] Koohang, Alex, Carol Springer Sargent, Jeretta Horn Nord, and Joanna Paliszkiewicz. 2022. "Internet of Things (IoT): From Awareness to Continued Use." *International Journal of Information Management* 62. 10.1016/j.ijinfomgt.2021.102442.

[4] Kadhim, Kadhim Takleef, Ali M. Alsahlany, Salim Muhsin Wadi, and Hussein T. Kadhum. 2020. "An Overview of Patient's Health Status Monitoring System Based on Internet of Things (IoT)." *Wireless Personal Communications* 114 (3): 2235–2262. 10.1007/S11277-020-07474-0.

[5] Khan, Ibrahim Haleem, and Mohd Javaid. 2022. "Role of Internet of Things (IoT) in Adoption of Industry 4.0." *Journal of Industrial Integration and Management* 7 (4): 515–533. 10.1142/S2424862221500068.

[6] Thangam, Dhanabalan, Anil B. Malali, Gopalakrishnan Subramanian, and Jin Yong Park. 2022. "Transforming Healthcare through Internet of Things." *Cloud and Fog Computing Platforms for Internet of Things*, April 15–24. 10.1201/9781003213 888-2/TRANSFORMING-HEALTHCARE-INTERNET-THINGS-DHANABA-LAN-THANGAM-ANIL-MALALI-GOPALAKRISHNAN-SUBRAMANIAN-JIN-YONG-PARK.

[7] Olmedo-Aguirre, José Oscar, Josimar Reyes-Campos, Giner Alor-Hernández, Isaac Machorro-Cano, Lisbeth Rodríguez-Mazahua, and José Luis Sánchez-Cervantes. 2022. "Remote Healthcare for Elderly People Using Wearables: A Review." *Biosensors*. 10.3390/bios12020073.

[8] Defranco, Joanna F., and Michael J. Metro. 2022. "Internet of Telemedicine." *Computer* 55 (4): 56–59. 10.1109/MC.2022.3143625.

[9] Rodrigues, Vinicius Facco, Rodrigo Da, Rosa Righi, Cristiano André Da Costa, and Rodolfo Stoffel Antunes. 2022. "Smart Hospitals and IoT Sensors: Why Is QoS Essential Here?" *Mdpi.Com*. 10.3390/jsan11030033.

[10] Bots, Sophie H., Rolf H.H. Groenwold, and Olaf M. Dekkers. 2022. "Using Electronic Health Record Data for Clinical Research: A Quick Guide." *European Journal of Endocrinology* 186 (4). 10.1530/EJE-21-1088.

[11] Pravin Renold, A., and K. V. Ranjith Kumar. 2022. "Design of Internet of Things Enabled Personalized Healthcare Device for Vital Signs Monitoring." *Journal of Ambient Intelligence and Smart Environments* 14 (5): 375–384. 10.3233/AIS-220098.

[12] Vincent, Raj, Gutierrez Reina, Francisco Luna-Perejón, Lourdes Miró Amarante, Francisco Gómez-Rodríguez, A. Angel Nancy, Dakshanamoorthy Ravindran, P. M. Durai Raj Vincent, Kathiravan Srinivasan, and Daniel Gutierrez Reina. 2022. "IoT-Cloud-Based Smart Healthcare Monitoring System for Heart Disease Prediction via Deep Learning." *Mdpi.Com.* 10.3390/electronics11152292.

[13] Mohbey, Krishna Kumar, and Sunil Kumar. 2022. "The Impact of Big Data in Predictive Analytics towards Technological Development in Cloud Computing." *International Journal of Engineering Systems Modelling and Simulation* 13 (1): 61–75. 10.1504/IJESMS.2022.122732.

[14] Prashar, Anupama. 2022. "Quality Management in Industry 4.0 Environment: A Morphological Analysis and Research Agenda." *International Journal of Quality and Reliability Management.* 10.1108/IJQRM-10-2021-0348/FULL/HTML.

[15] Mahfuz, Shad, Hong Seok Mun, Muhammad Ammar Dilawar, and Chul Ju Yang. 2022. "Applications of Smart Technology as a Sustainable Strategy in Modern Swine Farming." *Sustainability (Switzerland).* 10.3390/su14052607.

[16] Obaideen, K., B. A. A. Yousef, M. N. AlMallahi, Y. C. Tan, M. Mahmoud, H. Jaber, and M. Ramadan. 2022. "An Overview of Smart Irrigation Systems Using IoT." *Elsevier.* Accessed February 21, 2023. https://www.sciencedirect.com/science/article/pii/S2772427122000791.

[17] Obaidur Rahman, Md., Mohammod Abul Kashem, Al-Akhir Nayan, Most. Fahmida Akter, Fazly Rabbi, Marzia Ahmed, and Mohammad Asaduzzaman. n.d. "Internet of Things (IoT) Based ECG System for Rural Health Care." *Arxiv.Org* 12 (6): 2021. Accessed February 21, 2023. https://arxiv.org/abs/2208.02226.

[18] Bharany, Salil, Sandeep Sharma, Osamah Ibrahim Khalaf, Ghaida Muttashar Abdulsahib, Abeer S. al Humaimeedy, Theyazn H. H. Aldhyani, Mashael Maashi, and Hasan Alkahtani. 2022. "A Systematic Survey on Energy-Efficient Techniques in Sustainable Cloud Computing." *Mdpi.Com.* 10.3390/su14106256.

# Index

Printed in the United States
by Baker & Taylor Publisher Services